PENGUIN CLASSICS

THE LOSS OF THE SHIP *ESSEX*, SUNK BY A WHALE

OWEN CHASE was born on Nantucket Island in 1796. He was first mate of the whaleship *Essex* when she was rammed and sunk by a whale in November 1820. His account of the sinking and of the crew's ordeal in the open boats was published the following year. One of island's most successful whaling captains, he retired from the sea in 1840. He died on Nantucket in 1869.

At fourteen years old, THOMAS NICKERSON was the youngest member of the *Essex*'s crew when the whaleship departed from Nantucket for the last time in August 1819. After a career in the whale fishery and merchant service, Nickerson become a shipping broker in Brooklyn, New York. He retired to Nantucket in the 1870s and became the proprietor of a boardinghouse. At the encouragement of one of his guests, the professional writer Leon Lewis, he wrote an account of the *Essex* disaster that was not published until 1984. Nickerson died in 1883.

NATHANIEL PHILBRICK is the author of the National Book Award–winning *New York Times* bestseller *In the Heart of the Sea*. His newest book, *Sea of Glory*, will be available from Viking in November 2003. A leading authority on the history of Nantucket, he is director of the Egan Institute of Maritime Studies and a research fellow at the Nantucket Historical Association. A champion sailboat racer, he lives in Nantucket, Massachusetts.

THOMAS PHILBRICK is Professor Emeritus of English at the University of Pittsburgh and a lifelong small boat sailor. He is the author of *James Fenimore Cooper and the Development of American Sea Fiction* and the study *St. John de Crèvecoeur*. He has edited five of Cooper's novels and travel books for the Cooper Edition, as well as Dana's *Two Years Before the Mast* for Penguin Classics.

THE LOSS OF THE SHIP *ESSEX*, SUNK BY A WHALE

THOMAS NICKERSON, OWEN CHASE, AND OTHERS

EDITED WITH AN INTRODUCTION
AND NOTES BY NATHANIEL PHILBRICK
AND THOMAS PHILBRICK

PENGUIN BOOKS

PENGUIN BOOKS

Published by the Penguin Group

Penguin Putnam Inc., 375 Hudson Street, New York, New York 10014, U.S.A.

Penguin Books Ltd, 27 Wrights Lane, London W8 5TZ, England

Penguin Books Australia Ltd, Ringwood, Victoria, Australia

Penguin Books Canada Ltd, 10 Alcorn Avenue, Toronto, Ontario, Canada M4V 3B2

Penguin Books (N.Z.) Ltd, 182-190 Wairau Road, Auckland 10, New Zealand

Penguin Books Ltd, Registered Offices: Harmondsworth, Middlesex, England

This volume first published in Penguin Books 2000

10 9 8 7 6 5 4

The publication of Thomas Nickerson's "Desultory Sketches" is by arrangement with the Nantucket Historical Association. Address inquiries concerning the reprinting of portions of this text to Penguin Putnam Inc. Queries regarding other uses should be addressed to the Nantucket Historical Association, 2 Whalers Lane, P.O. Box 1016, Nantucket, Massachusetts 02554.

Illustrations and Thomas Nickerson's letter to Leon Lewis courtesy of the Nantucket Historical Association.

Herman Melville's annotations in his copy of Owen Chase's *Narrative* (*AC85 M4977 R821c (B)) reprinted by permission of the Houghton Library, Harvard University.

Excerpt from the *Journal of the Ship Surry* reprinted by permission of Mitchell Library, State Library of New South Wales, Sydney, Australia.

Excerpt from letter from Phebe B. Chase to Winnifred Battie reprinted by permission of James Chase.

LIBRARY OF CONGRESS CATALOGING IN PUBLICATION DATA
The loss of the ship Essex, sunk by a whale: first-person accounts/Thomas Nickerson, Owen Chase, and others; edited with an introduction and notes by Nathaniel Philbrick and Thomas Philbrick.
p.   cm.—(penguin classics)
Includes biographical references.
ISBN 0 14 04.3796 7
1. Essex (Whaleship)   2. Survival after airplane accidents, shipwrecks, etc.
3. Shipwrecks—pacific Ocean. I. Nickerson, Thomas, 1805–1883.   II. Philbrick, Nat.
III. Philbrick, Thomas.   IV. Series
G530.E77 L67   2000
910'.9164—dc21   00–020147

Printed in the United States of America
Set in Stempel Garamond

CONTENTS

INTRODUCTION

ON 20 NOVEMBER 1820 the Nantucket whaleship *Essex* was cruising the Pacific Ocean, almost a thousand miles from the nearest land, when it was repeatedly rammed by an eighty-five-foot sperm whale. The ship rapidly filled with water and capsized. The men were able to salvage some casks of bread and water from the wreck, along with several Galapagos tortoises. Fearing cannibals on the islands to the west, the twenty-man crew set out in three small whaleboats for South America, 3,000 miles away, stopping only for a six-day respite on barren Henderson Island in mid-Pacific. Within three months of the wreck, more than half the men were dead, starvation having forced the survivors to enact the very fate they had sailed all that distance to escape.

On 23 February 1820, a whaleboat containing the *Essex*'s Captain Pollard and another crew member was picked up by a Nantucket ship almost within sight of the Chilean coast. That night Captain Aaron Paddack recorded Pollard's account of the ordeal. Paddack's letter would be the first word of the disaster to reach the *Essex*'s home port of Nantucket Island, in June of that year. In November, another survivor, the *Essex*'s first mate, Owen Chase, published a much more detailed narrative. Two decades later, a young whaleman by the name of Herman Melville read Chase's account. Melville eventually procured his own copy of Chase's narrative before publishing *Moby-Dick* (1851), in which a whaleship is rammed by a whale.

For the next 130 years, the *Essex* disaster would be known almost exclusively in the context of Melville's use of Chase's narrative. Further, mostly fragmentary, accounts based on the testimony of other *Essex* crew members would come to light, but these lacked the authority and scope of Chase's narrative. In 1935, Robert

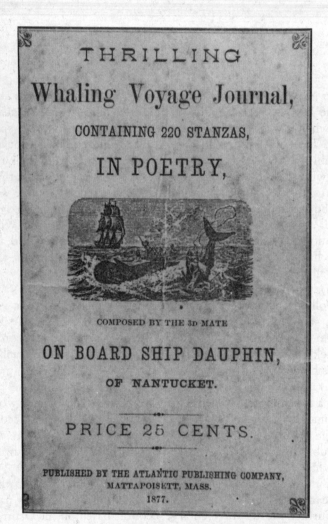

THRILLING
Whaling Voyage Journal,

CONTAINING 220 STANZAS,

IN POETRY,

COMPOSED BY THE 3D MATE

ON BOARD SHIP DAUPHIN,

OF NANTUCKET.

PRICE 25 CENTS.

PUBLISHED BY THE ATLANTIC PUBLISHING COMPANY,
MATTAPOISETT, MASS.
1877.

The cover of the poem by Charles Murphy

Gibbings published an edition of Chase's narrative that included two other sources: a pamphlet written by Thomas Chappel, one of the *Essex*'s boatsteerers, and a brief account written by a missionary who had spoken to Captain Pollard about the disaster. In 1963, B. R. McElderry, Jr., published an edition of Chase's narrative that added yet another source to the collection, the detailed notes that Melville had written on blank pages sewn into his copy of Chase's book. In 1981 Thomas Heffernan published *Stove by a Whale: Owen Chase and the Essex*, which reprinted everything contained in Gibbings and McElderry, plus several other important sources: Aaron Paddack's letter, an account written by Commodore Charles Goodwin Ridgely after seeing several of the survivors in Valparaiso, Chile; a manuscript at the Mitchell Library in Sydney, Australia, based on the testimony of the survivors who chose to stay on uninhabited Henderson Island; and, perhaps most important, Charles Wilkes's detailed account of his conversation with Captain Pollard. Despite the impressive number of sources Heffernan assembled for his volume, as well as the breadth of research he brought to bear on his chapters of analysis, Chase's narrative remained the book's centerpiece.

Then, in 1980, a notebook containing an account of the *Essex* disaster came to the attention of the Nantucket whaling expert Edouard Stackpole. Stackpole quickly realized that the 35,000-word narrative had been written by the ship's cabin boy, Thomas Nickerson, and represented a new, potentially revelatory look at the ordeal. In 1984 the Nantucket Historical Association published an abridged version of the Nickerson narrative edited by Stackpole and Helen Winslow Chase.

As Stackpole observed, Nickerson's account of the ordeal in the open boats adds relatively little to the Chase narrative. This is not true, however, of his description of the voyage prior to the sinking of the ship. Whereas Chase dedicates only a few pages to the events that preceded the whale attack, Nickerson devotes entire chapters to the voyage from Nantucket into the Pacific. Nickerson's narrative adds significantly not only to our understanding of what happened aboard the *Essex* in the fifteen months prior to the sinking but also to our general knowledge of whaling in the early nineteenth century.

What follows is the most complete collection to date of existing

Essex narratives. An attempt has been made to limit the materials to the known firsthand accounts of the ordeal; when the narrative is not written by the survivor himself, it is the work of a person who interviewed a survivor. An exception is Melville's commentary in Chase's narrative. Given the importance the author of *Moby-Dick* would have in influencing later approaches to the *Essex,* it was felt that Melville should have his say, particularly since he would, in 1851, speak with Captain Pollard.

The narratives have been arranged around the testimonies of four survivors: Owen Chase, Thomas Nickerson, Captain George Pollard, Jr., and the boatsteerer, Thomas Chappel. Two letters—one based on Pollard's testimony, the other on Chase's—have been given priority as the first known accounts of the disaster from the ship's officers. Ending the book is a section titled "Extracts: Memories and Apocrypha," a collection of anecdotes and rumors that demonstrates how the disaster impacted the lives of the survivors and continued to capture the imagination of the Nantucket community.

If nothing else, this collection of narratives demonstrates the importance of point of view in determining how an event is remembered. First there is Pollard's spare recitation of the devastating facts (as transcribed by Paddack), providing an unshrinking account of the execution of his young cousin, Owen Coffin, so that the rest of them might live. Brought back from the edge of the abyss, Pollard has told his story in one compulsive rush. Interestingly, Pollard's subsequent accounts retain a confessional quality that may help explain his ability to withstand the psychological shock of events that might have easily overwhelmed him. Published here for the first time is a portion of a recently discovered letter written by the Nantucketer Jethro Macy, who spoke to Owen Chase within days of his return to the island. The Macy letter gives a moving account of Chase's tortured attempts to recount the ordeal and is a natural companion to the Paddack letter.

Chase's *Narrative,* written with the help of a skilled ghostwriter, is something else altogether. It is more than a gripping survival tale; it is also an excellent work of self-promotion, depicting the author as a forceful and compassionate leader while glossing over his key role in pushing forward a plan that would doom most of the crew to a slow and terrible death.

NARRATIVE

OF THE

MOST EXTRAORDINARY AND DISTRESSING

SHIPWRECK

OF THE

WHALE-SHIP ESSEX,

OF

NANTUCKET;

WHICH WAS ATTACKED AND FINALLY DESTROYED BY A LARGE

SPERMACETI-WHALE,

IN THE PACIFIC OCEAN;

WITH

AN ACCOUNT

OF THE

UNPARALLELED SUFFERINGS

OF THE CAPTAIN AND CREW

DURING A SPACE OF NINETY-THREE DAYS AT SEA, IN OPEN BOATS,

IN THE YEARS 1819 & 1820.

BY

OWEN CHASE,

OF NANTUCKET, FIRST MATE OF SAID VESSEL.

NEW-YORK:

PUBLISHED BY W. B. GILLEY, 92 BROADWAY.

J. SEYMOUR, Printer.

1821.

The title page of Owen Chase's Narrative

Thomas Nickerson, writing many years after the ordeal, was careful to fill in some of the gaps left by the first mate. Nickerson reveals that, contrary to what Chase implies, the officers did not always agree. After the whale attack, Captain Pollard suggested that they sail for the Society Islands. Instead of sticking with his initial decision (which would have probably resulted in the deliverance of the entire crew), Pollard yielded to the objections of Chase and second mate Matthew Joy, who advocated sailing for South America. Nickerson was guilty of his own equivocations. Contradicting Chase's graphic description of how he, Nickerson, and Benjamin Lawrence consumed the body of Isaac Cole, Nickerson claims that they were never reduced to cannibalism. It was the extra rations made available by Cole's death, Nickerson insists, that enabled them to survive. Writing in a comfortable and quiet old age, Nickerson did not want to be remembered as a cannibal.

The religious tract based on the testimony of Thomas Chappel, the English boatsteerer who, along with William Wright and Seth Weeks, elected to remain on Henderson Island rather than continue on to South America, provides a detailed account of the three men's confinement on the island as well as several new details about the whale attack. Chappel, whom Nickerson remembered as "very wild and fond of fun at whatever expense," appears to have undergone a religious conversion on Henderson. Unfortunately, his newfound piety sometimes threatens to smother his extraordinary tale beneath a fog of spiritual platitudes.

The collection's final section, "Extracts: Memories and Apocrypha," reveals how Nantucketers, despite their public unwillingness to talk about the disaster, continued to gossip about the *Essex* throughout the nineteenth century. Even though Pollard was the victim of several unfounded rumors, he appears to have reconciled himself to his role in the disaster and enjoyed a happy and fulfilling life as a night watchman on Nantucket. Owen Chase, on the other hand, was plagued in his later years by memories of the ordeal even though he had enjoyed the professional success as a whaling captain that had eluded George Pollard.

By combining, for the first time, the accounts of four survivors in a single volume, this collection gives the reader an unparalleled opportunity to get at, if not the truth of the *Essex* disaster, the complex combination of sometimes contradictory testimonies that must serve in its stead. Read in their entirety, these narratives provide us with the closest possible approximation of what really happened in the days and months that preceded and followed the extraordinary tragedy that overtook the men of the *Essex*.

NATHANIEL PHILBRICK
THOMAS PHILBRICK

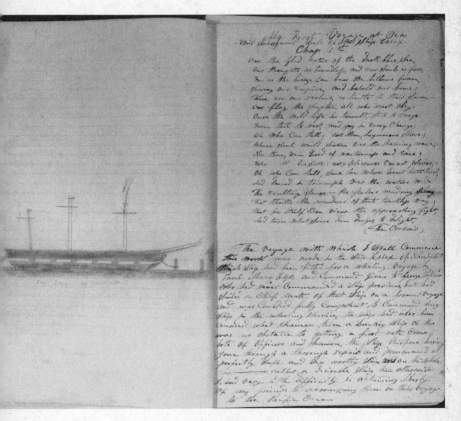

Thomas Nickerson's sketch of the Essex *at wharf*

SUGGESTIONS FOR FURTHER READING

Carlisle, Henry. *The Jonah Man.* New York: Alfred A. Knopf, 1984.

Ellis, Richard. *Men and Whales.* New York: Alfred A. Knopf, 1991.

Heffernan, Thomas Farel. *Stove by a Whale: Owen Chase and the Essex.* Middletown, CT: Wesleyan University Press, 1981.

Melville, Herman. *Moby-Dick.*

Philbrick, Nathaniel. *In the Heart of the Sea.* New York: Viking, 2000.

Stackpole, Edouard A. *The Sea Hunters: New England Whalemen during Two Centuries, 1635–1835.* Philadelphia: Lippincott, 1953.

THE *ESSEX* NARRATIVES

FIRST REPORTS

The Paddack Letter

Written the same day Captain Pollard and Charles Ramsdell were rescued by the whaleship *Dauphin,* the so-called Paddack letter provides a surprisingly detailed account of the disaster. Nantucket historian Edouard Stackpole attributed the letter to Aaron Paddack, Captain of the *Diana,* a whaleship from New York. Paddack visited, or gammed, with the *Dauphin*'s captain, Zimri Coffin, and presumably was witness to Captain Pollard's account of the ordeal. He then returned to his ship and committed what he had heard to paper. Paddack's account would make its way to several whaleship captains, most notably Captain Zephaniah Wood, who would be the first to bring the story back to New Bedford. A copy of Paddack's letter also reached Nantucket prior to the arrival of the first *Essex* survivors on the island. As Thomas Heffernan has pointed out, Owen Chase's narrative depends on Paddack's letter for information regarding the fate of the captain's and second mate's whaleboats after Chase was separated from them on 12 January 1820. The Penguin text is a transcription of a photocopy in the Nantucket Historical Association of the manuscript letter. The location of the original is unknown.

Off St. Maria
    Pacific Ocean

At 5 PM spake and boarded the Ship Dauphin,[1] Capt. Zimri
Coffin; on board of this ship I heared the most distressing narrative,
that ever came to my knowledge.

Capt. Coffin had that morning taken up a whale-boat, in which
was Capt. George Pollard Jun[r]. & Charles Ramesdell, who are believed to be the only survivors of the crew of Ship Essex* of Nantucket. That ship on the 20th November was in Latitude 40 miles[2]
South & Long[d]. 120 Degrees West of Greenwich, & while two
boats ware at a distance from the vessell at work on Whales, the
ship was attacked in a most deliberated manner by a large sperma-
cetia Whale which made two such violent onsets with his head that
the whole bow was stoven & the ship sunk to the waters edge
amedeately. With great exertions & by scutling[3] the deck in many
places they were enabled to get out 600 [lbs] bread & a few Tooles,
Nails & other small articles together with as much water as could be
taken in the boats & after laying by the wreck in their three Boats
two days, without being able to procure anything more they left
her & proceeded Southward. Four days after leaving the ship two
of the boats ware near failing by reason of their being heavyly
loaded. They ware however strengthened by the Nails &[c] that had
been saved & they continued to make what progress they could to
the Southward. On the 28[th] the Captn[s] boat was attacked in the
night by an unknown fish which stove two s[t]reaks[4] & split the
stem, but was at last beat off by the sprit pole. On the 20[th] December they accidentally fell in with Ducies Island[5] in Lat[d] 24°30′ &
Long 124°30′ as laid down. On this Island the whole ship's company landed, hauled the boats onto the beach & renailed them, &

------

*with the exception of those on the Island.

remained six days. The water they obtained at this Island was very brackish & was found to spring up through a rock at near low-water mark. A few fowl & Fish was the only sustinance that could be got & not sufficient to subsist a fourth part of their number. Three of their number chose to remain on the Island & the others (Seventeen) again took to the Boats with the hope of being able to reach Easter-Island, but by adverse winds & being too much exhausted to make exertions they ware drove far South of it.

January 10th 1821. Mathew P. Joy (second officer) Died through debility & costivnes and *his corps* was commited to the ocean. The 12th being in Latitude 31°:0' & Longitude about 117°:00 the first officer's Boat was seperated from the others in the night—The 14th the provisions of the second officer's Boat was intirely expended. The 20th one of their crew (a black man) died & became food for the remainder. 21st the provisions being all gone in the Capts Boat, they ware glad to pertake of the wretched fare with the other crew—The 23d another (collered) man died in the 3d boat & was disposed of in the same way.—27th another died in the same boat, & the 28th one died (also black) in the Capts Boat and in the night following the 3d Boat was seperated from the other then in Latd 35°:00' and Longd about 100°:00. The 6th of February having intirely consumed the last morsel of sustinance, the Capt. & the three others that remained with him ware reduced to the deplorable necessity of casting Lots to see who should be sacraficed to prolong the existance of the others. The lot fell to Owen Coffin, who with composure & resignation submitted to his fate, then in Latd 39°:00' & about the Longd of 90°:00'. The 11th Barzillai Ray died being intirely exhausted. By his death the Capt & Ramesdell ware kept alive 'till taken up as before stated.

[One leaf of the letter is missing at this point.]

NB. Capt Pollard, though very low when first taken up had amediatly revived. I regret to say that young Ramesdell has appeared to fail since taken up.

---

*who it is needless to add has administered all in his power to their wants. [A footnote evidently referring to Captain Zimri Coffin of the *Dauphin*, which rescued Pollard and Ramesdell.]

The Essex's crew at the time of the ship-wreck

George Pollard Jun[r].   Master
Owen Chase   1st Oficer
Mathew P. Joy   2[d] D[itt]°
Obed Hendricks   }   3 & 4th D°
Tho[s] Chaplin
Benj[n] Lawrence
Charles Ramesdell
Barzillia Roy
Owen Coffin
Isaac Cole
Thomas Nickason
Joseph West
W[m] Wright
Seth Wicks, & Six Blacks. In all 20.

At leaving Ducies Island the crew was disposed of as follows

With the Master	With the 1st Officer	With the 2d Officer
Owen Coffin	Benj Lawrence	O Hendricks
Barzillia Ray	Isaac Cole	Jo West
Charles Ramesdell	Tho[s] Nickerson	W[m] Bon & three other
& one Black—5	& Richd Peterson	Blacks. 7
	(Black) 5	

Left on the Island. Tho[s] Chaplin, W[m] Wright, & Seth Wicks

The Macy Letter

Not until December 1999 did this letter come to the attention of anyone beyond the descendants of Barnabas and Hannah Sears of South Yarmouth, Massachusetts, on Cape Cod. It was then that one of those descendants, Rosemary Heaman, generously informed Nathaniel Philbrick of its existence. Although the letter is unsigned, Philbrick has determined that the writer, who describes himself as the widower of Barzillai Ray's sister, was Jethro Macy of Nantucket. Macy married Barzillai's older sister Lydia in 1812. After bearing three children, Lydia died in 1818.

Macy spoke to Chase in the days after his arrival on Nantucket on 11 June 1819 and recorded his impressions on the 17th. Macy states that Chase possesses a copy of the Paddack letter, and then proceeds to quote from it, almost in its entirety. In addition to explaining why the men did not sail to Pitcairn Island (only a few days sail from Henderson Island, the uninhabited island where they found some water but insufficient supplies of food to feed twenty men), he points out that the second mate's whaleboat was (unlike Pollard's and Chase's) without any navigational equipment. Finally, he records what he knows of Chase's account of the disaster, information that the first mate would amplify in his own narrative.

The Macy letter was passed down from Barnabas Sears to his granddaughter Ruth Hinckley Stetson. The Penguin text is a transcription of selected passages from the manuscript letter owned by Stetson's granddaughter, Rosemary Heaman.

Dear Cousins B. & H. Sears

With an aching heart and quivering hand I take up the pen to answer to the substance of your letter by giving some account of the
loss of the ship Essex formerly of this place commanded by George
Pollard Junr. On board of that ship was Barzillai Ray a likely young
man of 20 years of age and brother to my deceased wife, he is no
more. I will give the information as I rec'd it[.] I got it from the
mate who has arrived here with all the men who were saved except
the Capt[ain,] he being too unwell to proceed here from Valparaiso[.] The name of the mate is Owen Chase a man of firm mind
and strong constitution of body but whose sufferings have been
such that it is impossible for him to talk much about it; even the
parts most distant from the worst start the tears, his voice falters
and strong efforts mixed with smiles mark his disjointed sentences.
His own story I know but little of after he separated from the Capts
boat. I got the following information from him of the Capt[.] It was
written by Capt *Paddack*—of the ship_____of New York who
went on board the Dauphin the same day the Capt was picked up[;]
it is as follows [*The letter now presents a slightly imperfect copy of
the Paddack account supplemented by bits of information evidently
provided by Chase, among them the identification of Weeks and
Wright as residents of Barnstable, Massachusetts, and Chappel as belonging to Plymouth, England. As the boats set out from Henderson
Island (called Ducier's in this letter) for Easter Island, the following
interpolation appears:*] Here it may be proper to make a few observations. Should it be asked why did they not go to Pitcairns Island
which lies 6 degrees to the west of Ducier's I answer that at the time
the ship saild which was August 12th 1819 our fleet were not in the
habit of going so far to the west in search for whales and consequently they had no chart of that vast western ocean and Pitcairns
Island not being laid down in their navigators[1] which was all the
books they had in the boat they knew not its Latt or long. [*The let-*

ter picks up the Paddack account once more, continuing past the point at which the surviving pages of the Paddack letter break off as follows:] On the 11th Feby Barzillai Ray died, being entirely exhausted, by his death the Capt and Charles Ramsdell were kept alive till taken up as before stated making 95 days since they were wrecked six of which they were on Duciers Island. [*The quotation of the Paddack letter ends here.*]

The following relates to the mates boat after her separation Jan 12 1821 at 11. 0 clk[; she] was separated from the other boats in a squall[.] Jany 20th Richard Peterson a black man died; his corpse was committed to the ocean[.] Feby 8th Isaac Cole died[;] our provisions being very nearly expended his body became food for the survivors[.] Feby 18th in the morning was taken by the brig Indian of London Capt Wm Crozier[,] the Island of Massafuero bearing E by N 14 leagues dist[.] Feby 25th arrived at Valparaiso. The mate states that they immediately allowanced themselves one quarter of a cake of bread pr day and about a teacup full of water for 24 hours[.] their suffering with heat and thirst when down about the line were intolerable[.] the ship was driven to the north of the line before they left her. he was obliged to keep a pistol loaded to keep them from the provisions[.] they saved but 2 compasses and quadrants[.] the boat which has not been heard of had neither[.] she was left in care of a boatsteerer after the 2nd mate died—tis possible they are picked up.

THE MATE'S STORY

Chase's *Narrative of the Most Extraordinary and Distressing Shipwreck of the Whale-Ship Essex*

Chase's *Narrative* was published in the fall of 1821, just a year after the sinking of the *Essex*. Scholars have generally agreed that Chase worked with a ghostwriter, although there is no solid proof as to his or her identity. One theory proposes that it was Samuel Jenks, editor of the newly established weekly the *Nantucket Inquirer*. As Thomas Heffernan has pointed out, however, Jenks's busy schedule that summer (the *Inquirer* began publication in June 1821), as well as stylistic evidence, suggests that the writer was someone else.

Heffernan has proposed an alternative candidate: Jenks's father-in-law, William Coffin, a merchant, barber, and Nantucket's first postmaster, whose authorship of a pamphlet concerning the robbery of the Nantucket Bank in 1795 proves that he was a skilled writer. Nathaniel Philbrick has proposed yet another possibility— Coffin's son, William Coffin, Jr. A graduate of Harvard College, Coffin, who was almost precisely Owen Chase's age, would become a well-known teacher and temperance advocate on Nantucket, penning several pamphlets with stylistic similarities to the *Essex* narrative. Thirteen years later, Coffin would be enlisted by Obed Macy to ghostwrite his magisterial *History of Nantucket* (1834). It has been suggested by the Nantucket historian Helen Winslow Chase that Coffin was also the ghostwriter for William Lay and Cyrus Hussey's *Mutiny on Board the Whaleship Globe* (1828).

The Penguin text of the *Narrative* reproduces that of the original edition (New York: W. B. Gilley, 1821), incorporating the seven corrections called for by its errata list.

TO THE READER.

I AM AWARE THAT the public mind has been already nearly sated with the private stories of individuals, many of whom had few, if any, claims to public attention; and the injuries which have resulted from the promulgation of fictitious histories, and in many instances, of journals entirely fabricated for the purpose, has had the effect to lessen the public interest in works of this description, and very much to undervalue the general cause of truth. It is, however, not the less important and necessary, that narratives should continue to be furnished that have their foundations in fact; and the subject of which embraces new and interesting matter in any department of the arts or sciences. When the motive is worthy, the subject and style interesting, affording instruction, exciting a proper sympathy, and withal disclosing new and astonishing traits of human character:—this kind of information becomes of great value to the philanthropist and philosopher, and is fully deserving of attention from every description of readers.

On the subject of the facts contained in this little volume, they are neither so extravagant, as to require the exercise of any great credulity to believe, nor, I trust, so unimportant or uninteresting, as to forbid an attentive perusal. It was my misfortune to be a considerable, if not a principal, sufferer, in the dreadful catastrophe that befell us; and in it, I not only lost all the little I had ventured, but my situation and the prospects of bettering it, that at one time seemed to smile upon me, were all in one short moment destroyed with it. The hope of obtaining something of remuneration, by giving a short history of my sufferings to the world, must therefore constitute my claim to public attention.

PREFACE.

THE INCREASING ATTENTION WHICH is bestowed upon the whale fishery in the United States, has lately caused a very considerable commercial excitement; and no doubt it will become, if it be not at present, as important and general a branch of commerce as any belonging to our country. It is now principally confined to a very industrious and enterprising portion of the population of the States, many individuals of whom have amassed very rapid and considerable fortunes. It is a business requiring that labour, economy, and enterprise, for which the people of Nantucket are so eminently distinguished. It has enriched the inhabitants without bringing with it the usual corruptions and luxuries of a foreign trade; and those who are now most successful and conspicuous in it, are remarkable for the primitive simplicity, integrity, and hospitality of the island. This trade, if I may so call it, took its rise amongst the earliest settlers, and has gradually advanced to the extended, important, and lucrative state in which it now is, without any material interruption, and with very little competition until the present time. The late war temporally, but in a great degree affected its prosperity, by subjecting numerous fine vessels with their cargoes to capture and loss; but in its short continuance, it was not sufficient to divert the enterprise of the whalemen, nor to subdue the active energies of the capatalists embarked in it. At the conclusion of peace, those energies burst out afresh; and our sails now almost whiten the distant confines of the Pacific. The English have a few ships there; and the advantages which they possess over ours, it may be feared will materially affect our success, by producing in time a much more extensive and powerful competition. They are enabled to realize a greater profit from the demand and price of oil in their markets; and the encouragement afforded by parliament, not only in permitting the importation of it free of duty, but in granting a liberal bounty.[1] It is to be hoped that the wisdom of Congress will be extended to this subject; and that our present decided supremacy will not be lost for the want of a deserved government patronage.

Recent events have shown that we require a competent naval

force in the Pacific, for the protection of this important and lucrative branch of commerce; for the want of which, many serious injuries and insults have been lately received, which have a tendency to retard its flourishing progress, and which have proved of serious consequence to the parties concerned.

During the late war, the exertions and intrepidity of Capt. Porter,[2] were the means of saving a great deal of valuable property, which otherwise must have fallen into the hands of the enemy. His skilful, spirited, and patriotic conduct, on all occasions where he was called upon to act, imparted a protection and confidence to our countrymen, which completely fulfilled their expectations of him, and without doubt those of the government in sending him there.

Our ships usually occupy from two to three years in making a voyage. Occasionally, necessity obliges them to go into port for provisions, water, and repairs; in some cases, amongst mere savages, and in others, inhospitable people, from whom they are liable to every species of fraud, imposition, and force, which require some competent power to awe and redress. As long as the struggle between the patriots and royalists[3] continues, or even should that speedily end—as long as young and instable governments, as there naturally must be for many years to come, exist there, our whalemen will continue to require that countenance and support which the importance and prosperity of the trade to them, and to the country, eminently entitle them. It is, undoubtedly, a most hazardous business; involving many incidental and unavoidable sacrifices, the severity of which it seems cruel to increase by the neglect or refusal of a proper protection.

The seamen employed in the fishery, and particularly those from Nantucket, are composed of the sons and connexions of the most respectable families on the island; and, unlike the majority of the class or profession to which they belong, they labour not only for their temporary subsistence, but they have an ambition and pride among them which seeks after distinguishment and promotion. Almost all of them enter the service with views of a future command; and submit cheerfully to the hardships and drudgery of the intermediate stations, until they become thoroughly acquainted with their business.

There are common sailors, boat-steerers, and harpooners:[4] the last of these is the most honourable and important. It is in this station, that all the capacity of the young sailor is elicited; on the dexterous management of the harpoon, the line, and the lance, and in the adventurous positions which he takes alongside of his enemy, depends almost entirely the successful issue of his attack; and more real chivalry is not often exhibited on the deck of a battle-ship, than is displayed by these hardy sons of the ocean, in some of their gallant exploits among the whales. Nursed in the dangers of their business, and exposed to the continual hazards and hardships of all seasons, climates, and weathers, it will not be surprising if they should become a fearless set of people, and pre-eminent in all the requisites of good seamen. Two voyages are generally considered sufficient to qualify an active and intelligent young man for command; in which time, he learns from experience, and the examples which are set him, all that is necessary to be known.

While on this subject, I may be allowed to observe that it would not be an unprofitable task in a majority of our respectable shipmasters in the merchant service, to look into the principles of conduct, and study the economical management of the captains of our whale-ships. I am confident many serviceable hints could be gathered from the admirable system by which they regulate their concerns. They would learn, also, what respect is due to the character and standing of a captain of a whale-ship, which those of the merchant service affect so much to undervalue. If the post of danger be the post of honour; and if merit emanates from exemplary private character, uncommon intelligence, and professional gallantry, then is it due to a great majority of the shipmasters of Nantucket, that they should be held above the operations of an invidious and unjust distinction. It is a curious fact that one does exist; and it is equally an illiberal, as an undeserved reproach upon them, which time and an acquaintance with their merits must speedily wipe away.

NARRATIVE.

CHAPTER I.

THE TOWN OF NANTUCKET, in the State of Massachusetts, contains about eight thousand inhabitants; nearly a third part of the population are quakers, and they are, taken together, a very industrious and enterprising people. On this island are owned about one hundred vessels, of all descriptions, engaged in the whale trade, giving constant employment and support to upwards of sixteen hundred hardy seamen, a class of people proverbial for their intrepidity. This fishery is not carried on to any extent from any other part of the United States, except from the town of New-Bedford, directly opposite to Nantucket, where are owned probably twenty sail. A voyage generally lasts about two years and a half, and with an entire uncertainty of success. Sometimes they are repaid with speedy voyages and profitable cargoes, and at others they drag out a listless and disheartening cruise, without scarcely making the expenses of an outfit. The business is considered a very hazardous one, arising from unavoidable accidents, in carrying on an exterminating warfare against those great leviathans of the deep; and indeed a Nantucket man is on all occasions fully sensible of the honour and merit of his profession; no doubt because he knows that his laurels, like the soldier's, are plucked from the brink of danger. Numerous anecdotes are related of the whalemen of Nantucket; and stories of hair-breadth 'scapes, and sudden and wonderful preservation, are handed down amongst them, with the fidelity, and no doubt many of them with the characteristic fictions of the ancient legendary tales. A spirit of adventure amongst the sons of other relatives of those immediately concerned in it, takes possession of their minds at a very early age; captivated with the tough stories of the elder seamen, and seduced, as well by the natural desire of seeing foreign countries, as by the hopes of gain, they launch forth six or eight thousand miles from home, into an almost untraversed ocean, and spend from two to three years of their lives in scenes of constant peril, labour, and watchfulness. The profession is one of great ambition, and full of honourable excitement: a tame man is never known amongst them; and the coward is marked with that peculiar aversion, that distinguishes our public naval service. There are perhaps no people of superior corporeal powers; and it has been truly said of them, that they possess a natural aptitude, which seems rather the lineal spirit of their fathers, than the effects of any experience. The town itself, during the war, was (naturally to have been expected,) on the decline; but with the return of peace it took a fresh start, and a spirit for carrying on the fishery received a renewed and very considerable excitement. Large capitals are now embarked; and some of the finest ships that our country can boast of are employed in it. The increased demand, within a few years past, from the spermaceti manufactories, has induced companies and individuals in different parts of the Union to become engaged in the business; and if the future consumption of the manufactured article bear any proportion to that of the few past years, this species of commerce will bid fair to become the most profitable and extensive that our country possesses. From the accounts of those who were in the early stages of the fishery concerned in it, it would appear, that the whales have been driven, like the beasts of the forest, before the march of civilization, into remote and more unfrequented seas, until now, they are followed by the enterprise and perseverance of our seamen, even to the distant coasts of Japan.

The ship Essex, commanded by captain George Polland, junior, was fitted out at Nantucket, and sailed on the 12th day of August, 1819, for the Pacific Ocean, on a whaling voyage. Of this ship I was first mate. She had lately undergone a thorough repair in her upper works, and was at that time, in all respects, a sound, substantial vessel: she had a crew of twenty-one men, and was victualled and provided for two years and a half. We left the coast of America with a fine breeze, and steered for the Western Islands.[5] On the second day out, while sailing moderately on our course in the Gulf Stream, a sudden squall of wind struck the ship from the SW. and knocked her completely on her beam-ends,[6] stove one of our boats, entirely destroyed two others, and threw down the cambouse.[7] We distinctly saw the approach of this gust, but miscalculated altogether as to the strength and violence of it. It struck the ship about three points off the weather quarter, at the moment that the man at the helm was in the act of putting her away to run before it. In an instant she was knocked down with her yards in the water; and before hardly a moment of time was allowed for reflection, she gradually came to the wind, and righted. The squall was accompanied with vivid flashes of lightning, and heavy and repeated claps of thunder. The whole ship's crew were, for a short time, thrown into the utmost consternation and confusion; but fortunately the violence of the squall was all contained in the first gust of the wind, and it soon gradually abated, and became fine weather again. We repaired our damage with little difficulty, and continued on our course, with the loss of the two boats. On the 30th of August we made the island of Floros,[8] one of the western group called the Azores. We lay off and on the island for two days, during which time our boats landed and obtained a supply of vegetables and a few hogs: from this place we took the NE. trade-wind, and in sixteen days made the Isle of May, one of the Cape de Verds. As we were sailing along the shore of this island, we discovered a ship stranded on the beach, and from her appearance took her to be a whaler. Having lost two of our boats, and presuming that this vessel had probably some belonging to her that might have been saved, we determined to ascertain the name of the ship, and endeavour to supply if possible the loss of our boats from her. We accordingly stood in towards the port, or landing place. After a short time three men were discovered coming out to us in a whale boat. In a few moments they were alongside, and informed us that the wreck was the Archimedes of New-York, captain George B. Coffin, which vessel had struck on a rock near the island about a fortnight previously; that all hands were saved by running the ship on shore, and that the captain and crew had gone home. We purchased the whale boat of these people, obtained some few more pigs, and again set sail. Our passage thence to Cape Horn was not distinguished for any incident worthy of note. We made the longitude of the Cape about the 18th of December, having experienced head winds for nearly the whole distance. We anticipated a moderate time in passing this noted land, from the season of the year at which we were there, being considered the most favourable; but instead of this, we experienced heavy westerly gales, and a most tremendous sea, that detained us off the Cape five weeks, before we had got sufficiently to the westward to enable us to put away. Of the passage of this famous Cape it may be observed; that strong westerly gales and a heavy sea are its almost universal attendants:

the prevalence and constancy of this wind and sea necessarily produce a rapid current, by which vessels are set to leeward; and it is
not without some favourable slant of wind that they can in many
cases get round at all. The difficulties and dangers of the passage are
proverbial; but as far as my own observation extends, (and which
the numerous reports of the whalemen corroborate,) you can always rely upon a long and regular sea; and although the gales may
be very strong and stubborn, as they undoubtedly are, they are not
known to blow with the destructive violence that characterizes
some of the tornadoes of the western Atlantic Ocean. On the 17th
of January, 1820, we arrived at the island of St. Mary's, lying on the
coast of Chili, in latitude 36° 69' S. longitude 73° 41' W. This island
is a sort of rendezvous for whalers, from which they obtain their
wood and water, and between which and the main land (a distance
of about ten miles) they frequently cruise for a species of whale
called the right whale. Our object in going in there was merely to
get the news. We sailed thence to the island of Massafuera, where
we got some wood and fish, and thence for the cruising ground
along the coast of Chili, in search of the spermaceti whale. We took
there eight, which yielded us two hundred and fifty barrels of oil;
and the season having by this time expired, we changed our cruising
ground to the coast of Peru. We obtained there five hundred and
fifty barrels. After going into the small port of Decamas,[9] and re-
plenishing our wood and water, on the 2d October we set sail for
the Gallipagos Islands. We came to anchor, and laid seven days off
Hood's Island,[10] one of the group; during which time we stopped a
leak which we had discovered, and obtained three hundred turtle.
We then visited Charles Island,[11] where we procured sixty more.
These turtle are a most delicious food, and average in weight generally about one hundred pounds, but many of them weigh upwards
of eight hundred. With these, ships usually supply themselves for a
great length of time, and make a great saving of other provisions.
They neither eat nor drink, nor is the least pains taken with them;
they are strewed over the deck, thrown under foot, or packed away
in the hold, as it suits convenience. They will live upwards of a year
without food or water, but soon die in a cold climate. We left
Charles Island on the 23d of October, and steered off to the westward, in search of whales. In latitude 1° 0' S. longitude 118° W. on
the 16th of November, in the afternoon, we lost a boat during our

work in a shoal of whales. I was in the boat myself, with five others, and was standing in the fore part, with the harpoon in my hand, well braced, expecting every instant to catch sight of one of the shoal which we were in, that I might strike; but judge of my astonishment and dismay, at finding myself suddenly thrown up in the air, my companions scattered about me, and the boat fast filling with water. A whale had come up directly under her, and with one dash of his tail, had stove her bottom in, and strewed us in every direction around her. We, however, with little difficulty, got safely on the wreck, and clung there until one of the other boats which had been engaged in the shoal, came to our assistance, and took us off. Strange to tell, not a man was injured by this accident: Thus it happens very frequently in the whaling business, that boats are stove; oars, harpoons, and lines broken; ancles and wrists sprained; boats upset, and whole crews left for hours in the water, without any of these accidents extending to the loss of life. We are so much accustomed to the continual recurrence of such scenes as these, that we become familiarized to them, and consequently always feel that confidence and self-possession, which teaches us every expedient in danger, and inures the body, as well as the mind, to fatigue, privation, and peril, in frequent cases exceeding belief. It is this danger and hardship that makes the sailor; indeed it is the distinguishing qualification amongst us; and it is a common boast of the whaleman, that he has escaped from sudden and apparently inevitable destruction oftener than his fellow. He is accordingly valued on this account, without much reference to other qualities.

CHAPTER II.

I HAVE NOT BEEN able to recur to the scenes which are now to become the subject of description, although a considerable time has elapsed, without feeling a mingled emotion of horror and astonishment at the almost incredible destiny that has preserved me and my surviving companions from a terrible death. Frequently, in my reflections on the subject, even after this lapse of time, I find myself shedding tears of gratitude for our deliverance, and blessing God, by whose divine aid and protection we were conducted through a series of unparalleled suffering and distress, and restored to the bosoms of our families and friends. There is no knowing what a stretch of pain and misery the human mind is capable of contemplating, when it is wrought upon by the anxieties of preservation; nor what pangs and weaknesses the body is able to endure, until they are visited upon it; and when at last deliverance comes, when the dream of hope is realized, unspeakable gratitude takes possession of the soul, and tears of joy choke the utterance. We require to be taught in the school of some signal suffering, privation, and despair, the great lessons of constant dependence upon an almighty forbearance and mercy. In the midst of the wide ocean, at night, when the sight of the heavens was shut out, and the dark tempest came upon us; then it was, that we felt ourselves ready to exclaim, "Heaven have mercy upon us, for nought but that can save us now." But I proceed to the recital.—On the 20th of November, (cruising in latitude 0° 40′ S. longitude 119° 0′ W.) a shoal of whales was discovered off the lee-bow. The weather at this time was extremely fine and clear, and it was about 8 o'clock in the morning, that the man at the mast-head gave the usual cry of, "there she blows." The ship was immediately put away, and we ran down in the direction for them. When we had got within half a mile of the place where they were observed, all our boats were lowered down, manned, and we started in pursuit of them. The ship, in the mean time, was brought to the wind, and the main-top-sail hove aback, to wait for us. I had the harpoon in the second boat; the captain preceded me in the first. When I arrived at the spot where we calculated they were, nothing was at first to be seen. We lay on our oars in anxious expectation of discovering them come up somewhere near us. Presently one rose, and spouted a short distance ahead of my boat; I made all speed towards it, came up with, and struck it; feeling the harpoon in him, he threw himself, in an agony, over towards the boat, (which at that time was up alongside of him,) and giving a severe blow with his tail, struck the boat near the edge of the water, amidships, and stove a hole in her. I immediately took up the boat hatchet, and cut the line, to disengage the boat from the whale, which by this time was running off with great velocity. I succeeded in getting clear of him, with the loss of the harpoon and line; and finding the water to pour fast in the boat, I hastily stuffed three or four of our jackets in the hole, ordered one man to keep constantly bailing, and the rest to pull immediately for the ship; we succeeded in keeping the boat free, and shortly gained the ship. The captain and the second mate, in the other two boats, kept up the pursuit, and soon struck another whale. They being at this time a considerable distance to leeward, I went forward, braced around the main-yard, and put the ship off in a direction for them; the boat which had been stove was immediately hoisted in, and after examining the hole, I found that I could, by nailing a piece of canvass over it, get her ready to join in a fresh pursuit, sooner than by lowering down the other remaining boat which belonged to the ship. I accordingly turned her over upon the quarter, and was in the act of nailing on the canvass, when I observed a very large spermaceti whale, as well as I could judge, about eighty-five feet in length; he broke water about twenty rods off our weather-bow, and was lying quietly, with his head in a direction for the ship. He spouted two or three times, and then disappeared. In less than two or three seconds he came up again, about the length of the ship off, and made directly for us, at the rate of about three knots. The ship was then going with about the same velocity. His appearance and attitude gave us at first no alarm; but while I stood watching his movements, and observing him but a ship's length off, coming down for us with great celerity, I involuntarily ordered the boy at the helm to put it hard up; intending to sheer off and avoid him. The words were scarcely out of my mouth, before he came down upon us with full speed, and struck the ship with his head, just forward of the fore-chains;[12] he gave us such an appalling and tremendous jar, as nearly threw us all on our faces. The ship brought up as suddenly and violently as if she had struck a rock, and trembled for a few seconds like a leaf. We looked at each other with perfect amazement, deprived almost of the power of speech. Many minutes elapsed before we were able to realize the dreadful accident; during which time he passed under the ship, grazing her keel as he went along, came up alongside of her to leeward, and lay on the top of the water, (apparently stunned with the violence of the blow,) for the space of a minute; he then suddenly started off, in a direction to leeward. After a few moments' reflection, and recovering, in some measure, from the sudden consternation that had seized us, I of course concluded that he had stove a hole in the ship, and that it would be necessary to set the pumps going. Accordingly they were rigged, but had not been in operation more than one minute, before I perceived the head of the ship to be gradually settling down in the water; I then ordered the signal to be set for the other boats, which, scarcely had I despatched, before I again discovered the whale, apparently in convulsions, on the top of the water, about one hundred rods to leeward. He was enveloped in the foam of the sea, that his continual and violent thrashing about in the water had created around him, and I could distinctly see him smite his jaws together, as if distracted with rage and fury. He remained a short time in this situation, and then started off with great velocity, across the bows of the ship, to windward. By this time the ship had settled down a considerable distance in the water, and I gave her up as lost. I however, ordered the pumps to be kept constantly going, and endeavoured to collect my thoughts for the occasion. I turned to the boats, two of which we then had with the ship, with an intention of clearing them away, and getting all things ready to embark in them, if there should be no other resource left; and while my attention was thus engaged for a moment, I was aroused with the cry of a man at the hatch-way, "here he is—he is making for us again." I turned around, and saw him about one hundred rods directly ahead of us, coming down apparently with twice his ordinary speed, and to me at that moment, it appeared with tenfold fury and vengeance in his aspect. The surf flew in all directions about him, and his course towards us was marked by a white foam of a rod in width, which he made with the

continual violent thrashing of his tail; his head was about half out of
water, and in that way he came upon, and again struck the ship. I
was in hopes when I descried him making for us, that by a dexterous movement of putting the ship away immediately, I should be
able to cross the line of his approach, before he could get up to us,
and thus avoid, what I knew, if he should strike us again, would
prove our inevitable destruction. I bawled out to the helmsman,
"hard up!" but she had not fallen off more than a point, before we
took the second shock. I should judge the speed of the ship to have
been at this time about three knots, and that of the whale about six.
He struck her to windward, directly under the cat-head,[13] and completely stove in her bows. He passed under the ship again, went off
to leeward, and we saw no more of him. Our situation at this juncture can be more readily imagined than described. The shock to our
feelings was such, as I am sure none can have an adequate conception of, that were not there: the misfortune befel us at a moment
when we least dreamt of any accident; and from the pleasing anticipations we had formed, of realizing the certain profits of our
labour, we were dejected by a sudden, most mysterious, and overwhelming calamity. Not a moment, however, was to be lost in endeavouring to provide for the extremity to which it was now certain
we were reduced. We were more than a thousand miles from the
nearest land, and with nothing but a light open boat, as the resource
of safety for myself and companions. I ordered the men to cease
pumping, and every one to provide for himself; seizing a hatchet at
the same time, I cut away the lashings of the spare boat, which lay
bottom up, across two spars directly over the quarter deck, and
cried out to those near me, to take her as she came down. They did
so accordingly, and bore her on their shoulders as far as the waist of
the ship.[14] The steward had in the mean time gone down into the
cabin twice, and saved two quadrants, two practical navigators, and
the captain's trunk and mine; all which were hastily thrown into the
boat, as she lay on the deck, with the two compasses which I
snatched from the binnacle. He attempted to descend again; but the
water by this time had rushed in, and he returned without being
able to effect his purpose. By the time we had got the boat to the
waist, the ship had filled with water, and was going down on her
beam-ends: we shoved our boat as quickly as possible from the
plank-shear[15] into the water, all hands jumping in her at the same

time, and launched off clear of the ship. We were scarcely two boat's lengths distant from her, when she fell over to windward, and settled down in the water.

Amazement and despair now wholly took possession of us. We contemplated the frightful situation the ship lay in, and thought with horror upon the sudden and dreadful calamity that had overtaken us. We looked upon each other, as if to gather some consolatory sensation from an interchange of sentiments, but every countenance was marked with the paleness of despair. Not a word was spoken for several minutes by any of us; all appeared to be bound in a spell of stupid consternation; and from the time we were first attacked by the whale, to the period of the fall of the ship, and of our leaving her in the boat, more than ten minutes could not certainly have elapsed! God only knows in what way, or by what means, we were enabled to accomplish in that short time what we did; the cutting away and transporting the boat from where she was deposited would of itself, in ordinary circumstances, have consumed as much time as that, if the whole ship's crew had been employed in it. My companions had not saved a single article but what they had on their backs; but to me it was a source of infinite satisfaction, if any such could be gathered from the horrors of our gloomy situation, that we had been fortunate enough to have preserved our compasses, navigators, and quadrants. After the first shock of my feelings was over, I enthusiastically contemplated them as the probable instruments of our salvation; without them all would have been dark and hopeless. Gracious God! what a picture of distress and suffering now presented itself to my imagination. The crew of the ship were saved, consisting of twenty human souls. All that remained to conduct these twenty beings through the stormy terrors of the ocean, perhaps many thousand miles, were three open light boats. The prospect of obtaining any provisions or water from the ship, to subsist upon during the time, was at least now doubtful. How many long and watchful nights, thought I, are to be passed? How many tedious days of partial starvation are to be endured, before the least relief or mitigation of our sufferings can be reasonably anticipated. We lay at this time in our boat, about two ship's lengths off from the wreck, in perfect silence, calmly contemplating her situation, and absorbed in our own melancholy reflections, when the other boats were discovered rowing up to us. They had but shortly before discovered that some accident had befallen us, but of the nature of which they were entirely ignorant. The sudden and mysterious disappearance of the ship was first discovered by the boat-steerer in the captain's boat, and with a horror-struck countenance and voice, he suddenly exclaimed, "Oh, my God! where is the ship?" Their operations upon this were instantly suspended, and a general cry of horror and despair burst from the lips of every man, as their looks were directed for her, in vain, over every part of the ocean. They immediately made all haste towards us. The captain's boat was the first that reached us. He stopped about a boat's length off, but had no power to utter a single syllable: he was so completely overpowered with the spectacle before him, that he sat down in his boat, pale and speechless. I could scarcely recognise his countenance, he appeared to be so much altered, awed, and overcome, with the oppression of his feelings, and the dreadful reality that lay before him. He was in a short time however enabled to address the inquiry to me, "My God, Mr. Chase, what is the matter?" I answered, "We have been stove by a whale." I then briefly told him the story. After a few moment's reflection he observed, that we must cut away her masts, and endeavour to get something out of her to eat. Our thoughts were now all accordingly bent on endeavours to save from the wreck whatever we might possibly want, and for this purpose we rowed up and got on to her. Search was made for every means of gaining access to her hold; and for this purpose the lanyards[16] were cut loose, and with our hatchets we commenced to cut away the masts, that she might right up again, and enable us to scuttle her decks. In doing which we were occupied about three quarters of an hour, owing to our having no axes, nor indeed any other instruments, but the small hatchets belonging to the boats. After her masts were gone she came up about two-thirds of the way upon an even keel. While we were employed about the masts the captain took his quadrant, shoved off from the ship, and got an observation. We found ourselves in latitude 0° 40′ S. longitude 119° W. We now commenced to cut a hole through the planks, directly above two large casks of bread, which most fortunately were between decks, in the waist of the ship, and which being in the upper side, when she upset, we had strong hopes was not wet. It turned out according to our wishes, and from these casks we obtained six hundred pounds of hard bread. Other parts of the deck

were then scuttled, and we got without difficulty as much fresh water as we dared to take in the boats, so that each was supplied with
about sixty-five gallons; we got also from one of the lockers a musket, a small canister of powder, a couple of files, two rasps, about
two pounds of boat nails, and a few turtle. In the afternoon the
wind came on to blow a strong breeze; and having obtained every
thing that occurred to us could then be got out, we began to make
arrangements for our safety during the night. A boat's line was
made fast to the ship, and to the other end of it one of the boats was
moored, at about fifty fathoms to leeward; another boat was then
attached to the first one, about eight fathoms astern; and the third
boat, the like distance astern of her. Night came on just as we had
finished our operations; and such a night as it was to us! so full of
feverish and distracting inquietude, that we were deprived entirely
of rest. The wreck was constantly before my eyes. I could not, by
any effort, chase away the horrors of the preceding day from my
mind: they haunted me the live-long night. My companions—some
of them were like sick women; they had no idea of the extent of
their deplorable situation. One or two slept unconcernedly, while
others wasted the night in unavailing murmurs. I now had full
leisure to examine, with some degree of coolness, the dreadful circumstances of our disaster. The scenes of yesterday passed in such
quick succession in my mind that it was not until after many hours
of severe reflection that I was able to discard the idea of the catastrophe as a dream. Alas! it was one from which there was no awaking; it was too certainly true, that but yesterday we had existed as it
were, and in one short moment had been cut off from all the hopes
and prospects of the living! I have no language to paint out the horrors of our situation. To shed tears was indeed altogether unavailing, and withal unmanly; yet I was not able to deny myself the relief
they served to afford me. After several hours of idle sorrow and re-
pining I began to reflect upon the accident, and endeavoured to realize by what unaccountable destiny or design, (which I could not
at first determine,) this sudden and most deadly attack had been
made upon us: by an animal, too, never before suspected of premed-
itated violence, and proverbial for its insensibility and inoffensive-
ness. Every fact seemed to warrant me in concluding that it was any
thing but chance which directed his operations; he made two several
attacks upon the ship, at a short interval between them, both of

which, according to their direction, were calculated to do us the most injury, by being made ahead, and thereby combining the speed of the two objects for the shock; to effect which, the exact manœuvres which he made were necessary. His aspect was most horrible, and such as indicated resentment and fury. He came directly from the shoal which we had just before entered, and in which we had struck three of his companions, as if fired with revenge for their sufferings. But to this it may be observed, that the mode of fighting which they always adopt is either with repeated strokes of their tails, or snapping of their jaws together; and that a case, precisely similar to this one, has never been heard of amongst the oldest and most experienced whalers. To this I would answer, that the structure and strength of the whale's head is admirably designed for this mode of attack; the most prominent part of which is almost as hard and as tough as iron; indeed, I can compare it to nothing else but the inside of a horse's hoof, upon which a lance or harpoon would not make the slightest impression. The eyes and ears are removed nearly one-third the length of the whole fish, from the front part of the head, and are not in the least degree endangered in this mode of attack. At all events, the whole circumstances taken together, all happening before my own eyes, and producing, at the time, impressions in my mind of decided, calculating mischief, on the part of the whale, (many of which impressions I cannot now recall,) induce me to be satisfied that I am correct in my opinion. It is certainly, in all its bearings, a hitherto unheard of circumstance, and constitutes, perhaps, the most extraordinary one in the annals of the fishery.

CHAPTER III.

NOVEMBER 21ST. THE MORNING dawned upon our wretched company. The weather was fine, but the wind blew a strong breeze from the SE. and the sea was very rugged. Watches had been kept up during the night, in our respective boats, to see that none of the spars or other articles (which continued to float out of the wreck,) should be thrown by the surf against, and injure the boats. At sunrise, we began to think of doing something; what, we did not know: we cast loose our boats, and visited the wreck, to see if any thing more of consequence could be preserved, but every thing looked cheerless and desolate, and we made a long and vain search for any useful article; nothing could be found but a few turtle; of these we had enough already; or at least, as many as could be safely stowed in the boats, and we wandered around in every part of the ship in a sort of vacant idleness for the greater part of the morning. We were presently aroused to a perfect sense of our destitute and forlorn condition, by thoughts of the means which we had for our subsistence, the necessity of not wasting our time, and of endeavouring to seek some relief wherever God might direct us. Our thoughts, indeed, hung about the ship, wrecked and sunken as she was, and we could scarcely discard from our minds the idea of her continuing protection. Some great efforts in our situation were necessary, and a great deal of calculation important, as it concerned the means by which our existence was to be supported during, perhaps, a very long period, and a provision for our eventual deliverance. Accordingly, by agreement, all set to work in stripping off the light sails of the ship, for sails to our boats;[17] and the day was consumed in making them up and fitting them. We furnished ourselves with masts and other light spars that were necessary, from the wreck. Each boat was rigged with two masts, to carry a flying-jib, and two sprit-sails; the sprit-sails were made so that two reefs could be taken in them, in case of heavy blows. We continued to watch the wreck for any serviceable articles that might float from her, and kept one man dur-

ing the day, on the stump of her foremast, on the look out for vessels. Our work was very much impeded by the increase of the wind
and sea, and the surf breaking almost continually into the boats,
gave us many fears that we should not be able to prevent our provisions from getting wet; and above all served to increase the constant
apprehensions that we had, of the insufficiency of the boats themselves, during the rough weather that we should necessarily experience. In order to provide as much as possible against this, and
withal to strengthen the slight materials of which the boats were
constructed, we procured from the wreck some light cedar boards,
(intended to repair boats in cases of accidents,) with which we built
up additional sides, about six inches above the gunwale; these, we
afterwards found, were of infinite service for the purpose for which
they were intended; in truth, I am satisfied we could never have
been preserved without them; the boats must otherwise have taken
in so much water that all the efforts of twenty such weak, starving
men as we afterwards came to be, would not have sufficed to keep
her free; but what appeared most immediately to concern us, and to
command all our anxieties, was the security of our provisions from
the salt water. We disposed of them under a covering of wood, that
whale-boats have at either end of them, wrapping it up in several
thicknesses of canvass. I got an observation to-day, by which I
found we were in latitude 0° 6′ S. longitude 119° 30′ W. having been
driven by the winds a distance of forty-nine miles the last twenty-
four hours; by this it would appear that there must have been a
strong current, setting us to the NW. during the whole time. We
were not able to finish our sails in one day; and many little things
preparatory to taking a final leave of the ship were necessary to be
attended to, but evening came and put an end to our labours. We
made the same arrangements for mooring the boats in safety, and
consigned ourselves to the horrors of another tempestuous night.
The wind continued to blow hard, keeping up a heavy sea, and
veering around from SE. to E. and E.SE. As the gloom of night approached, and obliged us to desist from that employment, which
cheated us out of some of the realities of our situation, we all of us
again became mute and desponding: a considerable degree of
alacrity had been manifested by many the preceding day, as their attention had been wholly engaged in scrutinizing the wreck, and in
constructing the sails and spars for the boats; but when they ceased

to be occupied, they passed to a sudden fit of melancholy, and the miseries of their situation came upon them with such force, as to produce spells of extreme debility, approaching almost to fainting. Our provisions were scarcely touched—the appetite was entirely gone; but as we had a great abundance of water, we indulged in frequent and copious draughts, which our parched mouths seemed continually to need. None asked for bread. Our continued state of anxiety during the night, excluded all hopes of sleep; still, (although the solemn fact had been before me for nearly two days,) my mind manifested the utmost repugnance to be reconciled to it; I laid down in the bottom of the boat, and resigned myself to reflection; my silent prayers were offered up to the God of mercy, for that protection which we stood so much in need of. Sometimes, indeed, a light hope would dawn, but then, to feel such an utter dependence on and consignment to chance alone for aid and rescue, would chase it again from my mind. The wreck—the mysterious and mortal attack of the animal—the sudden prostration and sinking of the vessel—our escape from her, and our then forlorn and almost hapless destiny, all passed in quick and perplexing review in my imagination; wearied with the exertion of the body and mind, I caught, near morning, an hour's respite from my troubles, in sleep.

November 22d. The wind remained the same, and the weather continued remarkably fine. At sunrise, we again hauled our boats up, and continued our search for articles that might float out. About 7 o'clock, the deck of the wreck began to give way, and every appearance indicated her speedy dissolution; the oil had bilged in the hold, and kept the surface of the sea all around us completely covered with it; the bulk-heads were all washed down, and she worked in every part of her joints and seams, with the violent and continual breaking of the surf over her. Seeing, at last, that little or nothing further could be done by remaining with the wreck, and as it was all important that while our provisions lasted, we should make the best possible use of time, I rowed up to the captain's boat, and asked him what he intended to do. I informed him that the ship's decks had bursted up, and that in all probability she would soon go to pieces; that no further purpose could be answered, by remaining longer with her, since nothing more could be obtained from her; and that it was my opinion, no time should be lost in making the best of our way towards the nearest land. The captain observed, that he would go once more to the wreck, and survey her, and after waiting until 12 o'clock for the purpose of getting an observation, would immediately after determine. In the mean time, before noon all our sails were completed, and the boats otherwise got in readiness for our departure. Our observation now proved us to be in latitude 0° 13′ N. longitude 120° 00′ W. as near as we could determine it, having crossed the equator during the night, and drifted nineteen miles. The wind had veered considerably to the eastward, during the last twenty-four hours. Our nautical calculations having been completed, the captain, after visiting the wreck, called a council, consisting of himself and the first and second mates, who all repaired to his boat, to interchange opinions, and devise the best means for our security and preservation. There were, in all of us, twenty men; six of whom were blacks, and we had three boats. We examined our navigators, to ascertain the nearest land, and found it was the Marquesas Islands. The Society Islands were next; these islands we were entirely ignorant of; if inhabited, we presumed they were by savages, from whom we had as much to fear, as from the elements, or even death itself. We had no charts from which our calculations might be aided, and were consequently obliged to govern ourselves by the navigators alone; it was also the captain's opinion, that this was the season of the hurricanes which prevail in the vicinity of the Sandwich Islands;[18] and that consequently it would be unsafe to steer for them. The issue of our deliberations was, that, taking all things into consideration, it would be most advisable to shape our course by the wind, to the southward, as far as 25° or 26° S. latitude, fall in with the variable winds, and then, endeavour to get eastward to the coast of Chili or Peru. Accordingly, preparations were made for our immediate departure; the boat which it was my fortune, or rather misfortune to have, was the worst of the three; she was old and patched up, having been stove a number of times, during the cruise. At best, a whale-boat is an extremely frail thing; the most so of any other kind of boat; they are what is called clinker built,[19] and constructed of the lightest materials, for the purpose of being rowed with the greatest possible celerity, according to the necessities of the business for which they are intended. Of all species of vessels, they are the weakest, and most fragile, and possess but one advantage over any other—that of lightness and buoyancy, that enables them to keep above the dash of the

sea, with more facility than heavier ones. This qualification is, however, preferable to that of any other, and, situated as we then were, I
would not have exchanged her, old and crazy as she was, for even a
ship's launch. I am quite confident, that to this quality of our boats
we most especially owed our preservation, through the many days
and nights of heavy weather, that we afterwards encountered. In
consideration of my having the weakest boat, six men were allotted
to it; while those of the captain and second mate, took seven each,
and at half past 12 we left the wreck, steering our course, with
nearly all sail set, S.SE. At four o'clock in the afternoon we lost
sight of her entirely. Many were the lingering and sorrowful looks
we cast behind us.

It has appeared to me often since to have been, in the abstract, an
extreme weakness and folly, on our parts, to have looked upon our
shattered and sunken vessel with such an excessive fondness and regret; but it seemed as if in abandoning her we had parted with all
hope, and were bending our course away from her, rather by some
dictate of despair. We agreed to keep together, in our boats, as
nearly as possible, to afford assistance in cases of accident, and to
render our reflections less melancholy by each other's presence. I
found it on this occasion true, that misery does indeed love company; unaided, and unencouraged by each other, there were with us
many whose weak minds, I am confident, would have sunk under
the dismal retrospections of the past catastrophe, and who did not
possess either sense or firmness enough to contemplate our approaching destiny, without the cheering of some more determined
countenance than their own. The wind was strong all day; and the
sea ran very high, our boat taking in water from her leaks continually, so that we were obliged to keep one man constantly bailing.
During the night the weather became extremely rugged, and the sea
every now and then broke over us. By agreement, we were divided
into two watches; one of which was to be constantly awake, and
doing the labours of the boat, such as bailing; setting, taking in, and
trimming the sails. We kept our course very well together during
this night, and had many opportunities of conversation with the
men in the other boats, wherein the means and prospects of our deliverance were variously considered; it appeared from the opinions
of all, that we had most to hope for in the meeting with some vessel,
and most probably some whale ship, the great majority of whom, in

those seas, we imagined were cruising about the latitude we were then steering for; but this was only a hope, the realization of which did not in any degree depend on our own exertions, but on chance alone. It was not, therefore, considered prudent, by going out of our course, with the prospect of meeting them, to lose sight, for one moment, of the strong probabilities which, under Divine Providence, there were of our reaching land by the route we had prescribed to ourselves; as that depended, most especially, on a reasonable calculation, and on our own labours, we conceived that our provision and water, on a small allowance, would last us sixty days; that with the trade-wind, on the course we were then lying, we should be able to average the distance of a degree a day, which, in 26 days, would enable us to attain the region of the variable winds, and then, in thirty more, at the very utmost, should there be any favour in the elements, we might reach the coast. With these considerations we commenced our voyage; the total failure of all which, and the subsequent dismal distress and suffering, by which we were overtaken, will be shown in the sequel. Our allowance of provision at first consisted of bread; one biscuit, weighing about one pound three ounces, and half a pint of water a day, for each man. This small quantity, (less than one third which is required by an ordinary person,) small as it was, we however took without murmuring, and, on many an occasion afterwards, blest God that even this pittance was allowed to us in our misery. The darkness of another night overtook us; and after having for the first time partook of our allowance of bread and water, we laid our weary bodies down in the boat, and endeavoured to get some repose. Nature became at last worn out with the watchings and anxieties of the two preceding nights, and sleep came insensibly upon us. No dreams could break the strong fastenings of forgetfulness in which the mind was then locked up; but for my own part, my thoughts so haunted me that this luxury was yet a stranger to my eyes; every recollection was still fresh before me, and I enjoyed but a few short and unsatisfactory slumbers, caught in the intervals between my hopes and my fears. The dark ocean and swelling waters were nothing; the fears of being swallowed up by some dreadful tempest, or dashed upon hidden rocks, with all the other ordinary subjects of fearful contemplation, seemed scarcely entitled to a moment's thought; the dismal looking wreck, and the horrid aspect and revenge of the whale, wholly engrossed my reflections, until day again made its appearance.

November 23d. In my chest, which I was fortunate enough to preserve, I had several small articles, which we found of great service to us; among the rest, some eight or ten sheets of writing paper, a lead pencil, a suit of clothes, three small fish hooks, a jack-knife, a whetstone, and a cake of soap. I commenced to keep a sort of journal with the little paper and pencil which I had; and the knife, besides other useful purposes, served us as a razor. It was with much difficulty, however, that I could keep any sort of record, owing to the incessant rocking and unsteadiness of the boat, and the continual dashing of the spray of the sea over us. The boat contained, in addition to the articles enumerated, a lantern, tinder-box, and two or three candles, which belonged to her, and with which they are kept always supplied, while engaged in taking whale. In addition to all which, the captain had saved a musket, two pistols, and a canister, containing about two pounds of gunpowder; the latter he distributed in equal proportions between the three boats, and gave the second mate and myself each a pistol. When morning came we found ourselves quite near together, and the wind had considerably increased since the day before; we were consequently obliged to reef our sails; and although we did not apprehend any very great danger from the then violence of the wind, yet it grew to be very uncomfortable in the boats, from the repeated dashing of the waves, that kept our bodies constantly wet with the salt spray. We, however, stood along our course until twelve o'clock, when we got an observation, as well as we were able to obtain one, while the water flew all over us, and the sea kept the boat extremely unsteady. We found ourselves this day in latitude 0° 58′ S. having repassed the equator. We abandoned the idea altogether of keeping any correct longitudinal reckoning, having no glass, nor log-line.[20] The wind moderated in the course of the afternoon a little, but at night came on to blow again almost a gale. We began now to tremble for our little barque; she was so ill calculated, in point of strength, to withstand the racking of the sea, while it required the constant labours of one man to keep her free of water. We were surrounded in the afternoon with porpoises that kept playing about us in great numbers, and continued to follow us during the night.

November 24th. The wind had not abated any since the preced-

ing day, and the sea had risen to be very large, and increased, if possible, the extreme uncomfortableness of our situation. What added
more than any thing else to our misfortunes, was, that all our efforts
for the preservation of our provisions proved, in a great measure,
ineffectual; a heavy sea broke suddenly into the boat, and, before
we could snatch it up, damaged some part of it; by timely attention,
however, and great caution, we managed to make it eatable, and to
preserve the rest from a similar casualty. This was a subject of extreme anxiety to us; the expectation, poor enough of itself indeed,
upon which our final rescue was founded, must change at once to
utter hopelessness, deprived of our provisions, the only means of
continuing us in the exercise, not only of our manual powers, but in
those of reason itself; hence, above all other things, this was the object of our utmost solicitude and pains.

We ascertained, the next day, that some of the provisions in the
captain's boat had shared a similar fate during the night; both which
accidents served to arouse us to a still stronger sense of our slender
reliance upon the human means at our command, and to show us
our utter dependence on that divine aid which we so much the more
stood in need of.

November 25th. No change of wind had yet taken place, and we
experienced the last night the same wet and disagreeable weather of
the preceding one. About eight o'clock in the morning we discovered that the water began to come fast in our boat, and in a few
minutes the quantity increased to such a degree as to alarm us considerably for our safety; we commenced immediately a strict search
in every part of her to discover the leak, and, after tearing up the
ceiling or floor of the boat near the bows, we found it proceeded
from one of the streaks or outside boards having bursted off there;
no time was to be lost in devising some means to repair it. The great
difficulty consisted in its being in the bottom of the boat, about six
inches from the surface of the water; it was necessary, therefore, to
have access to the outside, to enable us to fasten it on again: the leak
being to leeward, we hove about, and lay to on the other tack,
which brought it then nearly out of water; the captain, who was at
the time ahead of us, seeing us manœuvring to get the boat about,
shortened sail, and presently tacked, and ran down to us. I informed him of our situation, and he came immediately alongside to
our assistance. After directing all the men in the boat to get on one

side, the other, by that means, heeled out of the water a considerable distance, and, with a little difficulty, we then managed to drive in a few nails, and secured it, much beyond our expectations. Fears of no ordinary kind were excited by this seemingly small accident. When it is recollected to what a slight vessel we had committed ourselves; our means of safety alone consisting in her capacity and endurance[21] for many weeks, in all probability, yet to come, it will not be considered strange that this little accident should not only have damped our spirits considerably, but have thrown a great gloominess over the natural prospects of our deliverance. On this occasion, too, were we enabled to rescue ourselves from inevitable destruction by the possession of a few nails, without which, (had it not been our fortune to save some from the wreck,) we would, in all human calculation, have been lost: we were still liable to a recurrence of the same accident, perhaps to a still worse one, as, in the heavy and repeated racking of the swell, the progress of our voyage would serve but to increase the incapacity and weakness of our boat, and the starting of a single nail in her bottom would most assuredly prove our certain destruction. We wanted not this additional reflection, to add to the miseries of our situation.

November 26th. Our sufferings, heaven knows, were now sufficiently increased, and we looked forward, not without an extreme dread, and anxiety, to the gloomy and disheartening prospect before us. We experienced a little abatement of wind and rough weather to-day, and took the opportunity of drying the bread that had been wet the day previously; to our great joy and sati[s]faction also, the wind hauled out to E.NE. and enabled us to hold a much more favourable course; with these exceptions, no circumstance of any considerable interest occurred in the course of this day.

The 27th of November was alike undistinguished for any incident worthy of note; except that the wind again veered back to E. and destroyed the fine prospect we had entertained, of making a good run for several days to come.

November 28th. The wind hauled still further to the southward, and obliged us to fall off our course to S. and commenced to blow with such violence, as to put us again under short sail; the night set in extremely dark, and tempestuous, and we began to entertain fears that we should be separated. We however, with great pains, managed to keep about a ship's length apart, so that the white sails of our boats could be distinctly discernable. The captain's boat was but a short distance astern of mine, and that of the second mate a few rods to leeward of his. At about 11 o'clock at night, having laid down to sleep, in the bottom of the boat, I was suddenly awakened by one of my companions, who cried out, that the captain was in distress, and was calling on us for assistance. I immediately aroused myself, and listened a moment, to hear if any thing further should be said, when the captain's loud voice arrested my attention. He was calling to the second mate, whose boat was nearer to him than mine. I made all haste to put about, ran down to him, and inquired what was the matter; he replied, "I have been attacked by an unknown fish, and he has stove my boat." It appeared, that some large fish had accompanied the boat for a short distance, and had suddenly made an unprovoked attack upon her, as nearly as they could determine, with his jaws; the extreme darkness of the night prevented them from distinguishing what kind of animal it was, but they judged it to be about twelve feet in length, and one of the killer-fish species.[22] After having struck the boat once, he continued to play about her, on every side, as if manifesting a disposition to renew the attack, and did a second time strike the bows of the boat, and split her stem. They had no other instrument of offence, but the sprit-pole, (a long slender piece of wood, by which the peak of the sail is extended,) with which, after repeated attempts to destroy the boat, they succeeded in beating him off. I arrived, just as he had discontinued his operations, and disappeared. He had made a considerable breach in the bows of the boat, through which the water had began to pour fast; and the captain, imagining matters to be considerably worse than they were, immediately took measures to remove his provisions into the second mate's boat and mine, in order to lighten his own, and by that means, and constant bailing, to keep her above water until daylight should enable him to discover the extent of the damage, and to repair it. The night was spissy[23] darkness itself; the sky was completely overcast, and it seemed to us as if fate was wholly relentless, in pursuing us with such a cruel complication of disasters. We were not without our fears that the fish might renew his attack, some time during the night, upon one of the other boats, and unexpectedly destroy us; but they proved entirely groundless, as he was never afterwards seen. When daylight came, the wind again favoured us a little, and we all lay to, to repair the broken boat; which was effected by nailing on thin strips of boards in the inside; and having replaced the provisions, we proceeded again on our course. Our allowance of water, which in the commencement, merely served to administer to the positive demands of nature, became now to be insufficient; and we began to experience violent thirst, from the consumption of the provisions that had been wet with the salt water, and dried in the sun; of these we were obliged to eat first, to prevent their spoiling; and we could not, nay, we did not dare, to make any encroachments on our stock of water. Our determination was, to suffer as long as human patience and endurance would hold out, having only in view, the relief that would be afforded us, when the quantity of wet provisions should be exhausted. Our extreme sufferings here first commenced. The privation of water is justly ranked among the most dreadful of the miseries of our life; the violence of raving thirst has no parallel in the catalogue of human calamities. It was our hard lot, to have felt this in its extremest force, when nececessity subsequently compelled us to seek resource from one of the offices of nature.[24] We were not, at first, aware of the consequences of eating this bread; and it was not until the fatal effects of it had shown themselves to a degree of oppression, that we could divine the cause of our extreme thirst. But, alas! there was no relief. Ignorant, or instructed of the fact, it was alike immaterial; it composed a part of our subsistence, and reason imposed upon us the necessity of its immediate consumption, as otherwise it would have been lost to us entirely.

November 29th. Our boats appeared to be growing daily more frail and insufficient; the continual flowing of the water into them, seemed increased, without our being able to assign it to any thing else, than a general weakness, arising from causes that must in a short time, without some remedy or relief, produce their total failure. We did not neglect, however, to patch up and mend them, according to our means, whenever we could discover a broken or weak part. We this day found ourselves surrounded by a shoal of dolphins; some, or one of which, we tried in vain a long time to take. We made a small line from some rigging that was in the boat, fastened on one of the fish-hooks, and tied to it a small piece of white rag; they took not the least notice of it, but continued playing around us, nearly all day, mocking both our miseries and our efforts.

November 30th. This was a remarkably fine day; the weather not exceeded by any that we had experienced since we left the wreck. At one o'clock, I proposed to our boat's crew to kill one of the turtle; two of which we had in our possession. I need not say, that the proposition was hailed with the utmost enthusiasm; hunger had set its ravenous gnawings upon our stomachs, and we waited with impatience to suck the warm flowing blood of the animal. A small fire was kindled in the shell of the turtle, and after dividing the blood, (of which there was about a gill,) among those of us who felt disposed to drink it, we cooked the remainder, entrails and all, and enjoyed from it an unspeakably fine repast. The stomachs of two or three revolted at the sight of the blood, and refused to partake of it; not even the outrageous thirst that was upon them could induce them to taste it; for myself, I took it like a medicine, to relieve the extreme dryness of my palate, and stopped not to inquire whether it was any thing else than a liquid. After this, I may say exquisite banquet, our bodies were considerably recruited, and I felt my spirits now much higher than they had been at any time before. By observation, this day we found ourselves in latitude 7° 53′ S. our distance from the wreck, as nearly as we could calculate, was then about four hundred and eighty miles.

December 1st. From the 1st to the 3d of December, exclusive, there was nothing transpired of any moment. Our boats as yet kept admirably well together, and the weather was distinguished for its mildness and salubrity. We gathered consolation too from a favourable slant which the wind took to NE. and our situation was not at that moment, we thought, so comfortless as we had been led at first to consider it; but, in our extravagant felicitations upon the blessing of the wind and weather, we forgot our leaks, our weak boats, our own debility, our immense distance from land, the smallness of our stock of provisions; all which, when brought to mind, with the force which they deserved, were too well calculated to dishearten us, and cause us to sigh for the hardships of our lot. Up to the 3d of December, the raging thirst of our mouths had not been but in a small degree alleviated; had it not been for the pains which that gave us, we should have tasted, during this spell of fine weather, a species of enjoyment, derived from a momentary forgetfulness of our actual situation.

December 3d. With great joy we hailed the last crumb of our

damaged bread, and commenced this day to take our allowance of
healthy provisions. The salutary and agreeable effects of this change
were felt at first in so slight a degree, as to give us no great cause of
comfort or satisfaction; but gradually, as we partook of our small allowance of water, the moisture began to collect in our mouths, and
the parching fever of the palate imperceptibly left it. An accident
here happened to us which gave us a great momentary spell of uneasiness. The night was dark, and the sky was completely overcast,
so that we could scarcely discern each other's boats, when at about
ten o'clock, that of the second mate was suddenly missing. I felt for
a moment considerable alarm at her unexpected disappearance; but
after a little reflection I immediately hove to, struck a light as expe-
ditiously as possible, and hoisted it at the mast-head, in a lantern.
Our eyes were now directed over every part of the ocean, in search
of her, when, to our great joy, we discerned an answering light,
about a quarter of a mile to leeward of us; we ran down to it, and it
proved to be the lost boat. Strange as the extraordinary interest
which we felt in each other's company may appear, and much as our
repugnance to separation may seem to imply of weakness, it was the
subject of our continual hopes and fears. It is truly remarked, that
misfortune more than any thing else serves to endear us to our companions. So strongly was this sentiment engrafted upon our feelings, and so closely were the destinies of all of us involuntarily
linked together, that, had one of the boats been wrecked, and
wholly lost, with all her provisions and water, we should have felt
ourselves constrained, by every tie of humanity, to have taken the
surviving sufferers into the other boats, and shared our bread and
water with them, while a crumb of one or a drop of the other remained. Hard, indeed, would the case have been for all, and much
as I have since reflected on the subject, I have not been able to realize, had it so happened, that a sense of our necessities would have
allowed us to give so magnanimous and devoted a character to our
feelings. I can only speak of the impressions which I recollect I had
at the time. Subsequently, however, as our situation became more
straightened and desperate, our conversation on this subject took a
different turn; and it appeared to be an universal sentiment, that
such a course of conduct was calculated to weaken the chances of a
final deliverance for some, and might be the only means of consign-
ing every soul of us to a horrid death of starvation. There is no

question but that an immediate separation, therefore, was the most politic measure that could be adopted, and that every boat should take its own separate chance: while we remained together, should any accident happen, of the nature alluded to, no other course could be adopted, than that of taking the survivers into the other boats, and giving up voluntarily, what we were satisfied could alone prolong our hopes, and multiply the chances of our safety, or unconcernedly witness their struggles in death, perhaps beat them from our boats, with weapons, back into the ocean. The expectation of reaching the land was founded upon a reasonable calculation of the distance, the means, and the subsistence; all which were scanty enough, God knows, and ill adapted to the probable exigences of the voyage. Any addition to our own demands, in this respect, would not only injure, but actually destroy the whole system which we had laid down, and reduce us to a slight hope, derived either from the speedy death of some of our crew, or the falling in with some vesel. With all this, however, there was a desperate instinct that bound us together; we could not reason on the subject with any degree of satisfaction to our minds, yet we continued to cling to each other with a strong and involuntary impulse. This, indeed, was a matter of no small difficulty, and it constituted, more than any thing else, a source of continual watching and inquietude. We would but turn our eyes away for a few moments, during some dark nights, and presently, one of the boats would be missing. There was no other remedy than to heave to immediately and set a light, by which the missing boat might be directed to us. These proceedings necessarily interfered very much with our speed, and consequently lessened our hopes; but we preferred to submit to it, while the consequences were not so immediately felt, rather than part with the consolation which each other's presence afforded. Nothing of importance took place on the 4th of December; and on the 5th, at night, owing to the extreme darkness, and a strong wind, I again separated from the other boats. Finding they were not to be seen in any direction, I loaded my pistol and fired it twice; soon after the second discharge they made their appearance a short distance to windward, and we joined company, and again kept on our course, in which we continued without any remarkable occurrence, through the 6th and 7th of December. The wind during this period blew very strong, and much more unfavourably. Our boats continued to leak, and to take in a good deal of water over the gunwales.

December 8th. In the afternoon of this day the wind set in E.SE. and began to blow much harder than we had yet experienced it; by twelve o'clock at night it had increased to a perfect gale, with heavy showers of rain, and we now began, from these dreadful indications, to prepare ourselves for destruction. We continued to take in sail by degrees, as the tempest gradually increased, until at last we were obliged to take down our masts. At this juncture we gave up entirely to the mercy of the waves. The sea and rain had wet us to the skin, and we sat down, silently, and with sullen resignation, awaiting our fate. We made an effort to catch some fresh water by spreading one of the sails, but after having spent a long time, and obtained but a small quantity in a bucket, it proved to be quite as salt as that from the ocean: this we attributed to its having passed through the sail which had been so often wet by the sea, and upon which, after drying so frequently in the sun, concretions of salt had been formed. It was a dreadful night—cut off from any imaginary relief—nothing remained but to await the approaching issue with firmness and resignation. The appearance of the heavens was dark and dreary, and the blackness that was spread over the face of the waters dismal beyond description. The heavy squalls, that followed each other in quick succession, were preceded by sharp flashes of lightning, that appeared to wrap our little barge in flames. The sea rose to a fearful height, and every wave that came looked as if it must be the last that would be necessary for our destruction. To an overruling Providence alone must be attributed our salvation from the horrors of that terrible night. It can be accounted for in no other way: that a speck of substance, like that which we were, before the driving terrors of the tempest, could have been conducted safely through it. At twelve o'clock it began to abate a little in intervals of two or three minutes, during which we would venture to raise up our heads and look to windward. Our boat was completely unmanageable; without sails, mast, or rudder, and had been driven, in the course of the afternoon and night, we knew not whither, nor how far. When the gale had in some measure subsided we made efforts to get a little sail upon her, and put her head towards the course we had been steering. My companions had not slept any during the whole night, and were dispirited and broken down to such a degree as to appear to want some more powerful stimulus than the fears of death to enable them to do their duty. By great exertions, however, towards morning we again set a double-reefed mainsail and jib upon her, and began to make tolerable progress on the voyage. An unaccountable good fortune had kept the boats together during all the troubles of the night: and the sun rose and showed the disconsolate faces of our companions once more to each other.

December 9th. By twelve o'clock this day we were enabled to set all sail as usual; but there continued to be a very heavy sea running, which opened the seams of the boats, and increased the leaks to an alarming degree. There was, however, no remedy for this but continual bailing, which had now become to be an extremely irksome and laborious task. By observation we found ourselves in latitude 17° 40′ S. At eleven o'clock at night, the captain's boat was unexpect[ed]ly found to be missing. After the last accident of this kind we had agreed, if the same should again occur, that, in order to save our time, the other boats should not heave to, as usual, but continue on their course until morning, and thereby save the great detention that must arise from such repeated delays. We, however, concluded on this occasion to make a small effort, which, if it did not immediately prove the means of restoring the lost boat, we would discontinue, and again make sail. Accordingly we hove to for an hour, during which time I fired my pistol twice, and obtaining no tidings of the boat, we stood on our course. When daylight appeared she was to leeward of us, about two miles; upon observing her we immediately ran down, and again joined company.

December 10th. I have omitted to notice the gradual advances which hunger and thirst, for the last six days, had made upon us. As the time had lengthened since our departure from the wreck, and the allowance of provision, making the demands of the appetite daily more and more importunate, they had created in us an almost uncontrollable temptation to violate our resolution, and satisfy, for once, the hard yearnings of nature from our stock; but a little reflection served to convince us of the imprudence and unmanliness of the measure, and it was abandoned with a sort of melancholy effort of satisfaction. I had taken into custody, by common consent, all the provisions and water belonging to the boat, and was determined that no encroachments should be made upon it with my consent; nay, I felt myself bound, by every consideration of duty, by every dictate of sense, of prudence, and discretion, without which, in my situation, all other exertions would have been folly itself, to protect them, at the hazard of my life. For this purpose I locked up in my chest the whole quantity, and never, for a single moment, closed my eyes without placing some part of my person in contact with the chest; and having loaded my pistol, kept it constantly about me. I should not certainly have put any threats in execution as long as the most distant hopes of reconciliation existed; and was determined, in case the least refractory disposition should be manifested, (a thing which I contemplated not unlikely to happen, with a set of starving wretches like ourselves,) that I would immediately divide our subsistence into equal proportions, and give each man's share into his own keeping. Then, should any attempt be made upon mine, which I intended to mete out to myself, according to exigences, I was resolved to make the consequences of it fatal. There was, however, the most upright and obedient behaviour in this respect manifested by every man in the boat, and I never had the least opportunity of proving what my conduct would have been on such an occasion. While standing on our course this day we came across a small shoal of flying fish: four of which, in their efforts to avoid us, flew against the mainsail, and dropped into the boat; one, having fell near me, I eagerly snatched up and devoured; the other three were immediately taken by the rest, and eaten alive. For the first time I, on this occasion, felt a disposition to laugh, upon witnessing the ludicrous and almost desperate efforts of my five companions, who each sought to get a fish. They were very small of the kind, and constituted but an extremely delicate mouthful, scales, wings, and all, for hungry stomachs like ours. From the eleventh to the thirteenth of December inclusive, our progress was very slow, owing to light winds and calms; and nothing transpired of any moment, except that on the eleventh we killed the only remaining turtle, and enjoyed another luxuriant repast, that invigorated our bodies, and gave a fresh flow to our spirits. The weather was extremely hot, and we were exposed to the full force of a meridian sun, without any covering to shield us from its burning influence, or the least breath of air to cool its parching rays. On the thirteenth day of December we were blessed with a change of wind to the northward, that brought us a most welcome and unlooked for relief. We now, for the first time, actually felt what might be deemed a reasonable hope of our deliverance; and with hearts bounding with satisfaction, and bosoms swelling with joy, we made all sail to the eastward. We imagined we had run out of the trade-winds, and had got into the variables, and should, in all probability, reach the land many days sooner than we expected. But, alas! our anticipations were but a dream, from which we shortly experienced a cruel awaking. The wind gradually died away, and at night was succeeded by a perfect calm, more oppressive and disheartening to us, from the bright prospects which had attended us during the day. The gloomy reflections that this hard fortune had given birth to, were succeeded by others, of a no less cruel and discouraging nature, when we found the calm continue during the fourteenth, fifteenth, and sixteenth of December inclusive. The extreme oppression of the weather, the sudden and unexpected prostration of our hopes, and the consequent dejection of our spirits, set us again to thinking, and filled our souls with fearful and melancholy forebodings. In this state of affairs, seeing no alternative left us but to employ to the best advantage all human expedients in our power, I proposed, on the fourteenth, to reduce our allowance of provisions one half. No objections were made to this arrangement: all submitted, or seemed to do so, with an admirable fortitude and forbearance. The proportion which our stock of water bore to our bread was not large; and while the weather continued so oppressive, we did not think it adviseable to diminish our scanty pittance; indeed, it would have been scarcely possible to have done so, with any regard to our necessities, as our thirst had become now incessantly more intolerable than hunger, and the quantity then allowed was barely sufficient to keep the mouth in a state of moisture, for about one-third of the time. "Patience and long-suffering" was the constant language of our lips: and a determination, strong as the resolves of the soul could make it, to cling to existence as long as hope and breath remained to us. In vain was every expedient tried to relieve the raging fever of the throat by drinking salt water, and holding small quantities of it in the mouth, until, by that means, the thirst was increased to such a degree, as even to drive us to despairing, and vain relief from our own urine. Our sufferings during these calm days almost exceeded human belief. The hot rays of the sun beat down upon us to such a degree, as to oblige us to hang over the gunwale of the boat, into the sea, to cool our weak and fainting bodies. This expedient afforded us, however, a grateful relief, and was productive of a discovery of infinite importance to us. No sooner had one of us got on the outside of the gunwale than he immediately observed the bottom of the boat to be covered with a species of small clam, which, upon being tasted, proved a most delicious and agreeable food. This was no sooner announced to us, than we commenced to tear them off and eat them, for a few minutes, like a set of gluttons; and, after having satisfied the immediate craving of the stomach, we gathered large quantities and laid them up in the boat; but hunger came upon us again in less than half an hour afterwards, within which time they had all disappeared. Upon attempting to get in again, we found ourselves so weak as to require each other's assistance; indeed, had it not been for three of our crew, who could not swim, and who did not, therefore, get overboard, I know not by what means we should have been able to have resumed our situations in the boat.

On the fifteenth our boat continued to take in water so fast from her leaks, and the weather proving so moderate, we concluded to search out the bad places, and endeavour to mend them as well as we should be able. After a considerable search, and, removing the ceiling near the bows, we found the principal opening was occasioned by the starting of a plank or streak in the bottom of the boat, next to the keel. To remedy this, it was now absolutely necessary to have access to the bottom. The means of doing which did not immediately occur to our minds. After a moment's reflection, however, one of the crew, Benjamin Lawrence, offered to tie a rope around his body, take a boat's hatchet in his hand, and thus go under the water, and hold the hatchet against a nail, to be driven through from the inside, for the purpose of clenching it. This was, accordingly, all effected, with some little trouble, and answered the purpose much beyond our expectations. Our latitude was this day 21° 42' South. The oppression of the weather still continuing through the sixteenth, bore upon our health and spirits with an amazing force and severity. The most disagreeable excitements were produced by it, which, added to the disconsolate endurance of the calm, called loudly for some mitigating expedient,—some sort of relief to our prolonged sufferings. By our observations to day we found, in addition to our other calamities, that we had been urged back from our progress, by the heave of the sea, a distance of ten miles; and were still without any prospect of wind. In this distressing posture of our affairs, the captain proposed that we should commence rowing, which, being seconded by all, we immediately concluded to take a double allowance of provision and water for the day, and row, during the cool of the nights, until we should get a breeze from some quarter or other. Accordingly, when night came, we commenced our laborious operations: we made but a very sorry progress. Hunger and thirst, and long inactivity, had so weakened us, that in three hours every man gave out, and we abandoned the further prosecution of the plan. With the sunrise the next morning, on the seventeenth, a light breeze sprung up from the SE, and, although directly ahead, it was welcomed with almost frenzied feelings of gratitude and joy.

December 18th. The wind had increased this day considerably, and by twelve o'clock blew a gale; veering from SE. to E.SE. Again we were compelled to take in all sail, and lie to for the principal part of the day. At night, however, it died away, and the next day, the nineteenth, proved very moderate and pleasant weather, and we again commenced to make a little progress.

December 20th. This was a day of great happiness and joy. After having experienced one of the most distressing nights in the whole catalogue of our sufferings, we awoke to a morning of comparative luxury and pleasure. About 7 o'clock, while we were sitting dispirited, silent, and dejected, in our boats, one of our companions suddenly and loudly called out, "there is land!" We were all aroused in an instant, as if electrified, and casting our eyes to leeward, there indeed, was the blessed vision before us, "as plain and palpable" as could be wished for. A new and extraordinary impulse now took possession of us. We shook off the lethargy of our senses, and seemed to take another, and a fresh existence. One or two of my companions, whose lagging spirits, and worn out frames had begun to inspire them with an utter indifference to their fate, now immediately brightened up, and manifested a surprising alacrity and earnestness to gain, without delay, the much wished for shore. It appeared at first a low, white, beach, and lay like a basking paradise before our longing eyes. It was discovered nearly at the same time by the other boats, and a general burst of joy and congratulation now passed between us. It is not within the scope of human calculation, by a mere listener to the story, to divine what the feelings of our hearts were on this occasion. Alternate expectation, fear, gratitude, surprise, and exultation, each swayed our minds, and quickened our exertions. We ran down for it, and at 11 o'clock, A.M. we were within a quarter of a mile of the shore. It was an island, to all appearance, as nearly as we could determine it, about six miles long, and three broad; with a very high, rugged shore, and surrounded by rocks; the sides of the mountains were bare, but on the tops it looked fresh and green with vegetation. Upon examining our navigators, we found it was Ducie's Island, lying in latitude 24° 40′ S. longitude 124° 40′ W. A short moment sufficed for reflection, and we made immediate arrangements to land. None of us knew whether the island was inhabited or not, nor what it afforded, if any thing; if inhabited, it was uncertain whether by beasts or savages; and a momentary suspense was created, by the dangers which might possibly arise by proceeding without due preparation and care. Hunger and thirst, however, soon determined us, and having taken the musket and pistols, I, with three others, effected a landing upon some sunken rocks, and waded thence to the shore. Upon arriving at the beach, it was necessary to take a little breath, and we laid down for a few minutes to rest our weak bodies, before we could proceed. Let the reader judge, if he can, what must have been our feelings now! Bereft of all comfortable hopes of life, for the space of thirty days of terrible suffering; our bodies wasted to mere skeletons, by hunger and thirst, and death itself staring us in the face; to be suddenly and unexpectedly conducted to a rich banquet of food and drink, which subsequently we enjoyed for a few days, to our full satisfaction; and he will have but a faint idea of the happiness that here fell to our lot. We now, after a few minutes, separated, and went different directions in search of water; the want of which had been our principal privation, and called for immediate relief. I had not proceeded far in my excursion, before I discovered a fish, about a foot and a half in length, swimming along in the water close to the shore. I commenced an attack upon him with the breach of my gun, and struck him, I believe, once, and he ran under a small rock, that lay near the shore, from whence I took him with the aid of my ramrod, and brought him up on the beach, and immediately fell to eating. My companions soon joined in the repast; and in less than ten minutes, the whole was consumed, bones, and skin, and scales, and all. With full stomachs, we imagined we could now attempt the mountains, where, if in any part of the island, we considered water would be most probably obtained. I accordingly clambered, with excessive labour, suffering, and pain, up amongst the bushes, roots, and underwood, of one of the crags, looking in all directions in vain, for every appearance of water that might present itself. There was no indication of the least moisture to be found, within the distance to which I had ascended, although my strength did not enable me to get higher than about 20 feet. I was sitting down at the height that I had attained, to gather a little breath, and ruminating upon the fruitlessness of my search, and the consequent evils and continuation of suffering that it necessarily implied, when I perceived that the tide had risen considerably since our landing, and threatened to cut off our retreat to the rocks, by which alone we should be able to regain our boats. I therefore determined to proceed again to the shore, and inform the captain and the rest of our want of success in procuring water, and consult upon the propriety of remaining at the island any longer. I never for one moment lost sight of the main chance, which I conceived we still had, of either getting to the coast, or of meeting with some vessel at sea; and felt that every minute's detention, without some equivalent object, was lessening those chances, by a consumption of the means of our support. When I had got down, one of my companions informed me, that he had found a place in a rock some distance off, from which the water exuded in small drops, at intervals of about five minutes; that he had, by applying his lips to the rock, obtained a few of them, which only served to whet his appetite, and from which nothing like the least satisfaction had proceeded. I immediately resolved in my own mind, upon this information, to advise remaining until morning, to endeavour to make a more thorough search the next day, and with our hatchets to pick away the rock which had been discovered, with the view of increasing, if possible, the run of the water. We all repaired again to our boats, and there found that the captain had the same impressions as to the propriety of our delay until morning. We therefore landed; and having hauled our boats up on the beach, laid down in them that night, free from all the anxieties of watching and labour, and amid all our sufferings, gave ourselves up to an unreserved forgetfulness and peace of mind, that seemed so well to accord with the pleasing anticipations that this day had brought forth. It was but a short space, however, until the morning broke upon us; and sense, and feeling, and gnawing hunger, and the raging fever of thirst then redoubled my wishes and efforts to explore the island again. We had obtained, that night, a few crabs, by traversing the shore a considerable distance, and a few very small fish; but waited until the next day, for the labours of which, we considered a night of refreshing and undisturbed repose would better qualify us.

December 21st. We had still reserved our common allowance, but it was entirely inadequate for the purpose of supplying the raging demands of the palate; and such an excessive and cruel thirst was created, as almost to deprive us of the power of speech. The lips became cracked and swollen, and a sort of glutinous saliva collected in the mouth, disagreeable to the taste, and intolerable beyond expression. Our bodies had wasted away to almost skin and bone, and possessed so little strength, as often to require each other's assistance in performing some of its weakest functions. Relief, we now felt, must come soon, or nature would sink. The most perfect discipline was still maintained, in respect to our provisions; and it now became our whole object, if we should not be able to replenish our subsistence from the island, to obtain, by some means or other, a sufficient refreshment to enable us to prosecute our voyage.

Our search for water accordingly again commenced with the morning; each of us took a different direction, and prosecuted the examination of every place where there was the least indication of it; the small leaves of the shrubbery, affording a temporary alleviation, by being chewed in the mouth, and but for the peculiarly bitter taste which those of the island possessed, would have been an extremely grateful substitute. In the course of our rambles too, along the sides of the mountain, we would now and then meet with tropic birds, of a beautiful figure and plumage, occupying small holes in the sides of it, from which we plucked them without the least difficulty. Upon our approaching them they made no attempts to fly, nor did they appear to notice us at all. These birds served us for a fine repast; numbers of which were caught in the course of the day, cooked by fires which we made on the shore, and eaten with the utmost avidity. We found also a plant, in taste not unlike the peppergrass, growing in considerable abundance in the crevices of the rocks, and which proved to us a very agreeable food, by being chewed with the meat of the birds. These, with birds' nests, some of them full of young, and others of eggs, a few of which we found in the course of the day, served us for food, and supplied the place of our bread; from the use of which, during our stay here, we had restricted ourselves. But water, the great object of all our anxieties and exertions, was no where to be found, and we began to despair of meeting with it on the island. Our state of extreme weakness, and many of us without shoes or any covering for the feet, prevented us from exploring any great distance; test by some sudden faintness, or over exertion, we should not be able to return, and at night be exposed to attacks of wild beasts, which might inhabit the island, and be alike incapable of resistance, as beyond the reach of the feeble assistance that otherwise could be afforded to each. The whole day was thus consumed in picking up whatever had the least shape or quality of sustenance, and another night of misery was before us, to be passed without a drop of water to cool our parching tongues. In this state of affairs, we could not reconcile it to ourselves to remain longer at this place; a day, an hour, lost to us unnecessarily here, might cost us our preservation. A drop of the water that we then had in our possession might prove, in the last stages of our debility, the very cordial of life. I addressed the substance of these few reflections to the captain, who agreed with me in opinion, upon the necessity of taking some decisive steps in our present dilemma. After some considerable conversation on this subject, it was finally concluded, to spend the succeeding day in the further search for water, and if none should be found, to quit the island the morning after.

December 22d. We had been employed during the last night in various occupations, according to the feelings or the wants of the men; some continued to wander about the shore, and to short distances in the mountains, still seeking for food and water; others hung about the beach, near the edge of the sea, endeavouring to take the little fish that came about them. Some slept, insensible to every feeling but rest; while others spent the night in talking of their situation, and reasoning upon the probabilities of their deliverance. The dawn of day aroused us again to labour, and each of us pursued his own inclination, as to the course taken over the island after water. My principal hope was founded upon my success in picking the rocks where the moisture had been discovered the day before, and thither I hastened as soon as my strength would enable me to get there. It was about a quarter of a mile from what I may call our encampment; and with two men, who had accompanied me, I commenced my labours with a hatchet and an old chissel. The rock proved to be very soft, and in a very short time I had obtained a considerable hole, but, alas! without the least wished-for effect. I watched it for some little time with great anxiety, hoping that, as I increased the depth of the hole, the water would presently flow; but all my hopes and efforts were unavailing, and at last I desisted from further labour, and sat down near it in utter despair. As I turned my eyes towards the beach I saw some of the men in the act of carrying a keg along from the boats, with, I thought, an extraordinary spirit and activity; and the idea suddenly darted across my mind that they had found water, and were taking a keg to fill it. I quitted my seat in a moment, made the best of my way towards them, with a palpitating heart, and before I came up with them, they gave me the cheering news that they had found a spring of water. I felt, at that moment, as if I could have fallen down and thanked God for this signal act of his mercy. The sensation that I experienced was indeed strange, and such as I shall never forget. At one instant I felt an almost choking excess of joy, and at the next I wanted the relief of a flood of tears. When I arrived at the spot, whither I had hastened as fast as my weak legs would carry me, I found my companions had all taken their fill, and with an extreme degree of forbearance I then satisfied myself, by drinking in small quantities, and at intervals of two or three minutes apart. Many had, notwithstanding the remonstrances of prudence, and, in some cases, force, laid down and thoughtlessly swallowed large quantities of it, until they could drink no more. The effect of this was, however, neither so sudden nor bad as we had imagined; it only served to make them a little stupid and indolent for the remainder of the day.

Upon examining the place from whence we had obtained this miraculous and unexpected succour, we were equally astonished and delighted with the discovery. It was on the shore, above which the sea flowed to the depth of near six feet; and we could procure the water, therefore, from it only when the tide was down. The crevice from which it rose was in a flat rock, large surfaces of which were spread around, and composed the face of the beach. We filled our two kegs before the tide rose, and went back again to our boats. The remainder of this day was spent in seeking for fish, crabs, birds, and any thing else that fell in our way, that could contribute to satisfy our appetites; and we enjoyed, during that night, a most comfortable and delicious sleep, unattended with those violent cravings of hunger and thirst, that had poisoned our slumbers for so many previous ones. Since the discovery of the water, too, we began to entertain different notions altogether of our situation. There was no doubt we might here depend upon a constant and ample supply of it as long as we chose to remain, and, in all probability, we could manage to obtain food, until the island should be visited by some vessel, or time allowed to devise other means of leaving it. Our boats would still remain to us: a stay here might enable us to mend, strengthen, and put them in more perfect order for the sea, and get ourselves so far recruited as to be able to endure, if necessary, a more protracted voyage to the main land. I made a silent determination in my own mind that I would myself pursue something like this plan, whatever might be the opinion of the rest; but I found no difference in the views of any of us as to this matter. We, therefore, concluded to remain at least four or five days, within which time it could be sufficiently known whether it would be adviseable to make any arrangements for a more permanent abode.

December 23d. At 11 o'clock, A.M. we again visited our spring: the tide had fallen to about a foot below it, and we were able to procure, before it rose again, about twenty gallons of water. It was at first a little brackish, but soon became fresh, from the constant supply from the rock, and the departure of the sea. Our observations this morning tended to give us every confidence in its quantity and quality, and we, therefore, rested perfectly easy in our minds on the subject, and commenced to make further discoveries about the island. Each man sought for his own daily living, on whatsoever the mountains, the shore, or the sea, could furnish him with; and every day, during our stay there, the whole time was employed in roving about for food. We found, however, on the twenty-fourth, that we had picked up, on the island, every thing that could be got at, in the way of sustenance; and, much to our surprise, some of the men came in at night and complained of not having gotten sufficient during the day to satisfy the cravings of their stomachs. Every accessible part of the mountain, contiguous to us, or within the reach of our weak enterprise, was already ransacked, for birds' eggs and grass, and was rifled of all that they contained: so that we began to entertain serious apprehensions that we should not be able to live long here; at any rate, with the view of being prepared, as well as possible, should necessity at any time oblige us to quit it, we commenced, on the twenty-fourth, to repair our boats, and continued to work upon them all that and the succeeding day. We were enabled to do this, with much facility, by drawing them up and turning them over on the beach, working by spells of two or three hours at a time, and then leaving off to seek for food. We procured our water daily, when the tide would leave the shore: but on the evening of the twenty-fifth, found that a fruitless search for nourishment had not repaid us for the labours of a whole day. There was no one thing on the island upon which we could in the least degree rely, except the peppergrass, and of that the supply was precarious, and not much relished without some other food. Our situation here, therefore, now became worse than it would have been in our boats on the ocean; because, in the latter case, we should be still making some progress towards the land, while our provisions lasted, and the chance of falling in with some vessel be considerably increased. It was certain that we ought not to remain here unless upon the strongest assurances in our own minds, of sufficient sustenance, and that, too, in regular supplies, that might be depended upon. After much conver[s]ation amongst us on this subject, and again examining our navigators, it was finally concluded to set sail for Easter Island, which we found to be E.SE. from us in latitude 27° 9' S. longitude 109° 35' W. All we knew of this island was, that it existed as laid down in the books; but of its extent, productions, or inhabitants, if any, we were entirely ignorant; at any rate, it was nearer by eight hundred and fifty miles to the coast, and could not be worse in its productions than the one we were about leaving.

The twenty-sixth of December was wholly employed in preparations for our departure; our boats were hauled down to the vicinity of the spring, and our casks, and every thing else that would contain it, filled with water.

There had been considerable talk between three of our companions, about their remaining on this island, and taking their chance both for a living, and an escape from it; and as the time drew near at which we were to leave, they made up their minds to stay behind. The rest of us could make no objection to their plan, as it lessened the load of our boats, allowed us their share of the provisions, and the probability of their being able to sustain themselves on the island was much stronger than that of our reaching the main land. Should we, however, ever arrive safely, it would become our duty, and we so assured them, to give information of their situation, and make every effort to procure their removal from thence; which we accordingly afterwards did.

Their names were William Wright of Barnstable, Massachusetts, Thomas Chapple of Plymouth, England, and Seth Weeks of the former place. They had begun, before we came away, to construct a sort of habitation, composed of the branches of trees, and we left with them every little article that could be spared from the boats. It was their intention to build a considerable dwelling, that would protect them from the rains, as soon as time and materials could be provided. The captain wrote letters, to be left on the island, giving information of the fate of the ship, and that of our own; and stating that we had set out to reach Easter Island, with further particulars, intended to give notice (should our fellow-sufferers die there, and the place be ever visited by any vessel,) of our misfortunes. These letters were put in a tin case, enclosed in a small wooden box, and nailed to a tree, on the west side of the island, near our landing place. We had observed, some days previously, the name of a ship, "The Elizabeth,"[25] cut out in the bark of this tree, which rendered it indubitable that one of that name had once touched here. There was, however, no date to it, or any thing else, by which any further particulars could be made out.

December 27th. I went, before we set sail this morning, and procured for each boat a flat stone, and two arms-full of wood, with which to make a fire in our boats, should it become afterwards necessary in the further prosecution of our voyage; as we calculated we might catch a fish, or a bird, and in that case be provided with the means of cooking it; otherwise, from the intense heat of the weather, we knew they could not be preserved from spoiling. At ten o'clock, A. M. the tide having risen far enough to allow our boats to float over the rocks, we made all sail, and steered around the island, for the purpose of making a little further observation, which would not detain us any time, and might be productive of some unexpected good fortune. Before we started we missed our three companions, and found they had not come down, either to assist us to get off, nor to take any kind of leave of us. I walked up the beach towards their rude dwelling, and informed them that we were then about to set sail, and should probably never see them more. They seemed to be very much affected, and one of them shed tears. They wished us to write to their relations, should Providence safely direct us again to our homes, and said but little else. They had every confidence in being able to procure a subsistence there as long as they remained: and, finding them ill at heart about taking any leave of us, I hastily bid them "good-bye," hoped they would do well, and came away. They followed me with their eyes until I was out of sight, and I never saw more of them.

On the NW. side of the island we perceived a fine white beach, on which we imagined we might land, and in a short time ascertain if any further useful discoveries could be effected, or any addition made to our stock of provisions; and having set ashore five or six of the men for this purpose, the rest of us shoved off the boats and commenced fishing. We saw a number of sharks, but all efforts to take them proved ineffectual; and we got but a few small fish, about the size of a mackerel, which we divided amongst us. In this business we were occupied for the remainder of the day, until six o'clock in the afternoon, when the men, having returned to the shore from their search in the mountains, brought a few birds, and we again set sail and steered directly for Easter Island. During that night, after we had got quite clear of the land, we had a fine strong breeze from the NW.; we kept our fires going, and cooked our fish and birds, and felt our situation as comfortable as could be expected. We continued on our course, consuming our provisions and water as sparingly as possible, without any material incident, until the thirtieth, when the wind hauled out E.SE. directly ahead, and so continued until the thirty-first, when it again came to the northward, and we resumed our course.

On the third of January we experienced heavy squalls from the W.SW. accompanied with dreadful thunder and lightning, that threw a gloomy and cheerless aspect over the ocean, and incited a recurrence of some of those heavy and desponding moments that we had before experienced. We commenced from Ducies Island to keep a regular reckoning, by which, on the fourth of January, we found we had got to the southward of Easter Island, and the wind prevailing E.NE. we should not be able to get on to the eastward, so as to reach it. Our birds and fish were all now consumed, and we had begun again upon our short allowance of bread. It was necessary, in this state of things, to change our determination of going to Easter Island, and shape our course in some other direction, where the wind would allow of our going. We had but little hesitation in concluding, therefore, to steer for the island of Juan Fernandez, which lay about E.SE. from us, distant two thousand five hundred miles. We bent our course accordingly towards it, having for the two succeeding days very light winds, and suffering excessively from the intense heat of the sun. The seventh brought us a change of wind to the northward, and at twelve o'clock we found ourselves in latitude 30° 18′ S. longitude 117° 29′ W. We continued to make what progress we could to the eastward.

January 10th. Mathew P. Joy, the second mate, had suffered from debility, and the privations we had experienced, much beyond any of the rest of us, and was on the eighth removed to the captain's boat, under the impression that he would be more comfortable there, and more attention and pains be bestowed in nursing and endeavouring to comfort him. This day being calm, he manifested a desire to be taken back again; but at 4 o'clock in the afternoon, after having been, according to his wishes, placed in his own boat, he died very suddenly after his removal. On the eleventh, at six o'clock in the morning, we sewed him up in his clothes, tied a large stone to his feet, and, having brought all the boats to, consigned him in a solemn manner to the ocean. This man did not die of absolute starvation, although his end was no doubt very much hastened by his sufferings. He had a weak and sickly constitution, and complained of being unwell the whole voyage. It was an incident, however, which threw a gloom over our feelings for many days. In consequence of his death, one man from the captain's boat was placed in that from which he died, to supply his place, and we stood away again on our course.

On the 12th of Jan. we had the wind from the NW. which commenced in the morning, and came on to blow before night a perfect gale. We were obliged to take in all sail and run before the wind. Flashes of lightning were quick and vivid, and the rain came down in cataracts. As however the gale blew us fairly on our course, and our speed being great during the day, we derived, I may say, even pleasure from the uncomfortableness and fury of the storm. We were apprehensive that in the darkness of this night we should be separated, and made arrangements, each boat to keep an E.SE. course all night. About eleven o'clock my boat being ahead a short distance of the others, I turned my head back, as I was in the habit of doing every minute, and neither of the others were to be seen. It was blowing and raining at this time as if the heavens were separating, and I knew not hardly at the moment what to do. I hove my boat to the wind, and lay drifting about an hour, expecting every moment that they would come up with me, but not seeing any thing of them, I put away again, and stood on the course agreed upon, with strong hopes that daylight would enable me to discover them again. When the morning dawned, in vain did we look over every part of the ocean for our companions; they were gone! and we saw no more of them afterwards. It was folly to repine at the circumstance; it could neither be remedied, nor could sorrow secure their return; but it was impossible to prevent ourselves feeling all the poignancy and bitterness that characterizes the separation of men who have long suffered in each other's company, and whose interests and feelings fate had so closely linked together. By our observation, we separated in lat. 32° 16′ S. long. 112° 20′ W. For many days after this accident, our progress was attended with dull and melancholy reflections. We had lost the cheering of each other's faces, that, which strange as it is, we so much required in both our mental and bodily distresses. The 14th January proved another very squally and rainy day. We had now been nineteen days from the island, and had only made a distance of about 900 miles: necessity began to whisper us, that a still further reduction of our allowance must take place, or we must abandon altogether the hopes of reaching the land, and rely wholly on the chance of being taken up by a vessel. But how to reduce the daily quantity of food, with any regard to life itself, was a question of the utmost consequence. Upon our first leaving the wreck, the demands of the stomach had been circumscribed to the smallest possible compass; and subsequently before reaching the island, a diminution had taken place of nearly one-half; and it was now, from a reasonable calculation, become necessary even to curtail that at least one-half; which must, in a short time, reduce us to mere skeletons again. We had a full allowance of water, but it only served to contribute to our debility; our bodies deriving but the scanty support which an ounce and a half of bread for each man afforded. It required a great effort to bring matters to this dreadful alternative, either to feed our bodies and our hopes a little longer, or in the agonies of hunger to seize upon and devour our provisions, and coolly await the approach of death.

We were as yet, just able to move about in our boats, and slowly perform the necessary labours appertaining to her; but we were fast wasting away with the relaxing effects of the water, and we daily almost perished under the torrid rays of a meridian sun; to escape which, we would lie down in the bottom of the boat, cover ourselves over with the sails, and abandon her to the mercy of the waves. Upon attempting to rise again, the blood would rush into the head, and an intoxicating blindness come over us, almost to occasion our suddenly falling down again. A slight interest was still kept up in our minds by the distant hopes of yet meeting with the other boats, but it was never realized. An accident occurred at night, which gave me a great cause of uneasiness, and led me to an unpleasant rumination upon the probable consequences of a repetition of it. I had laid down in the boat without taking the usual precaution of securing the lid of the provision-chest, as I was accustomed to do, when one of the white men awoke me, and informed me that one of the blacks had taken some bread from it. I felt at the moment the highest indignation and resentment at such conduct in any of our crew, and immediately took my pistol in my hand, and charged him if he had taken any, to give it up without the least hesitation, or I should instantly shoot him!—He became at once very much alarmed, and, trembling, confessed the fact, pleading the hard necessity that urged him to it: he appeared to be very penitent for his crime, and earnestly swore that he would never be guilty of it again. I could not find it in my soul to extend towards him the least severity on this account, however much, according to the strict imposition which we felt upon ourselves it might demand it. This was the first infraction; and the security of our lives, our hopes of redemption from our sufferings, loudly called for a prompt and signal punishment; but every humane feeling of nature plead in his behalf, and he was permitted to escape, with the solemn injunction, that a repetition of the same offence would cost him his life.

I had almost determined upon this occurrence to divide our provisions, and give to each man his share of the whole stock; and should have done so in the height of my resentment, had it not been for the reflection that some might, by imprudence, be tempted to go beyond the daily allowance, or consume it all at once, and bring on a premature weakness or starvation: this would of course disable them for the duties of the boat, and reduce our chances of safety and deliverance.

On the 15th of January, at night, a very large shark was observed swimming about us in a most ravenous manner, making attempts every now and then upon different parts of the boat, as if he would devour the very wood with hunger; he came several times and snapped at the steering oar, and even the stern-post.[26] We tried in vain to stab him with a lance, but we were so weak as not to be able to make any impression upon his hard skin; he was so much larger than an ordinary one, and manifested such a fearless malignity, as to make us afraid of him; and our utmost efforts, which were at first directed to kill him for prey, became in the end self-defence. Baffled however in all his hungry attempts upon us, he shortly made off.

On the 16th of January, we were surrounded with porpoises in great numbers, that followed us nearly an hour, and which also defied all manœuvres to catch them. The 17th and 18th proved to be calm; and the distresses of a cheerless prospect and a burning hot sun, were again visited upon our devoted heads.

We began to think that Divine Providence had abandoned us at last; and it was but an unavailing effort to endeavour to prolong a now tedious existence. Horrible were the feelings that took possession of us!—The contemplation of a death of agony and torment, refined by the most dreadful and distressing reflections, absolutely prostrated both body and soul. There was not a hope now remaining to us but that which was derived from a sense of the mercies of our Creator. The night of the 18th was a despairing era in our sufferings, our minds were wrought up to the highest pitch of dread and apprehension for our fate, and all in them was dark, gloomy, and confused. About 6 o'clock, the terrible noise of whale-spouts near us sounded in our ears: we could distinctly hear the furious thrashing of their tails in the water, and our weak minds pictured out their appalling and hideous aspects. One of my companions, the black man, took an immediate fright, and solicited me to take out the oars, and endeavour to get away from them. I consented to his using any means for that purpose; but alas! it was wholly out of our power to raise a single arm in our own defence. Two or three of the whales came down near us, and went swiftly off across our stern, blowing and spouting at a terrible rate; they, however, after an hour or two disappeared, and we saw no more of them. The next day, the 19th of January, we had extremely boisterous weather, with rain, heavy thunder and lightning, which reduced us again to the necessity of taking in all sail and lying to. The wind blew from every point of the compass within the twenty-four hours, and at last towards the next morning settled at E.NE. a strong breeze.

January 20. The black man, Richard Peterson, manifested to day symptoms of a speedy dissolution; he had been lying between the seats in the boat, utterly dispirited and broken down, without being able to do the least duty, or hardly to place his hand to his head for the last three days, and had this morning made up his mind to die rather than endure further misery: he refused his allowance; said he was sensible of his approaching end, and was perfectly ready to die: in a few minutes he became speechless, the breath appeared to be leaving his body without producing the least pain, and at four o'clock he was gone. I had two days previously, conversations with him on the subject of religion, on which he reasoned very sensibly, and with much composure; and begged me to let his wife know his fate, if ever I reached home in safety. The next morning we committed him to the sea, in latitude 35° 07′ S. longitude 105° 46′ W. The wind prevailed to the eastward until the 24th of January, when it again fell calm. We were now in a most wretched and sinking state of debility, hardly able to crawl around the boat, and possessing but strength enough to convey our scanty morsel to our mouths. When I perceived this morning that it was calm, my fortitude almost forsook me. I thought to suffer another scorching day, like the last we had experienced, would close before night the scene of our miseries; and I felt many a despairing moment that day, that had well nigh proved fatal. It required an effort to look calmly forward, and contemplate what was yet in store for us, beyond what I felt I was capable of making; and what it was that buoyed me above all the terrors which surrounded us, God alone knows. Our ounce and a half of bread, which was to serve us all day, was in some cases greedily devoured, as if life was to continue but another moment; and at other times, it was hoarded up and eaten crumb by crumb, at regular intervals during the day, as if it was to last us for ever. To add to our calamities, biles[27] began to break out upon us, and our imaginations shortly became as diseased as our bodies. I laid down at night to catch a few moments of oblivious sleep, and immediately my starving fancy was at work. I dreamt of being placed near a splendid and rich repast, where there was every thing that the most dainty appetite could desire; and of contemplating the moment in which we were to commence to eat with enraptured feelings of delight; and just as I was about to partake of it, I suddenly awoke to the cold realities of my miserable situation. Nothing could have oppressed me so much. It set such a longing frenzy for victuals in my mind, that I felt as if I could have wished the dream to continue for ever, that I never might have awoke from it. I cast a sort of vacant stare about the boat, until my eyes rested upon a bit of tough cowhide, which was fastened to one of the oars; I eagerly seized and commenced to chew it, but there was no substance in it, and it only served to fatigue my weak jaws, and add to my bodily pains. My fellow sufferers murmured very much the whole time, and continued to press me continually with questions upon the probability of our reaching land again. I kept constantly rallying my spirits to enable me to afford them comfort. I encouraged them to bear up against all evils, and if we must perish, to die in our own cause, and not weakly distrust the providence of the Almighty, by giving ourselves up to despair. I reasoned with them, and told them that we would not die sooner by keeping up our hopes; that the dreadful sacrifices and privations we endured were to preserve us from death, and were not to be put in competition with the price which we set upon our lives, and their value to our families; it was, besides, unmanly to repine at what neither admitted of alleviation nor cure; and withal, that it was our solemn duty to recognise in our calamities an overruling divinity, by whose mercy we might be suddenly snatched from peril, and to rely upon him alone, "Who tempers the wind to the shorn lamb."[28]

The three following days, the 25th, 26th, and 27th, were not distinguished by any particular circumstances. The wind still prevailed to the eastward, and by its obduracy, almost tore the very hopes of our hearts away: it was impossible to silence the rebellious repinings of our nature, at witnessing such a succession of hard fortune against us. It was our cruel lot not to have had one bright anticipation realized—not one wish of our thirsting souls gratified. We had, at the end of these three days, been urged to the southward as far as latitude 36° into a chilly region, where rains and squalls prevailed; and we now calculated to tack and stand back to the northward: after much labour, we got our boat about; and so great was the fatigue attending this small exertion of our bodies, that we all gave up for a moment and abandoned her to her own course.—Not one of us had now strength sufficient to steer, or indeed to make one single effort towards getting the sails properly trimmed, to enable us to make any headway. After an hour or two of relaxation, during which the horrors of our situation came upon us with a despairing force and effect, we made a sudden effort and got our sails into such a disposition, as that the boat would steer herself; and we then threw ourselves down, awaiting the issue of time to bring us relief, or to take us from the scene of our troubles. We could now do nothing more; strength and spirits were totally gone; and what indeed could have been the narrow hopes, that in our situation, then bound us to life?

January 28. Our spirits this morning were hardly sufficient to allow of our enjoying a change of the wind, which took place to the westward.—It had nearly become indifferent to us from what quarter it blew: nothing but the slight chance of meeting with a vessel remained to us now: it was this narrow comfort alone, that prevented me from lying down at once to die. But fourteen days' stinted allowance of provisions remained, and it was absolutely necessary to increase the quantity to enable us to live five days longer: we therefore partook of it, as pinching necessity demanded, and gave ourselves wholly up to the guidance and disposal of our Creator.

The 29th and 30th of January, the wind continued west, and we made considerable progress until the 31st, when it again came ahead, and prostrated all our hopes. On the 1st of February, it changed again to the westward, and on the 2d and 3d blew to the eastward; and we had it light and variable until the 8th of February. Our sufferings were now drawing to a close; a terrible death appeared shortly to await us; hunger became violent and outrageous, and we prepared for a speedy release from our troubles; our speech and reason were both considerably impaired, and we were reduced to be at this time, certainly the most helpless and wretched of the whole human race. Isaac Cole, one of our crew, had the day before this, in a fit of despair, thrown himself down in the boat, and was determined there calmly to wait for death. It was obvious that he had no chance; all was dark he said in his mind, not a single ray of hope was left for him to dwell upon; and it was folly and madness to be struggling against what appeared so palpably to be our fixed and settled destiny. I remonstrated with him as effectually as the weakness both of my body and understanding would allow of; and what I said appeared for a moment to have a considerable effect: he made a powerful and sudden effort, half rose up, crawled forward and hoisted the jib, and firmly and loudly cried that he would not give up; that he would live as long as the rest of us—but alas! this effort was but the hectic fever of the moment, and he shortly again relapsed into a state of melancholy and despair. This day his reason was attacked, and he became about 9 o'clock in the morning a most miserable spectacle of madness: he spoke incoherently about every thing, calling loudly for a napkin and water, and then lying stupidly and senselessly down in the boat again, would close his hollow eyes, as if in death. About 10 o'clock, we suddenly perceived that he became speechless; we got him as well as we were able upon a board, placed on one of the seats of the boat, and covering him up with some old clothes, left him to his fate. He lay in the greatest pain and apparent misery, groaning piteously until four o'clock, when he died, in the most horrid and frightful convulsions I ever witnessed. We kept his corpse all night, and in the morning my two companions began as of course to make preparations to dispose of it in the sea; when after reflecting on the subject all night, I addressed them on the painful subject of keeping the body for food!! Our provisions could not possibly last us beyond three days, within which time, it was not in any degree probable that we should find relief from our present sufferings, and that hunger would at last drive us to the necessity of casting lots. It was without any objection agreed to, and we set to work as fast as we were able to prepare it so as to prevent its spoiling. We separated his limbs from his body, and cut all the flesh from the bones; after which, we opened the body, took out the heart, and then closed it again—sewed it up as decently as we could, and committed it to the sea. We now first commenced to satisfy the immediate cravings of nature from the heart, which we eagerly devoured, and then eat sparingly of a few pieces of the flesh; after which, we hung up the remainder, cut in thin strips about the boat, to dry in the sun: we made a fire and roasted some of it, to serve us during the next day. In this manner did we dispose of our fellow-sufferer; the painful recollection of which, brings to mind at this moment, some of the most disagreeable and revolting ideas that it is capable of conceiving. We knew not then, to whose lot it would fall next, either to die or be shot, and eaten like the poor wretch we had just dispatched. Humanity must shudder at the dreadful recital. I have no language to paint the anguish of our souls in this dreadful dilemma. The next morning, the 10th of February, we found that the flesh had become tainted, and had turned of a greenish colour, upon which we concluded to make a fire and cook it at once, to prevent its becoming so putrid as not to be eaten at all: we accordingly did so, and by that means preserved it for six or seven days longer; our bread during the time, remained untouched; as that would not be liable to spoil, we placed it carefully aside for the last moments of our trial. About three o'clock this afternoon a strong breeze set in from the NW. and we made very good progress, considering that we were compelled to steer the boat by management of the sails alone: this wind continued until the thirteenth, when it changed again ahead. We contrived to keep soul and body together by sparingly partaking of our flesh, cut up in small pieces and eaten with salt-water. By the fourteenth, our bodies became so far recruited, as to enable us to make a few attempts at guiding our boat again with the oar; by each taking his turn, we managed to effect it, and to make a tolerable good course. On the fifteenth, our flesh was all consumed, and we were driven to the last morsel of bread, consisting of two cakes; our limbs had for the last two days swelled very much, and now began to pain us most excessively. We were still, as near as we could judge, three hundred miles from the land, and but three days of our allowance on hand. The hope of a continuation of the wind, which came out at west this morning, was the only comfort and solace that remained to us: so strong had our desires at last reached in this respect, that a high fever had set in, in our veins, and a longing that nothing but its continuation could satisfy. Matters were now with us at their height; all hope was cast upon the breeze; and we tremblingly and fearfully awaited its progress, and the dreadful development of our destiny. On the sixteenth, at night, full of the horrible reflections of our situation, and panting with weakness, I laid down to sleep, almost indifferent whether I should ever see the light again. I had not lain long, before I dreamt I saw a ship at some distance off from us, and strained every nerve to get to her, but could not. I awoke almost overpowered with the frenzy I had caught in my slumbers, and stung with the cruelties of a diseased and disappointed imagination. On the seventeenth, in the afternoon, a heavy cloud appeared to be settling down in an E. by N. direction from us, which in my view, indicated the vicinity of some land, which I took for the island of Massafuera. I concluded it could be no other; and immediately upon this reflection, the life blood began to flow again briskly in my veins. I told my companions that I was well convinced it was land, and if so, in all probability we should reach it before two days more. My words appeared to comfort them much; and by repeated assurances of the favourable appearance of things, their spirits acquired even a degree of elasticity that was truly astonishing. The dark features of our distress began now to diminish a little, and the countenance, even amid the gloomy bodings of our hard lot, to assume a much fresher hue. We directed our course for the cloud, and our progress that night was extremely good. The next morning, before daylight, Thomas Nicholson, a boy about seventeen years of age, one of my two companions who had thus far survived with me, after having bailed the boat, laid down, drew a piece of canvass over him, and cried out, that he then wished to die immediately. I saw that he had given up, and I attempted to speak a few words of comfort and encouragement to him, and endeavoured to persuade him that it was a great weakness and even wickedness to abandon a reliance upon the Almighty, while the least hope, and a breath of life remained; but he felt unwilling to listen to any of the consolatory suggestions which I made to him; and, notwithstanding the extreme probability which I stated there was of our gaining the land before the end of two days more, he insisted upon lying down and giving himself up to despair. A fixed look of settled and forsaken despondency came over his face: he lay for some time silent, sullen, and sorrowful—and I felt at once satisfied, that the coldness of death was fast gathering upon him: there was a sudden and unaccountable earnestness in his manner, that alarmed me, and made me fear that I myself might unexpectedly be overtaken by a like weakness, or dizziness of nature, that would bereave me at once of both reason and life; but Providence willed it otherwise.

At about seven o'clock this morning, while I was lying asleep, my companion who was steering, suddenly and loudly called out

"There's a Sail!" I know not what was the first movement I made upon hearing such an unexpected cry: the earliest of my recollections are, that immediately I stood up, gazing in a state of abstraction and ecstasy upon the blessed vision of a vessel about seven miles off from us; she was standing in the same direction with us, and the only sensation I felt at the moment was, that of a violent and unaccountable impulse to fly directly towards her. I do not believe it is possible to form a just conception of the pure, strong feelings, and the unmingled emotions of joy and gratitude, that took possession of my mind on this occasion: the boy, too, took a sudden and animated start from his despondency, and stood up to witness the probable instrument of his salvation. Our only fear was now, that she would not discover us, or that we might not be able to intercept her course: we, however, put our boat immediately, as well as we were able, in a direction to cut her off; and found, to our great joy, that we sailed faster than she did. Upon observing us, she shortened sail, and allowed us to come up to her. The captain hailed us, and asked who we were. I told him we were from a wreck, and he cried out immediately for us to come alongside the ship. I made an effort to assist myself along to the side, for the purpose of getting up, but strength failed me altogether, and I found it impossible to move a step further without help. We must have formed at that moment, in the eyes of the captain and his crew, a most deplorable and affecting picture of suffering and misery. Our cadaverous countenances, sunken eyes, and bones just starting through the skin, with the ragged remnants of clothes stuck about our sun-burnt bodies, must have produced an appearance to him affecting and revolting in the highest degree. The sailors commenced to remove us from our boat, and we were taken to the cabin, and comfortably provided for in every respect. In a few minutes we were permitted to taste of a little thin food, made from tapiocha, and in a few days, with prudent management, we were considerably recruited. This vessel proved to be the brig Indian, captain William Crozier, of London; to whom we are indebted for every polite, friendly, and attentive disposition towards us, that can possibly characterize a man of humanity and feeling. We were taken up in latitude 33° 45′ S. longitude 81° 03′ W. At twelve o'clock this day we saw the island of Massafuera, and on the 25th of February, we arrived at Valparaiso in utter distress and poverty. Our wants were promptly relieved there.

The captain and the survivers of his boat's crew, were taken up by the American whale-ship, the Dauphin, Captain Zimri Coffin, of Nantucket, and arrived at Valparaiso on the seventeenth of March following: he was taken up in latitude 37°S. off the island of St. Mary. The third boat got separated from him on the 28th of January, and has not been heard of since. The names of all the survivers, are as follows:————Captain George Pollard, junr. Charles Ramsdale, Owen Chase, Benjamin Lawrence, and Thomas Nichol son, all of Nantucket. There died in the captain's boat, the following: Brazilla Ray of Nantucket, Owen Coffin of the same place, who was shot, and Samuel Reed, a black.

The captain relates, that after being separated, as herein before stated, they continued to make what progress they could towards the island of Juan Fernandez, as was agreed upon; but contrary winds and the extreme debility of the crew prevailed against their united exertions. He was with us equally surprised and concerned at the separation that took place between us; but continued on his course, almost confident of meeting with us again. On the fourteenth, the whole stock of provisions belonging to the second mate's boat, was entirely exhausted, and on the twenty-fifth, the black man, Lawson Thomas, died, and was eaten by his surviving companions. On the twenty-first, the captain and his crew were in the like dreadful situation with respect to their provisions; and on the twenty-third, another coloured man, Charles Shorter, died out of the same boat, and his body was shared for food between the crews of both boats. On the twenty-seventh, another, Isaac Shepherd, (a black man,) died in the third boat; and on the twenty-eighth, another black, named Samuel Reed, died out of the captain's boat. The bodies of these men constituted their only food while it lasted; and on the twenty-ninth, owing to the darkness of the night and want of sufficient power to manage their boats, those of the captain and second mate separated in latitude 35° S. longitude 100° W. On the 1st of February, having consumed the last morsel, the captain and the three other men that remained with him, were reduced to the necessity of casting lots. It fell upon Owen Coffin to die, who with great fortitude and resignation submitted to his fate. They drew lots to see who should shoot him: he placed himself firmly to receive his death, and was immediately shot by Charles Ramsdale, whose hard fortune it was to become his executioner. On the 11th Brazilla Ray died; and on these two bodies the captain and Charles Ramsdale, the only two that were then left, subsisted until the morning of the twenty-third, when they fell in with the ship Dauphin, as before stated, and were snatched from impending destruction. Every assistance and attentive humanity, was bestowed upon them by Capt. Coffin, to whom Capt. Pollard acknowledged every grateful obligation. Upon making known the fact, that three of our companions had been left at Ducies Island, to the captain of the U. S. frigate Constellation,[29] which lay at Valparaiso when we arrived, he said he should immediately take measures to have them taken off.

On the 11th of June following I arrived at Nantucket in the whale-ship the Eagle,[30] Capt. William H. Coffin. My family had received the most distressing account of our shipwreck, and had given me up for lost. My unexpected appearance was welcomed with the most grateful obligations and acknowledgments to a beneficent Creator, who had guided me through darkness, trouble, and death, once more to the bosom of my country and friends.

SUPPLEMENT

The following is a list of the whole crew of the ship, with their arrangements into the three several boats upon starting from the wreck: the names of those who died, were left on the island, or shot—with those also who survived, and who were in the third or second mate's boat at the time of separation—and whose fate is yet uncertain:—

Capt. James Pollard, jun.	1st boat	survived
Obed Hendricks,	do.	put in 3d boat
Brazilla Ray,	do.	died
Owen Coffin,	do.	shot
Samuel Reed, (black)	do.	died
Charles Ramsdale,	do.	survived
Seth Weeks,	do.	left on the island
Owen Chase,	2d boat	survived
Benjamin Lawrence,	do.	do.
Thomas Nicholson,	do.	do.
Isaac Cole,	do.	died
Richard Peterson, (black)	do.	do.
William Wright,	do.	left on the island
Matthew P. Joy,	3d boat	died
Thomas Chapple,	do.	left on the island
Joseph West,	do.	missing
Lawson Thomas, (black)	do.	died
Charles Shorter, (black)	do.	do.
Isaiah Shepherd, (black)	do.	do.
William Bond, (black.)	do	missing

FINIS.

Herman Melville's Annotation of Chase's Narrative

Although Melville first read Chase's *Narrative* as a young whale-man in the early 1840s, he did not acquire his own copy of the book until 1851. In April of that year, when Melville was in the final stages of writing *Moby-Dick,* his father-in-law Judge Shaw procured an imperfect copy for him from the Nantucketer Thomas Macy. On blank sheets of paper that had been bound into the book, Melville recorded a series of wide-ranging comments concerning the disaster. Also bound into the book was a letter from Thomas Macy addressed to Judge Shaw, which apologizes for the poor condition of that particular copy.

Almost all of Melville's remarks are written in ink. The only exceptions are some comments concerning his meeting with Captain Pollard on Nantucket in July 1852. These appear to have been recorded quite late in Melville's life when failing eyesight prompted him to write with a green crayon.

The Penguin text is a transcription of the annotations that Melville made in his copy of Chase's *Narrative,* now in the Houghton Library of Harvard University, shelf mark *AC85 M49// R821c(B); the annotations are published by permission of the library. Numbers within square brackets refer to Melville's numbering of the sheets. Problematic readings are also enclosed within brackets.

This thing of the Essex is found (stupidly abbreviated) in many compilations of nautical adventure made within the last 15 or 20 years.

The Englishman Bennett in his exact work ("Whaling Voyage round the Globe")[1] quotes the thing as an acknowledged fact.

Besides seamen, some landsmen (Judge Shaw[2] & others) acquainted with Nantucket, have evinced to me their unquestioning faith in the thing; having seen Captain Pollard himself, & being conversant with his situation in Nantucket since the disaster.

[3]   What I know of Owen Chace &C

When I was on board the ship Acushnet of Fairhaven, on the passage to the Pacific cruising-grounds, among other matters of forecastle conversation at times was the story of the Essex. It was then that I first became acquainted with her history and her truly astounding fate.

But what then served to specialize my interest at the time was the circumstance that the [4] Second mate of our ship, Mr. Hall,[3] an Englishman & Londoner by birth, had for two three-years voyages sailed with Owen Chace (then in command of the whaleship "William* Wirt" (I think it was) of Nantucket.) This Hall always spoke of Chace with much interest & sincere regard—but he did not seem to know anything more about him or the Essex affair than any body else. *See p. 19. of M.S.[4]

Somewhere about the latter part of A.D. 1841, in this same ship the Acushnet, we spoke the [5] "Wᵐ Wirt*" of Nantucket, & Owen Chace was the Captain,[5] & so it came to pass that I saw him. He was a large, powerful well-made man; rather tall; to all appearances something past forty-five or so; with a handsome face for a Yankee, & expressive of great uprightness & calm unostentatious courage. His whole appearance impressed me [pleasurably?]. He was the most prepossessing-looking whale-hunter I think I ever saw.

Being a mear foremast-hand I had no opportunity of conversing with Owen (tho' he was [6] on board our ship for two hours at a time) nor have I ever seen him since.

But I should have before mentioned, that before seeing Chace's ship, we spoke another Nantucket craft & *gammed* with her. In the forecastle I made the acquaintance of a fine lad of sixteen or thereabouts, a son of Owen Chace.[6] I questioned him concerning his father's adventure; and when I left his ship to return again the next morning (for the two vessels were to sail in company for a few days) [7] he went to his chest & handed me a complete copy (same edition as this one) of the *Narrative*. This was the first printed account of it I had ever seen, & the only copy of Chace's Narrative (regular & authentic) except the present one. The reading of this wondrous story upon the landless sea, & close to the very latitude of the shipwreck had a surprising effect upon me.

[14]   Authorship of the Book

There seems no reason to suppose that Owen himself wrote the Narrative. It bears obvious tokens of having been written for him; but at the same time, its whole air plainly evinces that it was carefully & conscientiously written to Owen's dictation of the facts.—It is almost as good as tho' Owen wrote it himself.

[15]   Another Narrative
                       of the Adventure

I have been told that Pollard the Captain, wrote, or caused to be wrote under his own name, his version of the story. I have seen extracts purporting to be from some such work. But I have never seen the work itself.—I should imagine Owen Chace to have been the fittest person to narrate the thing.

[16]   Note
                   Vide ante p.p. 4–5, m.s.

I was doubtful a little at the time of writing whether this ship was the Wm. Wirt. I am now certain that it was the *Charles Carroll* of which Owen Chace was captain for several voyages.[7]

[17] Since writing the foregoing I—sometime about 1850—3—[8]

saw Capt. Pollard on the island of Nantucket, and exchanged some
words with him. To the islanders he was a nobody—to me, the
most [18] impressive man, tho' wholly unassuming, even humble—
that I ever encountered.

[21]   Sequel

I can not tell exactly how many more pages the complete narrative contains—[9] but at any rate, very little more remains to be related.—The boat was picked up by the ship, & the poor fellows
were landed in Chili & in time sailed for home. Owen Chace returned to his business of whaling, & in due time became a Captain,
as related in the beginning.

Captain Pollard's boat (from which Chace's had become separated) was also after a miserable time, picked up by a ship, but not
[22] until two of its crew had died delirious, & furnished food for
the survivors.

The third boat, it does not appear, that it was ever heard of, after
its sub-separation from Pollard's.

Pollard himself returned to Nantucket, & subsequently sailed on
another whaling voyage to the Pacific, but he had not been in the
Pacific long, when one night, his ship went ashore on unknown
rocks, & was dashed to peices. The crew, with Pollard, put off in
their boats, & were soon picked up by [23] another whale-ship,
with which, the day previous, they had sailed in company.—I got
this from Hall, Second mate of the Acushnet.

Pollard, it seems, now took the hint & after reaching home from
this second shipwreck, vowed to abide ashore. He has ever since
lived in Nantucket. Hall told me that he became a butcher there. I
[believe?] he is still living. *A Night Watchman.*

Concerning the three men left on the island;—they were taken
off at last (in a sad state enough) by a ship, which [24] purposely
touched there for them, being advised of them, by their shipmates
who had been previously landed in Chili.

All the sufferings of these miserable men of the Essex might, in
all human probability, have been avoided had they, immediately after leaving the wreck, steered straight for Tahiti, from which they
were not very distant at the time, & *to* which, there was a fair Trade
wind. But they dreaded cannibals, & strange to tell knew not that

for more than 20 years, the English [25] [missionaries?] had been resident in Tahiti; & that in the same year of the shipwreck—1820— it was entirely safe for the [illegible][10] to touch at Tahiti.

But they chose to stem a head wind, & make a passage of several thousand miles (an unavoidably roundabout one too) in order to gain a civilized harbor on the coast of South America.

[26]   Further
                    Concerning Owen Chace

The miserable pertinaciousness of misfortune which pursued Pollard the Captain, in his second disastrous & entire shipwreck did likewise hunt poor Owen, tho' somewhat more dilatory in overtaking him, the second time.

For, while I was in the Acushnet we heard from some whale-ship that we spoke, that the Captain of the "*Charles* [27] *Carroll*"—that is Owen Chace—had recently received letters from home, informing him of the certain infidelity of his wife, the mother of several children, one of them being the lad of sixteen, whom I alluded to as giving me a copy of his father's narrative to read.[11] We also heard that this receipt of this news had told most heavily upon Chace, & that he was a prey to the deepest gloom.

THE BOY'S STORY

Nickerson's "Desultory Sketches"

At age fourteen, Thomas Nickerson was the youngest crew member of the *Essex* when the whaleship left Nantucket in August of 1819. Late in life, after a career as a whaleman and merchant captain, Nickerson wrote an account not only of the *Essex* disaster but also several other "sketches" describing colorful events from his many years at sea. In 1876, by which time he had returned to his native Nantucket after living in Brooklyn, New York, Nickerson sent the notebook containing his *Essex* narrative to the professional writer Leon Lewis in Penn Yan, New York. Lewis appears to have met Nickerson, who was by that time operating a boardinghouse on Nantucket, while summering on the island.

Although Edouard Stackpole believed that Nickerson wrote his account after being encouraged to do so by Lewis, the possibility exists that Nickerson had already written the narrative by the time he met Lewis. In a letter to Lewis (see below), he mentions that he has another story in which Lewis might be interested.

Lewis never prepared the manuscript for publication. Nickerson's obituary in the *Nantucket Inquirer and Mirror* in February 1883 mentioned that he had sent several manuscripts to Lewis, "who proposed to edit and publish them in book form . . . but Mr. Lewis abandoned the enterprise, and the book has not yet seen the light." As it turned out, the fall of 1876 was a difficult time for Lewis. His wife and literary collaborator Harriet was seriously ill and would ultimately die less than two years later at the age of thirty-eight. In 1880 Lewis remarried and moved to London, England, leaving Nickerson's *Essex* manuscript in the possession of a friend back in Penn Yan.

Around 1960 Nickerson's notebook was discovered by Ann Finch of Hamden, Connecticut, in the attic of a relative in Penn Yan. Not until 1980 did the notebook make its way to Stackpole, who confirmed that it was the work of the *Essex*'s cabin boy, Thomas Nickerson. Finch subsequently donated the manuscript to the Nantucket Historical Association, which in 1984 published an abridged version of the narrative.

The Penguin text of Thomas Nickerson's "Desultory Sketches

from a Seamans Log" is an edited version of the complete manuscript in the Nantucket Historical Association. The manuscript is
written in ink in Nickerson's hand on 105 leaves of ruled paper and
would seem to be a fair copy of an earlier draft that is no longer ex-
tant. Nickerson inserted a few additions and revisions in pencil, apparently in 1876 at the time when he turned the manuscript over to
Leon Lewis.

The only silent emendations in the Penguin text have to do with
Nickerson's capitalization and punctuation. In the manuscript
many letters (such as C, O, and S) are uniformly capitalized when
they occur at the beginning of a word, while proper nouns and
the first words of sentences are often left in the lower case. To
avoid confusion, this edition adopts the capitalization of general
nineteenth-century practice. Again, Nickerson uses the comma, the
period, and the dash interchangeably. The Penguin edition prints
his marks of punctuation in the form most appropriate to his syn-
tax. Where essential punctuation is missing altogether, it is supplied
within square brackets.

Nickerson's spellings are retained except in those few instances
in which his meaning is obscured by obvious slips of the pen or by
abbreviation unfamiliar to the modern reader. In those cases the
needed editorial emendations are made within square brackets. His
own penciled insertions are enclosed within curved brackets.

With these exceptions the Penguin edition faithfully reproduces
Nickerson's manuscript.

_____

MY FIRST VOYAGE AT SEA AND SUBSEQUENT LOSS OF THE SHIP ESSEX.

CHAP[TER] 1ST

Oer the glad waters of the dark blue sea,
Our thoughts as boundless, and our souls as free,
Far as the breeze can bear the billows foam,
Survey our empire, and behold our home!
These are our realms, no limits to their sway—
Our flag the sceptre all who meet obey.
Ours the wild life in tumult, still to range
From toil to rest, and joy in every change.
Oh who can tell? Not thou, luxurious slave!
Whose soul would sicken o'er the heaving wave;
Nor thou, vain lord of wantonness and ease!
Whom slumber soothes not,—pleasures cannot please,—
Oh who can tell, save he whose heart hath tried,
And danced in triumph o'er the waters wide
The exulting sense—the pulse's mad'ning play,
That thrills the wanderer of that trackless way?
That for itself can view the approaching fight,
And turn what some deem danger, to delight.

THE CORSAIR.[1]

THE VOYAGE WITH WHICH I shall commence this work was made in the ship Essex of Nantucket[,] which ship had been fitted for a whaling voyage by Paul Macy Esqr[2] and command given to George Pollard who had never commanded a ship previous, but had sailed as chief mate of that ship on a former voyage and was consider[d] fully competent to command any ship in the whaling service. The ship had also been consider[d] what seamen term a luckey ship, so there was no obstacle to getting a first rate crew both of officers and seamen. The ship therefore having gone through a thorough repair and pronounced a perfectly safe and sea worthy ship, was on the whole rather a desirable ship than otherwise[.]

I had very little difficulty in obtaining liberty of my friends to accompany them on their voyage to the Pacific Ocean and as I had been thus far brought up in that nursery for seamen where children from the time they can lisp are taught to look toward[s] Cape Horn for a support and to idolize the form of a ship, couldnot have been easily turned from my purpose. And it was perhaps the most pleasing moment of my life when I at the age of fourteen years went for the first time onboard that ship.

She was then lying at the wharf wholly unrigged and looked very much like the picture I have seen of Noah[s] ark, and from which one accustom[d] to the more modern built ship would have turned in disgust. Such however was to be my home in all probability for the coming three years and black and ugly as she was I wouldnot have exchanged her for a palace[.]

There was a custom at that time prevailing at Nantucket for all who were to make a voyage in a ship to assist in fitting the ship for sea, without any compensation save the privilige of going to sea in the ship. That practice I am told still continues at Nantucket, although all other whaling ports have abandoned it as unjust and overbearing. I know not with whom this custom originated but it is certainly very convenient for the ship owners and probably originated with themselves.

Thus after bestowing a donation of three weeks labour we succeeded in getting the ship rigged and over the bar,[3] there to await her loading and that too to be accomplished by our own men with the assistance of lighters[.] Here after six days more we find our vessel completely laden and fitted for sea and only waiting the arrival of a packet from Boston with half dozen negroes to complete our crew. She too, arrived the next day and our compliment of men, being complete[—] I willnot say seamen for I think we had few at that time that deserved the name—all was made ready for a start in quick time.

On the 12th of August 1819 our cap[t][ain] came onboard and gave orders to weigh the anchors and get the ship under way, an order that all were overjoyed to hear and hasten[d] to obey, little thinking that this stately ship with many of its cheerful crew would return to our native land no more forever. Perhaps it will be well to detain the reader a while and state that it is a custom to have landsmen or those who havenot been accustom^d to the sea to compose their crews in those whaling ships in preferance to practical seamen, and I think the former are far preferable to the latter as they can be formed to adhere to the discipline of a whaler with less trouble than the regular old salt. The latter are very much set in their ways on shipboard and find it hard to bend their minds to the rules of a whale ship, and as it is always the case that the mates and boatstearers have some considerable experience it doesnot matter much even though there should be none before the mast who could claim the title of an able seaman for as experience has since taught me that a few (months) onboard will make even the greenest capable of executing the general orders of the ship.

I wouldnot urge that they could be made seamen in that short time, but that with the direction of their officers can do all that will be necessary for the performance of such a voyage.

Let us return to the departure. Our anchors were soon hove up and secured to the bows and the hands turned too to make sail upon the ship, and it would certainly have been very amusing to seaman to have watched our motions whilst getting the ship under way[.] In fact all was bustle[,] confusion and awkwardness, that is, on part of the crew. The officers were smart active men, and were no doubt something piqued at having such a display of awkwardness, in full view of their native town[.]

Nor was it untill we had passed the eastern end of the island, that our topgallant sails were set and all sails trim^d to the breeze. Mean time many of us who were natives of the island, were found gaping and staring astern to catch the last glimpse of our native land, nor was it untill my ears received a slight pressure from the fingers of the chief mate, that I was reminded that a few ropes remain^d to be coiled up and the decks to be swept[,] a duty which generally devolves upon lads of my class[.]

And although but a few hours before I had been so eager to go this voyage, there seemed a sudden gloom to spread over me as the land receded from our view and sunk beneath a western horizon. Then it was that I for the first time realized that I was alone upon a wide and an unfeeling world even at that tender age without one relative or friend to bestow one kind word upon me. And to sanctify this to me and cause me to feel the full sacrifice that I had made

I was assailed by the hoarce voice of the mate calling to me in its
harshest tone, ["]You boy Tom, bring back your broom here and
sweep clean. The next time I have to speak to you, your hide shall
pay for it my lad.["] Here then was a stumper for me, a pleasing
prospect truly before me, that of a long voyage and a hard overseer.
This wasnot pleasing to a boy of my years who had never been used
to hear such language or threats before.

As night approached all hands were turned up, and call[d] aft upon
the quarterdeck, when the watches were selected and myself taken
into the larboard or mate's watch. After this proceeding the captain
made his appearance upon deck to lay down his rules and frame his
discipline for the voyage. This however was given without overbearing display or ungentelmanlike language, simply stating in substance, that as now we had commenced a long voyage togather,
much would depend upon the crew themselves as regarded their
comfort or success[.] All orders from himself or officers were to be
strictly obeyed. Those of his officers he should be particularly jeal-
ous of, and any who should wilfully disobey or offend either one of
them would be dealt with or punished even as though the insult had
been offered to himself.

After this harangue had been got over, the men were dismissed
and ordered forward to their duty and respective stations. Our crew
were divided into two messes, about two thirds of the crew occupying the forecastle including the negroes, and about one third occupying the steerage[.] In this latter number I was in mess, and
thought myself fortunate indeed to escape being so closely pent up
with so large a number of blacks.

We were now arraigned for supper, and indeed it was my first
supper upon the ocean, and it seemed truly a novelty to me. All
were seated in a circle around our kid or tub of salt meat, with each
man his tin cup of tea and holding in our hands a huge piece of salt
junk and cake of hard biscuit[.] All seemed to enjoy their meal as
well as though they had been seated at table in a palace groaning
under its weight of costly viands. Indeed I have often known the affairs of a nation as warmly and as ernestly discuss[d] as though our
whole country[s] destiny had depended upon the decision of their argument in that same little circle.

At eight oclock PM all hands were call[d] upon deck and the larboard watch chosen to take the first watch untill midnight when the

starboard watch were sent below and released from duty. I will state here for information of those who are not familiar with customs at sea, that all ships make it a rule to divide their crews into two watches[,] viz larboard or mates watch and starboard or 2nd mates watch, and for the sake of changing the watches everey night that each can have a fair chance[—]that is[,]they who have the first watch one night the next night may have the second watch—it has been found necessary to divide one four hour watch into two distinct watches of two hours each. The hours have been chosen between four and eight PM. This of course makes the desired change. They have been christened dog watches and are always distinguished by that name, but for what reason they have been called dog watches I am unable to explain, unless it may be said they have been cur-tailed.

As I have before stated the larboard watch now took charge of the deck and as all were new hands, the novelty of standing a watch for the first time at sea caused the time to slip lightly by. The night proved fine with a clear and beautiful sky and the hands were lounging about the decks during the night long after the watches had been relieved. At eight bells in the morning all hands were again turned too to clear the decks and prepare the ship for whaling, for should whales be seen, the boats must be launched upon the ocean and green and useless as the hands were they would be call^d upon to man the boats and persue them.

The men were now made to know that they had two hours each to spend at the mast head everey day during the voyage looking for whales. This was no pleasing news to some of our number who by this time began to feel that there was a certain process to be gone through with before they could become seaman[,] viz sea sickness, and many were rolling and tumbling about the decks almost readey or willing to die or be cast into the sea. To such this was certainly undesired news, that they should climb to the top of the mast and spend two hours looking for whales. Some said even should they succeed in getting aloft to the mast head they couldnot hold on for a moment and the idea of looking out for whales was altogether absurd and unreasonable. One of the lads said he shouldnot go and he hoped the captain wouldnot expect it of him, but a few soft words from the officers and some little challenging of their spirits brought them to their former good senses and they resolved to try and do the best in their power and finally succeeded beyond their expectation.

This day August the 13th found us in clear blue water with nothing to obstruct the sight save the small circle of the horizon stretching itself around our little bark which almost appears a little world of itself. Here we had the pleasing sight of a few dolphin[4] swimming around our ship and often playfully turning upon their sides and looking upwards as though they would bid us welcome. Their changable colours were plainly visible as they played about, a few feet beneath the surface of the deep. I have never thought as many have stated that the dolphin displays his hues so brilliantly after being taken from the water as they do whilst swimming in their own element[.] They may indeed show more variety of colours when dying, but a close observer will find great variety and elegance in their hues when playing as they often do around the ship.

It really seems that providence had designed me for a sailor for I have never been for a moment in my whole carreer the least sea sick, and upon this occasion I could readily join with those onboard who were not sick in laughing at those who were less fortunate than ourselves. All who have made a voyage at sea must know that for those who are sea sick there is not the least sympathy existing in their more fortunate shipmates for all know that however disagreeable it may be, there is no actual danger attending it, hence their lack of sympathy[.] It is nevertheless most perplexing to the sufferers.

August the 15[th][:] fell in with a ship steering like ourselves to the ESE and bearing the appearance of a whaler. This induced our cap[t]ain to steer more towards him and as we were the fastest sailer of the two soon came up with and spoke him. She proved to be the ship Midas of New Bedford[,] Captain Spooner[,] five days from New Bedford bound to the coast of Brazil[.] After passing the compliments of the day and comparing longitudes the ships separated. The weather now began to look dark and dreary with heavey clouds gathering in the southwest[.] The sea became very rough which caused the ship to roll and tumble heavily and seemed to threaten a storm. We however continued to carry a press of sail throughout the night and had no cause to disturb the hands except for their respective watches.

But on the next day as the ship had drawn out into the Gulf

Stream the weather became very thick with a steady rain. The hands had been call[d] to take in the fore and mizen top gallant sails, leaving the ship with the three top sails, courses, main top gallant sail, and fore top mast steering sail[5] set, when a violent squall struck the ship from the south east heaving the ship almost instantly upon her beam-ends which caused the utmost confusion and consternation amongst the crew. But the cool and undismayed countenance of the captain soon brought all to their sober senses, when all haulyards and sheets were let go, but the ship lay so far upon her side that nothing would run down as desired untill the ship again righted upon its bottom.

The ship righted up immediately when the first gust had past, but the sails were all aback with the yards very near square which press[d] the ship so far backward before the sails could be taken off that the ship was very near running under stern first, which everey seaman must know is a most dangerous position for a ship to be caught in, but by the skill of our captain and officers who exerted themselves to their utmost all appearance of danger soon vanished[.] The wind then changed to north west and blew moderately.

We had by this time had an opportunity of returning to our common senses and view the effects of the squall which we found to have been to us most serious. The first gust had taken away o[u]r new main top gallant sail and studding sail togather with our larboard quarter boat[,] the waist boat and stern boat togather with all our whaling apparatus attatched to them[.] The cook house togather with its apparatus had been carried away and broken up. When all was over we had only two boats left wherewith to obtain our cargo, although we had men sufficient to have man[d] out three. Nor can those voyages be obtain[d] by any other means than with their boats.

The first determination of the captain was to return home and get a supply of boats etc but after some little reflection and a consultation with his officers it was deemed most prudent to continue on our course and trust to fortune and a kind providence to make up our loss, which was accomplished in due season.

As I have before stated the wind had changed to north west which was directly against us to return. Their opinion was that it would remain in that quarter for a long time and greatly delay the prosecution of our voyage. That at least was their excuse, but I presume the fact was that they feared to return lest the men should have been discouraged and would avail themselves of the first opportunity to escape.

After this decision the ships head was again turned to the eastward and all possible sail set to expedite our passage. We passed almost daily many vessels bound toward the United States which would frequently draw forth the expression from some of our young sailors, ["]Oh how I wish I was onboard with them going home again for I am heartily sick of those whaling voyages,["] although as yet we hadnot seen anything in form of a whale. But alas poor fellows[,] many of them were never permitted to return to their home or friends again as will be shown hereafter.

All hands were kept daily at work fitting the ship and preparing all things which would be made useful towards the voyage, and our vessel steered directly towards the Azores or Western Islands with the hope of falling in with the spermaciti whales which abound in that sea and are frequently found very near the shores of those islands, and we were also compell^d to touch there for a supply of vegetables.

[CHAPTER 2ND]

ON THE AFTERNOON OF September th 2nd the man at mast head gave the joyful cry of ["]Land ho!["] but the wind falling off before night and leaving it quite calm, we didnot approach it untill the next day. This land was the islands of Corvo and Flores which are very near each other, and appearing in the distance like a cloud with its sides nearly perpendicular. Indeed, one not accustomed to seeing such land could very easily mistake it for a cloud hanging over the horizon. We had very light airs through the night, which by daylight had brought us plainly in view of the island Flores, but the wind again left us and finding to all appearance that it might remain calm throughout the day, the captain determined to take two boats and leave for the island. The cliffs about this island appear white in the distance and as the atmosphere at this time was very clear gave the land the appearance of being much nearer than it really was, all the officers agreeing that it wasnot more than ten or twelve miles distant.

The crews of the boats were selected to go onshore and all hands ordered below to take breakfast and be readey for further orders. The officers now suddenly disappeared for their breakfast, and by the time the cook had dealt out our cup of coffee to each man and we were seated to take our scanty meal, the hoarce voice of the mate was again hear^d at the steerage gangway[6] calling us to get the boats away. This seemed rather hard for us, the prospect of so long a row without breakfast[,] but hard as it was there was no alternative. All too well knew the discipline of the ship to stand a second call. Therefore the pots and pans were instantly drop^d and all sprang upon deck and hastened to prepare the boats. One barrel of whale oil was placed in each boat for the purpose of trade with the islanders and a small quantity of water to quench the burning thirst of the boatmen and being thus equip^d we started for the shore.

This custom of trading off oil for the vegetable produce of the island has prevailed for many years as the islanders prefer the oil to cash for their articles. Very often have ships obtain[d] a supply of their produce for a few gallons of oil which had they used Spanish dollars would have cost them from sixty to one hundred dollars. Indeed it requires considerable of a Yankee to trade the oil off to good advantage and make a profitable speculation for the ship. I will describe more particularly on an other page the mode of speculation thus carried on with the islanders.

I had been appointed to row at the after oar in the boat in which the captain embarked which certainly gave me much pleasure at the time as it would afford me a run onshore in a foreign land, but strange as it may seem I had an opportunity of regretting my appointment long before we reached the landing place. After rowing three hours and had sunk the hull of our ship entirely beneath the horizon[,] still the shores of the island looked as far distant as when first we had left the ship. For my own part I was completely worn down and exhausted and the captain was frequently compell[d] to indulge me by laying in my oar and giving me time to renew my strength, for it being a new business to me, I presume that I worked much harder than any man in the boat.

We continued on our rowing untill the tall masts and white sails of the ship had entirely disappeared beneath the horizon although the sky and atmosphere were clear as they could possibly have been. We finally succeeded in getting to the island and enterd the beautiful little harbour of [Sta] Cruz in the island of Flores. Here we found some few small crafts, as the seamen term them, moored to the rocks, which were used in passing about amongst those islands but were on the whole a miserable representation of a vessel.

I had now a little time given me to look about the town and I think I employed it tolerably well, for being quite worn out with having been so long cooped up onboard a ship, that it gave me the greatest satisfaction to rove about the town and stretch my limbs. The inhabitants too amused me so much. There seemed such a wildness about them in their manners and in their dress, that to one like myself wholly unaccustomed to anything foreign that all seemed to give a double charm. In their language there seemed that unnatural sharp squealing and sudden variations in their voices as they conversed amongst themselves gave a wildness to the whole scene not easily to be forgotten by any who visit them. The dress of

the men were very much like those of our own country as regards
pattern but mostly of the coarsest kind of cloth. The ladies too were
dressed in the coarsest kind of cloth with the skirts detached from
the waist and generally of different colours. But I am inclined to
think those which I had an opportunity of seeing during a stay of
but [a] few hours must have been of the common or lower order for
indeed I didnot see one which I thought could have any claim to
common decency. The men seemed without exception to be of the
meanest order possible for there was a continued quarrelling among
themselves even in the little traffic they held with us.

I will give you an idea of the manner in which trade is carried on
at those islands by our whaling ships that touch here for trade or
supplies. On first landing the captain of course will make a formal
report to the commandant of the port through the American consul
which is a mere matter of form when permission is immediately obtained to open a trade with the inhabitants for vegetation. Orders
are then sent to the officers in charge of the boat to make a commencement. The barrels of oil are then taken from the boat upon
the beach and tap^d readey for use. There is generally one of the
boatstearers chosen to act as clerk of the day.

Here seated with his quart pot and pint cup it is his buisness to
deal out to those who may favour him with their custom. This buisness requires a considerable fore knowledge of pedling for many
comes with a small bowl of potatoes which does not contain half
dozen and from that quantity up to a barrel is brought by various
persons, and then will come perhaps a few onions or some half
dozen fowls. And should the clerk be too liberal he will pay dear
for his whistle[7] and his oil casks will be empty before his boat is
laden with his trade.

It is amusing to see how eager the females are for the trade and
those who have nothing to offer in exchange are continually sitting
around with cups to catch the drops of oil that may chance to fall
from the tap, and very often I have seen them fighting and hauling
hair to see who should have the first opportunity to catch the drip-
pings untill the clerk, worn out with their confusion would drive
them all away together. In this way were we employed during the
day before spoken of at Flores, and at about four oclock finding our
boats well laden with potatoes, onions and poultry and our oil not

entirely sold out, what remained was dealt out to the poor old women of which there were many around us asking alms.

We had been surprised to find our capt willing to await untill so late an hour on shore, for we had expected our return to the ship would have been attended with an other long pull. But I presume the captain was aware that ship had catched a light breeze and made her way very near in towards the island, but as he was a man of few words he made no mention of it to anyone.

We who had been drifting about the town were still under the impression that the day had been calm and of course believed the ship to be far distant. Add to this our men had been kept all day without their dinner and of course had no desire to encounter such another regatta as in the morning. We presume our captain didnot go all day without food himself but as he couldnot feel the wants of others we presume he didnot heed them.

But after all I have no doubt but this little neglect of his has been of some service to many of us and kept us from falling into the same error ourselves[.] For it has so happened many times since when I have had command myself that I have had many excursions with my boat and men but I certainly have never forgotten to provide them with means of getting something to sustain them.

At about sunset we took our leave of the little harbour of ^Sta Cruz, and on passing around the point of rocks which form the entrance of the harbour our joy was unbounded at seeing the ship very near us and laying aback to recieve us onboard. We soon reached the ship and after taking our vegetation onboard hoisted up our boats and after spreading all sails to the breeze which was blowing lightly from the northward we again shaped our course to persue the voyage and bid adieu to the steep cliffs of Flores which were soon sunk beneath the horizon.

Perhaps our countrymen generally are not aware that those islands produce the finest vegetables in the world. The onions and potatoes are certainly the finest I have ever seen both as regards their flavour and size. Their onions will frequently measure four to six inches in diameter. The potatoes also grow to an enormous size and yet retain all their natural sweetness. There is nothing of that rank or bitter taste so often attending an overgrown vegetable.

Having now taken our departure from the land our watches were again set, and the general routine of ships duty carried on daily and our look out regularly kept at the mast head, yet we saw nothing to indicate whales, or to break in upon the dull monotony of a sea voyage. Tis true we had ocasionally a cry from the mast head of ["]Sail ho,["] which proved to be some passing vision of a vessel in the distance and rarely came near enough to be seen by those who were upon our ships deck.

NOTHING FURTHER TRANSPIRED TO break in upon the daily duties of the ship save now and then a passing squall when the top gallant studdingsails and perhaps the top gallant sails would call the attention of the new ship boys to stow them away for a few moments when they were again set after the gust would subside. We were now making very good progress towards the Cape Verd Islands, and in lattitude 29ᵈᵉᵍʳᵉᵉˢ north we took the north east trade wind which hastened our progress so much that on the fourteenth day after leaving the Western Isles we saw the island Bonavista, one of the Cape Verds, and on the following day saw the Isle of Mayo [Maio] at which we designed to stop to obtain a supply of hogs which may be had here in abundance at a trifling cost.

On approaching the shores of this island, I observed the captain and mates to be more cheerful than usual and alternately passing the spy glass about from one to the other seemed to look anxiously towards the beach near to which we were approaching. The cause of their glee did not remain long a secret from our seamen for we could soon discover without the aid of a glass that a large ship lay piled up, as the seamen term it, upon the beach[.] But the cause of their joy was that they had made her out to be a whaler and the prospect seemed to be that from her we should be able to make up our loss of boats. I wouldnot that the reader should think our captain was rejoiceing to find a fellow being in distress or that so noble a ship had become a wreck. But through her loss gleamed a hope of obtaining that which it were impossible to obtain a cargo for our ship without, for our readers will bear in mind the loss of our boats at the beginning of our voyage.

After running down near the beach we backed our sails with the view of going onshore to the wreck, but a boat shoved off from the beach and came to us. They reported the wreck to have been the ship Archimedes of New York bound on a whaling voyage to the Pacific Ocean and whilst steering along this shore had accidentally struck upon a sunken rock and caused the ship to leak so badly they were compell[d] to run the ship upon the beach to save the cargo.

Our acting consul came onboard in this boat, Ferdinand Gardner [Esq] of Hudson [N.Y.] who had purchased the wreck and her cargo. He couldnot spare us but one of the ships boats for they were of the utmost service to himself in forwarding his buisness around the island. But in our situation even one boat was a goodly prize and we were under many obligations to him for thus far supplying our need.

After taking our new boat onboard we again set sail for the harbour. This newly purchased boat proved to be the very one that so miraculously conveyed a part of our ships company togather with myself across the great Pacific Ocean and saved some of us at least from a watery grave. These boats are built of very light thin cedar boards not half an inch in thickness. They are about twenty feet in length and five feet wide but they are very buoyant and lively at sea, hence their safety.

A strong breeze soon brought us down in sight of the harbour, and the large pyrimidal hills looked very curious to us who were strangers, as they were perfectly white and all about one height. But on a near approach we could plainly discover that they were solid hills of salt which are brought in by the negroes from the surrounding salt ponds readey for shipment. This furnishes considerable trade with the island and I believe is the only article of export from the island.

We found laying at anchor in this harbour several American vessels taking onboard salt for the United States and also the whaling ship Atlantic of Nantucket, Captain Barzillai Coffin. This ship had been very successful and had obtain[d] in making his passage thus far more than 300 barrells of oil and had come here to ship it to the United States and we found them very buisy discharging and shipping it onboard an American brig.

We anchor[d] our ship and lay one and a half days during which time we had traded not oil as before but white beans, which are in great demand at those islands. We have traded away about one and half barrel of beans for about thirty hogs, when we again weighed anchor and took our leave of this barren spot of earth. The hogs that are taken from those islands are almost skeletons and when walking the bones seem to almost pierce through the skin.

The manner of taking off salt at this island to load the ships, is very tedious. Owing to the continual breaking in of the sea on the shores of this island no wharves or quays can be made to stand and they are compell[d] to lay an anchor off in the harbour with a large rope or stay attatched to it and thence taken to the top of the rock which I should judge may be about forty feet above the level of the sea. The ships long boat or perhaps a miserable lighter maybe obtain[d], is hauled at the end of the stay, and by means of small hauling lines the salt is conveyed onboard in bags[.] When the boat is laden it is taken to the ship. This process must necessarily cause a great delay of time as well as unusual trouble.

In attempting to land upon the beach whilst at this island and in the best part of the harbour our boat was instantly capsized or overset in the surf which breaks almost incessantly, and thrown upon the beach bottom upwards. The lads didnot much mind this for none were hurt but they were greatly amused to see the captain get so fine a ducking. I know of nothing that a sailor wouldnot encounter willingly where life wouldnot be too greatly endanger[d] if he can but turn the laugh upon his captain or officers.

After leaving this island we steered away to the south and made very good progress untill we reached the fourteenth degree of lattitude north of the equator after which we found our progress very much retarded in consequence of the long and frequent calms with which we met and frequent and hard rains which fell in torrents around us frequently falling so fast that our scuppers couldnot free the decks from the immense quantities of water and it would run over the plank shears into the sea. Our new sails actually became mildewed for want of an opportunity to dry them.

When in the lattitude of two degrees north we fell in with and spoke the ship Atlantic which we have before spoken of at the Isle of Mayo. We kept along in company with them for several days as we were both steering in one direction. And I well remember hearing the mate of that ship say upon one ocasion that although he had passed those lattitudes thirty different times, he had never been so long delayed in getting to the equator in consequence of such a succession of calms. We however succeeded eventually in crossing the equator having the wind to settle lightly in the south east[.] This caused us to keep close hauled by the wind untill past the lattitude of Cape St Augustine[ ][8]

As we anticipated we had crossed the equator too far to the westward, for we had no means of ascertaining our true position as our ship was sailed by what nautical men term ac[coun]t, or dead reckoning[.] The latter I think a very appropriate name and in this instance not misapplied. On a subsequently made voyage[9] with this same Capt Pollard he had made himself acquainted with the manner of working and practising lunar observations[10] and consequently made better passages and turned his corners much shorter than on our former voyage.

But let us return again. After having passed Cape St Augustine we steered away to the south west in order to pass between the Falkland Islands and Patagonia and on this route saw nothing worthy of note untill we were in lattitude 30deg:oo south when we fell in with a shoal of spermaciti whales which were the first we had seen since we had left home. Here was the prospect of a chance to display our skill, and for the uninnitiated to have some little practice.

The ship was drawn up in a suitable position for our purpose, and put under suitable canvass for the convenience of the ship keepers which were only three in number, when orders were given to lower away the boats. Each man had been anxiously watching at his post for this order and now that it was given the word had scarcely passed the lips of our captain ere the boats were set safely into the water, the tackles unhooked and each man set down to his oar in an instant. Now came the trial of skill and superiority in rowing and as we had about one mile to pull before we came up with the whales, we had an opportunity to test the capacities of each boat and their crews in point of speed and power. This trial more than any other during our voyag was the subject of much debate and excitement among our crews, for neither was willing to yield the palm to the other.

But the swimming qualities of the mates crew of which I was one, were soon called in requisition, for as we were in the very act of harpooning a whale our boat was stoven to pieces by a whale coming up under the boat, which we had not before seen. And this opperation was so suddenly performed that the first warning we had, was a cold bath for each man, but I presume the monster was as much frightened as ourselves, for he disappeared almost instantly after a slight flourish of his huge tail. The other boats were very near to us at the time and hastened to the rescue. After taking us all out of the water they proceeded to pick up the broken fragments which were floating around in every direction. The whales too had taken the hint and were making the best of their way to escape us by going directly to the windward, a direction which all species of whales seem to take when persued.

So we had to return to our ship in some measure disheartened by the loss of an other boat, which again seemed to threaten the destruction of our voyage. But necessity is the mother of invention. Our officers acting up to this, set themselves to work repairing the broken boat, and the project was successful.

After the stoven boat was taken upon deck we found one side remained entire, although the keel had been broken in two places. The first process was to splice the keel. This was done by introducing a middle piece and grooving the ends togather. This done the half boat was turned upright and the keel nailed firmly to the deck[.] They then proceeded to place timbers along corresponding with the whole side of the boat, after which she was replanked and nailed and soon again became a perfect model. This piece of workmanship would have done honour to a practical boatbuilder. I have spoken of this more particularly as I wish to show the ingenuity of seamen as I consider this a fair specimen.

Very soon after this we succeeded in taking a large whale without much trouble and as this was our first greasey work I will make some mention of it. It may be of service to some of our young men who may be about to begin the whaling buisness. It may be the means of saving to them hundreds of dollars at the end of those long voyages, for should they fall short of clothing they must go to the slop chest for a supply. Here they will have a large profit to pay to the owners of the goods. Many times they are charged one hundred p[e]r cent on the first cost.

As I donot design in this work to give a description of catching whales or reducing them to oil, I will briefly state that in this our first attempt the buisness being new to us, we didnot much like to have ourselves so filthy and greasey and as often as our watches changed we threw of[f] our old clothes and took new ones from our chests[.] And by the time the oil of our first whale was train[11] and run into casks nearly all our clothes was thrown aside upon deck and neglected untill it was nearly all spoiled and became unfit for use and finally thrown into the sea. By this means many of us were thrown upon the tender mercies of a slop chest to supply our wants during the remainder of our voyage and had we not have lost our ship there is reason to believe that at the end of the voyage our slop chest would have made a draft upon us to the amount of seven-eights of our earnings. This shouldnot have been.

Every man engaged in this buisness should select for himself on his outward passage two suits of clothing for cold weather whilst passing Cape Horn[.] He will then find himself comfortable whilst in that cold climate, and after passing into a more moderate climeate they should be closely examined and put in good order and placed in the bottom of his chest there to remain until the homeward passage, and not use them upon any ocasion untill he finds himself again in a cold region. By this means he can secure to himself health and vigour, and not be drawn up with rheumatic pains for want of a little timely precaution. His thin clothing should be divided into suits bearing a proportion to each years requisition.

If they will do this I think we shallnot hear so much of cheating amongst ship owners or outfitters, for I don't believe in all my knowledge of ship owners, that a single case has occurr[d] wherein the ship owner has knowingly cheated his men. In nine cases out of ten where this complaint has been made it can be traced to want of care on part of the seamen. I admit they are many times duped and robb[d] by those around them when they come on shore[.] Those land sharks can stuff[12] them and make them believe them their friends and all else are their enemies.

The name also of cruelty and hard usage onboard those ships has spread widely abroad. This I believe to be greatly exagerated and misplaced. I must say in one point I think the ship owners are somewhat to blame[.] Perhaps in many instances they are unconscious of it themselves. I will state my reasons for thinking so and trust I may be excused for my presumption. In the first instance they endeavour in obtaining a crew for their ship to get them for as small a lay or proportion of the voyage as possible which often times with ordinary success will scarcely pay for their outfits. By this means no doubt many a good ship has had their voyages ruined and the owners themselves became the sufferers for want of a little liberality on their part at the beginning[.]

It is well known that most of our young men from the country come down to the sea coast under great anticipations and considerable excitement with but little regard to the result of what their profits may be[.] They enter onboard those ship[s] for a whaling voyage and once at sea they find time to reflect upon what the proceeds of the voyage will probably be by which at best with the usual lays can be but very little and oftentimes nothing at all after deducting their outfits[.] They therfore make up their minds to cut stick[13] in the first port to which they may chance to arrive.

They wish to have some excuse for absconding for they donot wish their friends to know they have made such a thoughtless engagement[.] They therefore tell all with whom they meet that they left in consequence of hard usage onboard their ship. Let anyone who may think differently upon this subject ascertain the lays of each man onboard some one of these ships which may arrive and see what proportion is paid to her seamen. But let them not include captain nor officers; I think them sufficiently paid.

Again the charge of tyranny onboard those ships comes from another class and which is too often the case many young men who are so wild, insolent and dissipated that their parents cannot keep them at home and send them onboard a whale ship to reform them. Here then we see a task for the captain and officers to perform. Here is a young man who perhaps has been rear[d] with the most tender care, and has scarcely ever received a word in anger or a frown from the brow of his parents in opposition to his general conduct[.] He has been subject to his midnight revelry and perhaps almost every other kind of vice. Here we find him suddenly transferred from his debaucherey to the discipline of a ship, which in its mildest form is tyranny to him. Here I think it is but natural to think that he will recieve every check upon his conduct as an infringment upon his liberty and proclaim any one a tyrant who has dared to thwart him in his wild carreer. From such as this the cry often goes forth that the ship is worse than state prison and her captain and officers worse than negro drivers.

In many instances of this kind I have known the parents of such youths to enter suit against the captain and his officers and in many instances to have recover^d heavey damages, when they couldnot have kept the boy at home for their multiplicity of evil actions. To parents I would say who may chance to have such a lad in their family[,] keep them at home. A long voyage onboard a whaler will rarely benefit them if ever, and will be of the utmost disadvantage to the ship.

On the contrary, should this meet the eye of any young man of steadey and correct habits, who may wish to enjoy a change of climate and have some knowledge of sea life, let him make a voyage in a whaler around into the Pacific. He will find in it, although long, many pleasing scenes worthy a place in his memory in after years. And if he will throw off whatever of prejudice he may have entertaind previously he will find in it many pleasing scenes, and spend a very agreeable three years[.] He will meet with many kind and intelligent captains and officers who will instruct him in all he may wish to acquire.

But let us return again to the Essex. Nothing more broke in upon the dull monotony of a long passage at sea untill near the Falkland Islands which lies in the lattitude of 51^{deg}:00 south and longitude of 60^{deg}:00 west. Here one very dark night whilst we were reefing our topsails we were suddenly startled by a sharp shrill sound close alongside our ship[.] We at first thought it the cry from one of our men who had fallen overboard and were about to heave our ship too, when a second shriek followed which soon un-decieved us. We found it had been a penguin that had so seriously alarmed us, and it certainly very nearly resembled the human voice in its shrieks[.]

The next day we had a perfect calm[.] Not a breeze ruffled the bosom of the ocean during the day. This gave us a fine opportunity of viewing the different species of sea fowls which abound in those seas. Seals were also playing around our ship in great numbers plunging and swimming as though they desired our attention[.] We had also a fine opportunity of viewing the different kinds of penguins with which those seas abound. There are three kinds of penguin[,] viz the king[,] the macaroni and the jackass[.] The king penguin is about the size of a goose[.] The head and back nearly black[,] the breast is white with long strips of red feathers over its eyes resembling eye brows and running over upon its neck giving the bird a most beautiful appearance[.] The maccaroni penguin is not so large. It is very much like them except the colours which differs a little there being more white under the throat[.] It has long feathers over the eyes resembling the smellers of a cat. The jackass penguin derives its name from the noise it makes which very much resembles the braying of that animal[.] It is not so handsome as the others[.] They have no wings[;] their little flippers can only serve them to swim.

The albatross is also worthy of some notice. This is the largest bird that gets its living from the ocean. There are several kinds of them and of various colours[—]black, white and grey[—]across their wings. Their shape is like a sea gull, having a large head and beak. I have frequently caught them with hook and line baited with the rhind of pork and veered away astern of the ship. When caught and put togather upon deck they will bite and tear each other fearfully. I remember having measured one which we caught and which was the largest I have ever seen. It measured from the tip of each wing sixteen feet and was white as milk in everey part[.] It was webb footed as all sea fowls are and measured nine inches across its toes.

There were many gulls, shags, and gannets, flying around which proved to us that land was not far distant, for shags are seldom seen many leagues from the land.

The next day we caught a fine breeze of wind and steered off to the southward in order to pass Cape Horn.

[CHAPTER 4TH]

I WILL HERE RELATE a laughable little circumstance which took place during this passage which ever after served to amuse us whilst we were togather[.]

On going below one day to dine our men found in their dinner kid or tub so very small an allowance of meat for that number of men, that they held a hasty meeting and resolved that none should touch any of it, that when the captain came upon deck a man should act as spokesman and take the kid aft upon the quarterdeck. The men took up their stations upon the windward side of the forecastle readey to act in concert when the chosen one shoulderd the kid and walked aft towards the cabin gangway.

I had been set to work by the mate before dinner to tar the netting[14] of the main staysail, which not being finished gave me an opportunity of being out of the squabble and sufficiently elevated above deck to observe all that might be going on, and had hoped as I had taken no part in the affair that I shouldnot be seen or call'd upon, by the time the man had set his beef kid down upon the quarterdeck, all eyes being turned aft.

The captain made his appearance upon deck, and on looking into the kid before him, I could see him change colour from white to red[,] from red to blue and finally to almost black. By this time it was plain to discover that he felt his dignity intruded upon. Then turning forward he called out to the men in a voice of thunder, ["]Who brought this kid aft, come here you d[am]nd scoundrels and tell me.["] Here all hands walked aft each trying to hide himself behind the other.

The captain observing this cowardly spirit amongst them became himself brave as Caesar and commenced walking fore and aft the quarterdeck in double quick time, turning over his quid of tobacco and spitting freely upon deck, frequently muttering to himself, ["]You'll throw your kid in my face you dand scoundrels will you,["] and at length coming to a full stop upon the forward part of the quarter deck threw off his jacket and hat and stamped upon it. Then commenced his harangue[:] ["]You scoundrels[,] havenot I given you all the ship could afford, havenot I treated you like men, havenot you had plenty to eat and drink[?] What in he[ll] do you want more[?] Do you wish me to coax you to eat, or shall I chew your food for you[?"]. To all this the men made no reply[.] They were so terrified they darenot speak nor was one complaint urged by them during the whole time of his violence.

Here upon looking up the captain seeing me, in my perching place called out ["]Come down here, you young rascal I'll kill the whole bunch of you togather[*] then, bang up north west and go home.["] But as I came crawling down to be killed with my ship-mates I was overjoyed to hear him order all hands away forward to their duty, and all the satisfaction given them was ["]If I hear any more from you about provisions, I'll tie the whole of you up to-gather and whip it out of you[."] He then went muttering to him-self but loud enough to be heared all over the decks, what we afterwards termed his soliloquay[:]

> Thirty hogs in the Isle of May
> Duff[†] everey other day
> Butter and cheese as much as you could sway
> And now you want more beef d[n] you.

I wouldnot impress upon the mind of the reader that Pollard was a hard master. He was generally very kind where he could be so, but his supply of provisions for this voyage were very small, and in this he was touched on a tender point. The above show of violence was only one of his freaks, and passed off with the setting sun. The next morning found him as kind as before, and ever after the hands were satisfied to eat what they found before them, without grumbling.

A few more days brought us near to the coast of Patagonia and as the wind hauled more to the eastward there seemed a prospect of soon passing Cape Horn. At 8 AM on the 25 Nov[v] the cry of ["]Land ho,["] was heared from the mast head and {we} could soon see from the deck what we readily call[d] land and the captain with-

---

*This was a favourite expression of his which I never knew the meaning of.
†A sailors name for pudding.

out hesitation pronounced it to be Staten Island, or more commonly call^d Statten Land.

This appeared to show so distinctly that the high square bluffs were easily made out. We steered in towards the land until we were to all appearance sufficiently near then bore up, and run down along the eastern shore to the south. The air was something hazey but not thick and we continued to sail along untill noon, when all at once whilst looking towards it, the island disappeared. The haze had cleared away, and what we had been steering for all day mistaking it for land, had been but a fogg bank and the sun had driven it quite away. I have many times since seen fogg banks in the distance which bore something the appearance of land, but have never seen any thing wherby the mariner could have been so easily decieved as on that occasion.

The wind still continued from the north east and we were sailing with all our light sails spread when at 5 PM the sky began to thicken in the south west and it was but a few minutes ere the whole black mass of clouds were upon us, which looked as if the whole chain of the Andes Mountains were about to burst upon us, and bury us beneath its dark and frowning ridges.

All hands was call^d instantly upon deck but so rapid was its progress that we had only time to take in the top gallant sails without furling them and let our top sail haulyards run instantly when it struck the ship almost with the force of a cannon ball. The ship could scarcely stand up under even the little canvas she then had upon her and careened nearly upon her beam ends. A little quick work on part of the officers and men, soon reduced the ships sails to a close reefed main top sail and storm staysails[.] The sea soon got to a mountainous height but the ship rode over them as buoyantly as a sea gull without taking onboard one bucket of water[.]

This gale continued for ten days during which time the ship was compell^d to lay driving about almost at the mercy of the waves whilst it lasted. Here we continued driving about with adverse winds sometimes catching a few hours of moderate weather when we could show a little more sail and then again driven to our close reefs for the space of thirty days before we were far enough to the westward [to] pass clearly around the cape. We didnot experience serious gales so as to endanger our ship, but having blowed so long from WSW to WNW kept up a high rolling swell, which made time pass rather uncomfortable with us and served to delay us in our progress very much. The thermometer was never so low as the freezing point but the weather was generally bleak and the winds piercing. The daylight was rarely hid from our view and the finest print could at all times when the weather was clear, be read with ease upon deck {during the night}. Ships in passing this cape, cannot haul to the northward untill they have made considerable to westward of the land[.] Otherwise they would be in danger of being driven on shore by the violent and long continued gales which prevail from the westward.

As we progressed pretty rapidly to the northward the climate became mild and the weather pleasant. On the 2nd day of January we saw the tops of the lofty Cordilliere [Cordillera] Mountains in the lattitude of 37^{deg}:00 south and on the morning of the 3^{d} saw the island of S[an]ta Maria. We fell in a little south of the island as we wished to look into the bay. The wind along this shore prevails from the south the greatest part of the year. Therefore ships bound to any port on the coast of Chili will find it to their advantage to make the land a few miles to southward of their port.

After having passed the island we stood into the bay of Auroco [Arauco] as we observed ships laying there and from which we hoped to obtain the news, if any. We found several ships here catching right whales which frequent those bays at that season of the year[.] Those ships which we found at anchor here were the Francis, Paragon and Chili of Nantucket[,] the brig Ospray of New Bedford, and the Countess of Morley of London. They gave us a very unfavourable account of the prospects of whaling upon this coast. They had all been unfortunate themselves. After delivering what letters we had for them we again stood out to sea. Daylight the following morning found us far off at sea with nothing but the tops of the mountains in view.

It was at this port that the ships Hero of Nantucket and Perseverance {No. 2} of London[15] were taken and nearly their whole crews massacred. That of the Perseverance were all murdered except two who were left to work about town and subsequently made their escape to Talcahuano after suffering incredible hardships for want of food.

The crew of the ship Hero were more fortunate. The circumstances of her capture were these. This ship had been rather unfor-

tunate in obtaining a cargo of spermaciti oil and called at this bay
with the hope of getting a few right whales to complete her cargo[.]
They had been there a day or two and had caught one whale and
were boiling when the capture took place by the pirates[.]

Captain James Russel who commanded the Hero said to his mate
that as they had no vegetables onboard he would take one boat and
crew to the town and obtain a sufficiency for their present use.
During the time he had been laying at anchor there, they had held
no communication with the town as they were some considerable
distance from it laying on the ^{Sta} Maria side of the bay. Therefore
they had no knowledge of the piratical intention of the then governor of Auroco, Genl Benevido.[16]

They landed with the utmost confidence. They had no sooner
landed than they were seized by those lawless wretches and conveyed to prison. The boat of the Hero was then man^d out with their
own crew of robbers and sent to take possession of the ship. They
came near the ship at ten oclock at night when they stop^d rowing.
The ships crew knowing it to be their own boat hailed them[.] The
answer was made by fireing a whole volley of musketry onboard
the ship[.] The crew having no means of defence ran off below deck
to escape their shot. The pirates finding no opposition boarded the
ship and tied the crew[.] They tied the mate and locked him in the
captains state room.

At daylight they loosed them and caused them to run the ship
nearer in towards the town, and began to take out her cargo and
take it on shore[.] They compell^d the crew to work on the cargo by
day and tied them each night. The captain had a lad with him in the
boat, and thinking to save him told them it was his own son. They
however kept them both confined togather and probably both were
murder^d togather as there has been no account of the boy.

On the second day after they had begun to discharge the cargo
there was a brig seen to enter the harbour and stand directly over
toward the ship[.] On her nearer approach the Spaniards mistook
her for a man of war[.] They tied the ships crew and drove them below. The mate was not tied but locked up in the stateroom[.] They
next slip^d the ships cable[17] with the hope that she would drive upon
the rocks. They then left the ship. They were compell^d to make all
possible despatch as the brig by this time had got well into the bay.

Meantime the mate finding all quiet upon deck burst open his door and hastened to unloose the men that were confined[.] They cut adrift the sails that were furled and in less time than I have been relating it all sails were set upon the ship and her head turned once more to seaward. The brig proved to be a merchant vessel and on seeing the ship set sails so hastily supposed her to be some pirate and tacked again standing out to sea with all possible despatch.

After this manouvre the pirates were satisfied that she was no vessel of war and again started in persuit of the Hero. It so happened that the ship was compell[d] to haul nearly head towards the boats in persuit to clear a point of rocks which she had to pass and ere she was clear of it the boats were nearly within musket shot of the ship. At this time many of the crew came aft desiring the mate to heave too for the boats. ["]For["] said they ["]we are sure to be taken by them and if we stop they may spare our lives.["] The reply of this noble fellow was, ["]Well my lads if any wish to remain and enjoy their clemency they must take a plank and jump overboard. They will soon meet them. For my own part the ship cant be stop[ed]. If they shoot me, they must do it flying.["*]

A moment more and they had passed the rocks when the ship steered away before the wind. Having a fine strong breeze from the south they were soon out of the harbour and safely at sea but the ill fated captain with his boy and some of his crew were in prison to suffer death by their ruffian hands. As soon as the ship was found to have made her escape, the governer gave orders for the captain to be shot immidiately with part of his comrades from prison. The Hero arrived safely at Valparaiso after a passage of but few days. I was at that port on her arrival and recieved my information of the circumstanses as they had previously occurrd from the survivors.

The authorities of Chili very soon despatched a force to put down the band of pirates at Auroco, and very soon succeeded in dispersing or capturing them. The governor made his escape in an open canoe along the coast to the northward, and landed a little south of Valparaiso. Then being destitute of provisions and wishing to go farther north he asked alms of a muleteer who was hunting cattle. This fellow having seen him in his better days and remembering his countenance, having heard of the reward upon his head,

---

{*The chief mate that saved the Hero was since Capt Obed Starbuck who still
      survives 1876.}

immidiately threw his lassau over his head as he would have done a bullock and started his mule at full run, un[t]ill he had so far worn down His Excellency as to be able easily to tie him and bring him to town handing him over to justice and reaping his own reward. His head was struck off and his body quarter^d and distributed in four of the principal cities of Chili and hung in gibbets. Several years after the event spoken of I saw his head and one arm at the city of Conception.

[CHAPTER 5ᵀᴴ]

WE CRUISED ABOUT UPON the coast of Chili a few months and obtained about one hundred and fifty barrels of oil when finding some threats of the scurvy among our crew and our stock of firewood getting small we resolved to make for the island Massafuero for a supply. This island lies in the lattitude of 33:00 south and is uninhabited[.] It has been much frequented by sealing crews for many years past, but the seals having now become scarce either having been all killed, or forsaken the island it has been abandoned. It is about twentyfive miles in circumferance. It has a bold and rockey shore and the anchorage about no part of the island exceeds half a mile from shore. I have seen it in a very clear day from a ships deck 70 miles by a meridian observation.

We saw many goats upon the island but they were so wild that we couldnot get near them. There are many fine fish caught near the surrounding rocks. We filled two boats with them in a short time. They were not easily cured as the fisherman term it. They willnot recieve salt sufficiently quick to save them. We obtained several boat loads of wood in course of the day which we got by hauling it from the shore to the boats by means of long lines, there being too much sea for a boat to land upon the beach.

We picked up our wood along the shores, which had fallen from the mountains and dried apparently for many years in the sun. Much better could have been cut upon the hills but we hadnot time as we wished to remain no longer than one day upon the island[.] This island has been much injured by volcanoes and in most places wholly deprived of its soil, but wherever the soil remains seems thickly coverᵈ with wood and brush.

Our men whilst onshore found in a cave or fissure of a rock, a roughly made box. Impellᵈ by curiosity they hauled it out upon the rocks. They found it to contain the skeleton of a human being. There was no lid upon the box but they found laying upon the breast a very large stone which had broken in the breast bone and pressed it to the bottom of the coffin. This was undoubtedly the skeleton of some one of a sealing or fishing party who had died at this island, but there appears some little mystery as regards the stone found upon the breast.

All the wild birds that we saw here were a few hawks and sparrows with an abundan[ce] of the Mother Carys Chickens {or Petrel} surrounding the shores. There is streams of fresh water running down the sides of the mountains upo{n} the sea shores.

After leaving this island we made the best of our way towards the Bay of Concepcion and town of Talcahuano to obtain a supply of vegetables and recruit our men as we had now been a long time at sea[.] A few days brought us again in sight of the lofty Cordillieare Mountains and on the evening of that day we made the Paps of Bio Bio, or Dugs of Concepcion[.] Those two hills which stand connected take their name from the resemblance which they bear to a ladys breast. Those cannot be easily mistaken, and are an excellent guide in entering the harbour of Talcahuano.

We enter[d] this spacious bay and soon gaind the common anchorage in front of the town. It had now been five months since the anchor had been down in any harbour, and our men were overjoyed at looking around and finding that we were land lockd, or surrounded by land.

There now seemed a prospect of having a run onshore and we were promised by the mate to have plenty of liberty on shore if the men would hasten their work of painting ship and filling the water casks[,] a promise which he faithfully kept. On the morning of a beautiful day after having finished our work, orders came forward from the quarter deck, for the larboard watch to prepare themselves for the days liberty and with it came a desire from the captain that any who wished to have a little money would come aft upon the quarterdeck.

The messenger had scarcely gone ere there was a general rush of the larboard watch aft for fear that the captain would change his mind before they got the money. Seated upon the cabin gangway we found our captain tossing over and over in his hands some half dozen Spanish dollars which he seemed to wish to make as much display of as possible. Now came the first charge which we were to recieve preveous to landing on a foreign shore.

The harangue commenced on part of the captain—["]Well men

what want you here[?"]—["]Why Sir the steward told us, you had
sent for us to give us money.["] ["]Well how much do you want[?"]
["]We dont care Sir we will take all you may choose to give us.["]
["]Well then you shall have one dollar each but remember I shall
charge you fifty pr cent on every dollar you take so make a good
use of it, and mind you all come onboard sober when the sun sets,
or you have no more liberty this voyage. So go forward and prepare. The boat will be at the beach waiting for you at sun set.["]

The captain had alreadey trespass[d] upon our time by detaining us
so long, and we flew to make all despatch possible. Many of our
men now saw the need of our thin clothing so foolishly wasted in
the first of our voyage and they found it very difficult to dress
themselves with clothes suitable for their first visit. But after some
planning and contriving, a thing always foremost in a sailors mind,
with borrowing, lending[,] brushing and scraping we were soon in
readiness for a start[.] And thus prepared we seated ourselves in the
stern of the boat to get clear of rowing ourselves on shore, for
sailors are very much opposed to work of any kind when rigged in
a shore suit. We had two hands lent from the other watch to row us
on shore.

On our landing we were met by several renegadoes from the
town who had absconded from different ships which had touched
here for supplies who pretended to feel the greatest sympathy or interest for us, the truth of which was that they wished to share our
money whilst it lasted. Their first step was to take us all to the
dance house or fandango. There we found a few young women
seated around the hall upon wooden stools, and playing off some
Spanish airs upon their guitars to dance by. There didnot seem to be
either melody or music in their touch, but after such an interval of
confinement our men were ready to dance to anything had it even
been a corn stalk fiddle[.] With their guitars were an accompani-
ment of an old copper pan used as a tambourine. To this music did
our men dance apparently with as much satisfaction as though it
had been the finest music in the world.

I have since heard music from the fingers of a Spanish lady upon
the guitar of her country which did credit to the performer both for
taste and skill. But those of whom we were first describing, were
ladies from the lower order and looked more to getting Jacks
money than to the notes of her music. Many of our lads had got

clear of their cash before noon by frequently treating their partner and paying their fidler.

There was a young man in the watch with me who like myself didnot much relish this kind of amusement[.] We therfore agreed to take a stroll up into the country[.] We therfore left this den of infamy and vice, and started for the mountains. Here having gained the top of a high hill which gave a commanding view of the whole town and a large space of the surrounding country, we seated ourselves for several hours enjoying the beautiful scene which lay like a map spread out before us.

The town which is built upon a low flat ground seemed immidiately under our feet giving us a perfect birds-eye view of it. The waters of the bay too being scarcely ruffled by a breeze shone like a mirror with here and there a ship upon its bosom appearing in the distance seemed little more than a small dot upon the surface. In the distance and toward the sea lay the beautiful little island of Quirakina [Quriquina] forming the entrance to the bay and behind us the green tops of the mountains rising in majesty one above the other untill they mingled with the snow cap^t tops of the Cordilleares, and seemed almost to pierce the sky. Around us lay spread a beautiful plain which reaches to the city of Concepcion and as it were cover^d with velvet. Ocasionally would pass a rustic on his way to Concepcion with his caravan of donkeys, and pack of dogs. The whole gave to my young mind an impression which time only can efface. Indeed I think it was the most beautiful prospect I have ever enjoyed.

Sunset found us all at the boat agreeable to orders, and although some of our new tars were so well in for it they could scarcely get into the boat, yet none so far trespassed as to break their liberty and all returned onboard the ship good humourdly. During our stay each watch took their daily turns on shore so that when our ship was ready again for sea, all hands had been well recruited and ready for service.

Whilst at this place I became intimately acquainted with the aged priest or curate of the place. He seemed to evince the greatest interest for me and in my wellfare[.] This was probably owing to my age and being thus early engaged in sea service. Everey opportunity which I had onshore my first visit was sure to be at his house. There I was always treated kindly, and he became so attached to me that he shed tears, when I call^d upon him for the last time to say that we should sail in the morning. When ever I had paid the old man a visit he was sure to have some good thing put away for me. As he spoke the English language fluently he gave me much good advice, which I have placed with my hearts dearest treasure and shall strive to retain untill I shall cease to breathe.

Father Francesco de Rosa of whom we have been speaking was born in Seville in old Spain and emigrated to Chili in 1794 since which he had never met with one individual whom he could call a relative[.] In speaking of his friends at home I have seen him weep most bitterly but would chide himself by saying ["]Ah well, my sacrifice has been great tis true but if I have done any good my design has been accomplished. I leave the rest with God.["]

I donot believe the good old patriarch had an enemy in the world. I have since seen him at a very advanced age on the island of Tumaco on the coast of Peru in the full enjoyment of his health and faculties. I carenot what was the professed faith of this man. I believe if there is a Christian permitted to live upon earth, father Francisco was that man[.] He proved it to the world in his walk through life, and after his death I believe his reward will be that of the righteous.

The houses at this town are seldom built more than a storey and a half high, probably owing to the frequent shocks of earth quakes with which they are troubled[.] The town lies nine miles from the city of Concepcion in a north west direction through a beautiful and level plain[.] It is defended by two batteries or forts, one upon the east^n side of the port upon very low ground[,] the[y] being slightly elevated above the level of the sea, and I think are capable under ordinary managment of doing good execution upon an enemy's ships. The guns were of 24 lbs calibre but many of them were laying about the fort with broken carriages or dismounted. The other fort is to the north west and elevated about one hundred feet above the level of the sea and was fitted for eight guns, but most of them as at the other lay unfit for use.

They have a great trade with the leeward coast or Peru. I have in latter years seen seven ships loading with wheat, with which this country abounds[.] There is also timber, spars, and boards in abundance carried from this port. The surrounding country is tolerably well cultivated and abounds in excellent provisions[.] Bullocks[,] horses and sheep are abundent here and can be bought very cheap. The bay has many fish, but the inhabitants seem to prefer the mus-cle[,] a sort of shell fish which are caught here with great trouble. This buisness of getting muscles seems to {be} carried on principally by the women[.] It is very common to see them diving where there is six and eight feet water and fetching them up with their hands.

Amongst the upper circles in the city of Concepcion, I think their ladies exceed any in point of beauty and modesty that I have seen upon the coast although of later years I have been much upon that coast and had many opportunities of judging for myself. But it seems very strange in the great march of improvements about the world more especially amongst the ever changing fashions of the ladies, that some change of fashion hasnot taken place here, for here you still find midst their gayest circles, the old fashioned hoop dress as worn by their grandmothers a hundred years ago[.] This gives them the appearance of a wine cask sawed off in the middle and turned bottom upwards from their waist downwards, but they are very pleasing and agreeable in their manners. The inhabitants seem very much mixed up and you find but very few who maynot have a claim to Indian blood.

I visited Concepcion in 1834 in company with several American gentelmen and all seemed in the highest enjoyment of prosperity. How little could we know of what an awful fate awaited that noble but devoted city which was so soon to lay a heap of ruins.[18] We spent a few very plasant hours and formed some very pleasing ac-quaintances amongst the inhabitants[.]

In our way to town we were met by an old man bowed down with years who accompanied by his son was bearing a burthen upon their shoulders[.] This consisted of a long pole with a sort of bag suspended horizontally between them and seemed to contain a human body. As the old man beckoned us we stoppd our horses to find what he wished of us. He came to us with tears gushing down his furrowed cheeks and only wished us to aid him by giving him a trifle towards the burial of his daughter[.] He said this was the third day in which himself and son had laboured almost without food carrying around the dead body of his daughter, striving to obtain enough money by begging to satisfy the demand of their beastly priest to perform for them the burial service and suffer her to be laid in consecrated ground. Ah how unlike the good old Father Francisco who but a few years before occupied the very same situation now held by this wretch.

I asked the old man if he had known Father F. ["]Ah["] said he after crossing his forehead and uttering a few half broken sentences, ["]I knew him well but we find none like him now.["] We raised among us the amount the old man said was the demand and gave it to him. It gave us pleasure in seeing the countenance of the old man display the workings of his heart as we reached him the desired sum[.]

I dismounted to be sure they hadnot been decieving us and hauling open the shroud found it to be a face with which we had been familiar although something changed in death[.] We recognized it to have been a girl who used to attend in market and of whom we used to buy our vegetables. ["]Ah["] thought I ["]how little do we know what we enjoy in our own country untill we visit abroad.["] We turned our horses heads and rode to town followed no doubt with the blessings of the old man who could now return and demand of that haughty priest the burial which for want of a little paltry trash had been denied him. I shall ever cherish the remembrance of the eager desire displayed by my companions to join me in making up the amount of money requisite for the decent burial of the dead and to relieve the old man's wants.

But I have strayed from my subject and with your permission we will again return to the voyage of the Essex.

After having completed our recruits of vegetables &c we weighed anchor and stood out to sea, with the hope of meeting with good success for the reader will remember that our cargo was to be obtain^d from the bosom of the ocean. After being once more at sea, we took up our station upon the southern coast of Chili and ploug[h]ed to and fro with very little success and frequently meeting with ships, who like ourselves were seeking in vain the oily treasures of the deep. Here we used frequently to meet with Lord Cochrane's detatched fleet,[19] who were cruising for Spanish vessels, which at that time was very numerous, the most of the coast of Peru being then in posession of the Royalists or E[u]ropean Spaniards. We at one time fell in with one his prize sloops of war the Eagle, being entirely destitute of provisions and supplied them. Otherwise, being very far at sea their suffering must very soon have been great.

[CHAPTER 6TH]

WE CONTINUED TO CRUISE over that part of the ocean untill the season of whaling had terminated and having obtaind but 250 bbls of oil, which was a very small portion for the time occupied we steered to the northward for the milder coast of Peru. We didnot however make a direct course toward that climate for this being all considered a good whaling range of course the more distance sailed over by us the better chance of obtaining that which we most desired. We therefore steerd to the north west about twelve hours and north east for the same number of hours of each day, thereby passing over all possible distance, being plainly in sight of the land at one time and at others two hundred miles distant. This no doubt will seem a tedeous mode of making a passage but it will be borne in mind that we were searching for whales.

In working along this coast the lofty Andes Mountains frequently show their tops, but most of the time they are cover^d with a thick mist. In about the lattitude of 14 to 18 degrees south the weather is generally very gloomy as the sun is rarely in view, and it frequently occurs that a ship is many days without a meridian observation the sun being constantly obscured by a thick mist. The winds too are very boisterous in those regions notwithstanding it bears the name of Pacific Ocean and frequently whilst cruising for whales we have been compell^d to close reef our sails.

We were on the whole rather fortunate with our whaling and in two months had taken about four hundred and fifty barrells of oil, although it was very difficult to obtain in consequence of such a high and rolling sea that our boats were very much injured in hoisting them from the water and were on more than one occasion dashed in pieces by the heavey rolling of the ship.

We here fell in c^o[mpany] with the whaling ship Aurora from Nantucket Captain Daniel Russel[20] only five months from home[.] This to us was late very late news for we hadnot hear^d from home since we had sailed which had been ten months[.] They had brought

us plenty of letters and some news papers[,] a rich treat truly. After
the captain and officers had selected theirs the mail bag was sent
forward for the crew to overhaul and pick for themselves. What so
pleasing as to recieve letters from our friends after so long an absence from them; why, what young school miss, even at the short
distance of a boarding school in our own country cannot appreciate
our delightful occupation for a short time. Who but can realize how
much we enjoyed who found a letter in the package or the disappointment of those who had none.

It was amusing to watch those of our lads who had been disappointed and found no letters for them. They would follow us
around the decks and whilst we were reading our letters would seat
themselves beside us as though our letters could be of service to
them or convey news from their own friends. But as our family letters could be of no interest to them they were compell[d] to seek for
news in the careless folds of a newspaper.

This ship had also brought us a few of them which next to letters
was the greatest treat they could have given us. Many of us set up all
our next watch below to overhaul them, and although they didnot
contain any very important news, yet to us the whole was interesting, and I learned the contents so well by heart, that I could have repeated them six months afterwards.

The Aurora was direct from a town call[d] Arica[,] a small town
which lies in the 18th degree south lattitude, and as the prevailing
winds were from the S-east being in the trades lay directly to the
windward of us. But, as Captain Russel gave a very good account of
its facilities for recruiting our men and obtaining an easey supply of
water that our captain resolved to go there immidiately. We accordingly set all our sails, haul[d] too our tacks and commenced plying to
windward, and on the tenth day gain[d] an anchorage in the harbour
of Arica.

Here we found the ship Mary of London Captain Zenas Ford,
on a trading voyage which we consider[d] a fortunate circumstance as
they were afterward of much company for us. They had truly a fine
ships company being a fine class of young men, who seemed to feel
that they had a reputation to care for, and ever during our stay at
this place did they conduct themselves in a consistent and becoming
manner. The ship also showed to have excellent discipline with
good treatment to his men. Indeed the captain might well have been

proud of his little command. His chief mate was drowned soon afterward in the river of Guayaquil.

This town was at this time under government of the crown of Spain and remaind so untill a short time before the castles of Callao was evacuated by Genl Rodil.[21] It was not retain^d for its strength but left unmolested for its minor importance, serving only as a fit place for plunder whenever the army of Patriots came that way. It was taken and pillaged a short time preveous to our arrival there by the fleet under command of Cochrane[.] Even the churches wasnot respected but a general plunder of all its valuables. This however was contrary to the orders of the Admiral.

It is a town of but little trade and there may have been four or five thousand inhabitants and a garrison of eight hundred men. They were badly clothed and worse officer^d. This probably accounts for the town's having surrender^d so easily, for I was told that only three guns were fired from town when they surrender^d.

There are a few small mines in the interior but not much worked upon. Their houses are built of bamboo with the cracks fill^d with dried mud and in a few instances are white washed. The inhabitants are very much mixed up with the negro blood. They have a fort with about ten guns mounted upon it but pierced for a larger number, and there was also a fort upon the high headland south of the harbour[.] It has a flag staff and a small garrison kept there.

The anchorage is safe although it is an open harbour but as the wind never blows from the sea there is no danger in that direction. This harbour is much frequented by a species of whale call^d the hump back. They swim very near the ships at the common anchorage. Fresh water can be obtain^d at this place easily for you have only to take a shovel with you onshore and by digging a hole in the beach of two feet you can have a beautiful spring to fill any quantity you may require. The only obstacle you may meet with is the surf in rafting off your cask, but by catching a smoothe sea you can easily obviate this difficulty, and you may get of[f] three hundred barrels pr day if necsasary.

The markets at this place are badly supplied and but few vegetables are to be had. In fact the whole country in this vicinity is notorious for its barrenness and but very little produce can be looked for.

Whilst we were at this port there was a party came off given on-

board the Mary by the captain to the governor and suite to which
all the civil officers & aristocracy of the port were invited as well as
the captain of our ship[.] The ship was decorated with national and
private colours tastefully arranged, and being a handsome ship all
combin^d to make a very imposing appearance.

There was considerable amusement on part of the sailors whilst
taking the ladies onboard. There was a rope call^d a whip purchase
got upon the main yard with a cover^d chair attatched to the lower
end. The chair was lower^ed into the boat when a lady would be
seated and secured by means of a belt passing around the waist so
that they couldnot possibly fall out. When the word ["]Whip["]
was given the seamen would hoist them up in the twinkling of an
eye, and when the lady didnot appear to be much frighten^d, they
would lower her without delay upon deck. But when a timid one
occupied the chair, Jack was sure to run her up to the main yard a
distance of forty feet and hold them suspended in the air for several
minutes, to the great delight of their more fortunate friends who
had been safely landed upon deck.

Soon as all were onboard there was a grand national salute fired
from the ship which made all tremble with the unexpected shock.
After which an excellent dinner was served up, when all set to with
that natural gusto so familiar to a Spaniard. Indeed the guests
seemed to enjoy the whole, and especially did they do justice to the
captains wine and brandy[.] For in a short time the empty bottles
could be seen in a string for half a mile out to sea as they had been
rifled and thrown overboard the tide having taken them along like a
row of Indians marching single file.

The party broke up before night fall, and the commandant gave a
ball on the same evening at his house. There was amongst the company an old friar who was familiarly known by the cognomen of
Father Sidéacco. He was the life of Arica. No party could be complete without his presence. He created mirth wherever he came[.]
Even in the streets he was known as the jester[.] His long black
robes which caused him to appear so saint-like, screen^d him not
from the jests and jeers of the people.

And on the occasion of which we have been speaking as the
boats were returning to shore with the party and the two boats
which had taken in the ladies had succeeded in landing them safely
although the surf through which they had to pass was rolling very

high upon the beach, they had disembarked and from the beach was anxiously watching the boat which contain[d] the favourite priest. And whilst they were yet looking there came a towering high sea which completely overwhelmed the boat and she was upset instantly being then fifty yards from the shore.

The boat was turned upon the heads of the inmates and all very narrowly escaped being drowned, but after rescuing all that could be seen[,] our common friend the priest was still missing[.] At length his three corner[d]-hat was seen floating near the boat and amongs[t] the wild billows of the surf. There was upon this discovery a general burst of grief amongst the ladies. All had given him up for lost, and were about to turn from the dreadful scene in grief and mourning, when a loud shriek was hear[ed] from seaward[.]

The boat was still floating about upon the surface and amongst the breakers but nothing seen of the old man. The boats had ventured off to try and save the broken boat from the breakers when on turning it over lo there lay the priest apparently cool and collected. His first words were ["]Ah my friends you didnot look much to the old man but I hope the ladies are safe.["] On being assured such was the fact he again assumed his wonted cheerfulness.

The cause of his having been so long hidden from us was that he had been cover[d] by the boats having turn[d] directly upon him and as it had been raised by retaining a portion of wind beneath, he by laying upon his back and holding on upon the timbers had thus been enabled to breathe and sustain[d] life untill released by us as above stated. And as he couldnot swim he darenot let go his hold, hence the cause of being hidden so long from our view[.]

He didnot however favour the evening party with his presence, but the boats crews with myself had the pleasure of taking a parting draught of sherry at the parsonage and there we parted with the old man to many of us for the last time upon earth.

[CHAPTER 7TH]

As we had now finished the recruiting of our ship, this being the sole object for which we came to this port, we weighed our anchor on the next morning and steer^d out once more to sea, and remain near this port for some length of time. For the reader will not forget that ours was a whaling voyage and obtain^d but few whales which yealded but little oil, and after the season had expired, bore up and steered to the northward. We during this rout[e] coasted generally in sight of the land, and passed very near the Lobos Islands. These are two small islands laying about seven leagues distant from the main land of Peru.

Here we met with many native fishermen who came from the adjacent coast for fish around those islands. The form of their boats are very curious and call'd by them the cattemaran. It is formed with having a number of logs tied together or lashed as the sailor would have it, being a very light kind of wood and is perhaps as buoyant as cork. These logs are about thirty feet long and two feet diameter. They are secured by small cross sticks which are so lashed as to keep them a little distance apart, between which the water passes freely. Their masts are secured by a sort of raised work in the centre to the height of several feet, through which the mast leads down and secures to a bottom log. They have a large square sail something narrowed at the head, and set after the plan of the latin [lateen] sail. They are steered by means of a long strip of plank put between the logs at any convenient place near the stern and yet with this unwieldy cluster of logs do they work many miles along the coast often making a good way against the prevailing trade wind. This could scarcely be credited by a stranger at first sight, but it is nevertheless to[o] true.

There is vast numbers of sea fowls and many seals around this group of islands, but as we made no stop I shall not make any attempt to describe them. The whole coast from Arica to the Lobos

Islands presents to the eye a continued stretch of sunburnt and barren hills near the sea coast. The Lobos Islands are in the lattitude 6^d:30^m south long^d 80:40 west.

The town of Paita lays a short distance to the north of these islands and is a place of considerable note. We have an American consulate established there. It is on the south side of the bay of Colan which makes it an excellent harbour and a famous resort for our whaling ships which frequent these seas. Here they can obtain a good supply of sweet potatoes[,] onions and cabbages, with a few pumpkins but no water. Even the water used in the town is brot upon mules from the surrounding country.

The river Tumbez [Tumbes] is much frequented by whalers for water[.] This lies in latti^d of 3^deg and would be an excellent watering place were it not for there being a bar to cross before getting into the river which at times breaks very high and it often happens that the ships get their casks broken in pieces and come off with the loss of several men. There is some vegetation to be obtained at this place such as sweet potatoes[,] yams, & with a scanty supply of tropical fruits.

I was laying at this port in 1835 in a ship call^d the Samuel Wright of Salem ^Mass.22 taking onboard a supply of wood and water and had very nearly finished without accident, when on mustering our hands one morning found that our third mate togather with six of our best hands had stolen away one of our boats during the night and absconded. We immidiately saw the necessity of making some attempt to waylay and if possible to catch them.

So after having been onshore to the commander of the port and obtained a warrant to arrest them in case of finding them at some other part of the coast we set ourselves buisily at work fitting up one of our remaining boats for a long cruise, and after having fitted a schooner rig, and taken onboard a week's provision with plenty of ballast and selected one boatstearer ^Mr Zephaniah Wood and two trustworthy seamen I took charge of the boat and started for the Guayaquil River in persuit, thinking in all probability they would make this their land fall. The mouth of this river is about 70 miles to the north of our ships anchorage.

Thus equip^d, I started of[f] with a fair wind and very pleasant weather, but we hadnot proceeded more than twenty miles when

the sky became suddenly overcast with every appearance of an awful storm. The rain fell in torrents throughout the night and as we
had no covering to our boat we were soon wet through to the
skin[.] The rain continued to fall with unabated fury untill the next
morning and the thunder and lightning the most awful and vivid
that I have ever witness[d], which also kept up during the night. The
gusts of wind were very hard and the night very dark, but our little
whaleboat glided away like a thing of life. We continued on our
course under easey sail, when at daylight the storm clear[d] away
showing to us the island Puná, and that our position was very fair,
for we had only to haul too and sail directly into the harbour. But
certainly a more disagreeable night than the past cannot easily be
described and I presume should this meet the eye of any of my
shipmates of that dreadful night they will shrug their shoulders and
heave a passing thought upon that our first night{s experience}.

The island Puna is at the mouth of the Guayaquil River[.] It has
a small town containing about four hundred inhabitants[.] At this
town I landed and deliver[d] my message to the com[mande][r] of the
town. He recieved me very kindly and offer[d] me every facility in his
power to recover the lost men. He then despatched soldiers in all
directions in search but to no purpose for the men as we afterwards
learned pass[d] the island during the storm by mistake as they had intended to land there and b[y] that means they escaped but they suffer[d] every hardship[,] some of their number even death itself.

We found at this island two families residing upon a beautiful site
to appearance but very sickly being constantly visited with the
billous fever. Those families were one an American [Mr] John Swett
of Boston and [Mr] Cope British consul[.] They had sought an assy-
lum at this place to escape the tumult of war then waging at this
province.

General Flores[23] at this time held possession of the city of
Guayaquil and General Wright[24] had the island Puna as his resort
for his flotilla. He was in the service of Gen[l] Rocheforte,[25] and completely held the forces by sea of Flores at bay. His flotilla consisted
of about twelve schooners with some crafts of a smaller size with
which he used to annoy the enemy very much. He is an Irishman
by berth and a truly brave and humane general. There was a rumour
at this town of the general's having caught a musket ball in the hol-

low of his hand during his last engagement. He related the circumstance to me as it occur[d].

["]This battle["] said he ["]which by the way was a pretty severe one, was fought onboard the floatilla with an overwhelming number of Flores's troops[.] The contest had been long and trying[.] Many[,] very many of our number had fallen, and our men seem[d] to droop and appeard dishearten[d],["] when the gen[l] on moving from his position observed a spent bullet which had pass[d] through the bulwark and lodged upon the rail. He caught it up in a moment and a thought struck him, to take advantage of their superstition and turn the circumstance to his own advantage. He therfore holding it in the hollow of his hand and starting high upon the rail cried out to his men, ["]Look now look at this[.] I have caught one of their bullets in my hand and stop[d] it[.] Now["] said he ["]{we} are sure of them, for their powder is good for nothing.["] This gave them new spirits and after having cheer[d] lustily they renewed the fight with three fold vigour, and he declared to me on his honour, he believed that alone to have been the means of giving to them the victory which soon after followed and of deciding the contest so soon[.]

There was a little affair came off during my stay at his camp which convinced me that he was humane as well as brave. On a dark night one of his centinals who was posted without the camp, heard a sudden rustling amongst the bushes. The centinal challenged but recieving no answer to the third call fired and shot the intruder dead. On examineing he found it to have been a poor unfortunate cow who had been the innocent cause of her own destruction. The next morning there came a complaint to the general that the cow kill[d] was the only support of a poor widow. He enquired what a good cow would cost. On being informed that a cow such as had been kill[d] would cost thirty dollars, his reply was ["]Well I have just sixty dollars of my own[.] God knows when or where I shall get more but here[,] take half I have and get yourself a cow. You shall not suffer whilst I can prevent it.["]

I remain[d] three days at this place and finding my expedition a complete failure, we again embarked and made the best of our way to Tumbez to rejoin our ship, where we found all anxiously watching for our return and were overjoyed again to see us notwithstanding our expedition hadnot been crown[d] with success. Here we picked up two men who had absconded from other whale ships, and as there was no other men to be got here we put to sea, and in a few days, one of the two men we had taken at Tumbez died with a fever contracted at that river. We buried him at the island Puna on the premises of the British consul with all due respect to the dead, ^{Mr} Cope having the kindness to read the funeral service and conduct burial. The name of the deceased was Samuel Day a native of Philadelphia.

[CHAPTER 8ᵀᴴ]

LET US NOW RETURN to the voyage of the Essex[.] After having made a short stay at the Lobos Islands we steered away to the northward, making a sort of zig zag course, some times near the shore and at others far off at sea. We finally crossed the equator and made the best of our way for the town of Tacames [Atacames]. This town is very small[,] composed of bamboo huts with thatched roofs and built upon stakes raised about twenty feet from the ground[.] They are thus raised as well to keep them from mosquitoes as from the wild beasts which prowl about town during the night time. It is in latt 00:50ᵐⁱⁿᵘᵗᵉˢ north of the equator and contains about three hundred inhabitants[,] a mixture of the Spanish and Indians. They are a very kind and civil race to strangers but are extremely poor. I dont believe the whole town could produce one thousand dollars in cash[.] Everey requisite of food grows spontanious. Of meats they make but little use themselves keeping the most to sell to the shipping. Their food consists chiefly in plantains but they have abundance of excellent oranges. They raise some few potatoes and pine apples but as these require some labour they grow as few as possible.

Hither we made our way and gainᵈ an anchorage to lay in a store of wood and water for a long cruise to the westward. We found laying at this place the ship George of London Capᵗ Benneford from a long whaling voyage[,] having nearly all his men down with the scurvy[.] He was compellᵈ to hire a house on shore and make it {a} hospital for his whole ships company as he had but three men out of a lot of forty capable of doing duty. But under good managment they all recoverᵈ without the loss of a single man.

The whaling ship Lady Adams of Nantucket[26] arrived during our stay at this place, for the same purpose of ourselves[,] that of recruiting for a long season. Twas on one very pleasant day the captains of the two American ships got up a cruise in {the} woods for hunting of wild turkies. They had employed the cooks the day

preveous to baking pies etc for a long hunt[.] I being the youngest
boy onboard was chosen to make up the company in place of a
hunters dog.

We accordingly having every preparation, made our start on the
day appointed for the bush. We had travell[d] about three hours over
the meadows and through the woods toward the hunting grounds,
when we heard the most dismal howling set up before us, that
can be imagined. We continued on our way untill we seemed to
be approaching nearer and nearer the spot whence the dismal
sounds came, when the two captains came to a full stop, looked
at each other a few moments as though they wished to say something which each was ashamed to open first when they turned
simultaneously around making good their retreat simply re-
marking that the walking was so bad and the sun so extremly hot
they would return and take a cooler day for the excurcion. The fact
may easily be seen by the reader. They no doubt was afraid some
beast of pray would devour them and that I could not find my way
back, being too young to tell their anxious wives what became
of them.

I have since visited that town and found what sort of animal had
so seriously alarmed us. It is a small bird not larger than the hum-
mingbird of our country which keeps up a continued noise night
and day and may easily be mistaken for something more dangerous.
Although our hunt was put off to an other day, it was never proposed again and we were compell[d] to be satisfied with a few tame
turkies purchased in town instead of our game still roaming in the
woods, and like most of treasures we will leave them behind the
mountain.

After having obtain[d] a supply of wood and water[,] the main articles for which we came, we again set sail from this place. We now
directed our course for a groups of islands call[d] the Gallapagos with
the hope of getting a supply of terrapin with which those islands
abound and which have been so ably described by C[om][modore]
Porter[27] during our last war with England. After a passage of six
days we gain[d] an anchorage at Hoods [Española] Island. We caught
a few whales in making this passage which swell[d] our little quantity
of oil to about 700 barrels[.]

We anchor[d] in five fathoms water[.] On the northwest part of the island there is a small bay call[d] Stephens Bay[.] In this we came to anchor as the prevailing winds at this place is from SE. A ship could be hove down[28] in this harbour without danger. The surrounding beach upon this, as well as all the other islands are a beautiful snow white and in an evening appears like snow. There were many seals of the hair species but I saw no fur seals at this place. Those islands appear of volcanic origen[.] The rocks appear very much burn[d], and where there is soil it wears mostly the appearance of very dry snuff. In treading upon those rocks as you pass from one to the other they ring much like pot metal, and the whole lays so promiscously that in treading upon one you will tumble over a dozen pieces of the rocks at a time.

The method of taking terrapin by the seamen who touch at these islands is as follows. They first provide themselves with strips of canvass formed like suspenders, with small cords at each end[.] Thus prepared, they start off into the country from two to five miles, then divide into pairs or go singly as they may choose[,] keeping a sharp look out as they pass on under the trees for the object of their search and when any one finds more than he can carry to the boat alone, he cries out at the top of his voice[.] If any are in hearing that have no load of course they come to the sound untill they find him[.]

They then commence to harness their prisoner[.] They sieze him, turn him upon his back and place a large stone upon the shell, beneath the knee joint which prevents the terrapin from drawing in his legs during the operation of harnessing. They then tie those small cords which are attached to the belts, to the legs a little above the foot. The victim thus bound is thrown upon the back of the man in waiting passing the belts over his shoulders to secure him in that position. They then start for the boat beneath the powerful rays of a burning sun and trust me, when I tell you theirs is no enviable situation.

Their average weight is about eighty lbs but I have often seen them four hundred w[eigh]t. Their constant uneasiness whilst carrying them togather with add to the very uneven walking and constant giving way of stones beneath ones feet makes it I have often thought the hardest labour that can be given to man. And I have often seen an irritable seaman throw them from his back upon the rocks breaking in the whole top shell and sitting himself down upon the rocks, call down all the bitter curses he could think of upon the head of the poor unfortunate terrapin which lay bleeding at his feet. It is customary for each man to make three trips pr day into the woods, and bring each his load to the boat.

The shape of this animal resembles in some measure our small land tortoise which is found upon the uplands and is like it[,] high with round back[.] They have a very long neck which with their head resembles very much a snake and forms a very disagreeable appearance. I have often seen them with neck more than two feet in length.

They have a very novel, and yet harmless mode of combat. They will approach each other as nearly as possible[.] Then stretching out the necks from the shell to its utmost extremity with mouth open, they appear like the most spiteful reptile. They will stand in that position for a few moments, with their mouthes, head and neck quivering with rage, when the vanquished party will percieve the victor's head a little above his own and shrink back in an instant. That decides the contest. The vanquished will then draw his neck[,] head and legs as closely into the shell as possible and remain in that position untill the victor has taken himself away. And what seems more remarkable is, that although the combattants often meet upon the decks afterward I have never known them to renew the attack. This I believe to be their only mode of warfare. They have no teeth[,] their mouths being formed like a parrot's bill. When upon the islands they are very sagacious in taking care of themselves and secreting their eggs.

They are often kept for a long time onboard a ship, without food, or water. I have known them kept seven months without either, but it is certainly very cruel. Many people contend that they dont feel the knawings of hunger as other animals do, but of this I cannot be persuaded, for I have observed them when kept in that way, to be constantly moving around the decks tasting of every thing that lay within their reach. Their food is of the cabbage tree which is a very juicey tasteless tree peculiar to those islands.

During one of daily excurcions we missd one of our officers named Benjamin Lawrence[.] He had gone away from the boat in the morning and lost his way having gone too far across the island without noteceing his land-marks for return, and although we all set about looking him up, it was night when he return[d] to the boat. He was very much exhausted as he had passed the whole day without food or water under a burning sun of 110[deg].

He related to us his day's journey thus, that after having parted with his company in the woods, he had struck off in a s[out]h east direction untill he found a terrapin. This he harness[d] and threw upon his back and started in what he believed to be the direction of the ship, but it must have been quite an opposite direction[.] After walking for several hours and finding himself in an impassable thicket he let his back load go and climb[d] a tree to find if possible some clew to his position, but could see nothing to direct him. He now began to realize in some measure his situation as he remembered that the island produced no water[,] only at the rainy season.

He now renew[d] his march in search of the sea beach at any point of the island, determined to follow the beach untill he should see the ship. He now began to feel the need of a cooling stream and as he soon met with a terrapin he soon struck up a bargain with him for his blood. He therfore cut off the animals head and drank the warm blood as it came oozing from the wound. This was of some service in strengthening him for his journey and he again marched on.

A few hours travel brought him upon the sea shore, but from the tallest tree the ship couldnot be seen. He continued his march upon the beach amidst a burning sand for he felt quite certain that by doing so he must at some period meet with his friends. He finally after a long and weary march of it, saw the ship in the distance and began to dread the laugh which would be turned upon him if he return[d] to the boat empty handed. He therfore struck off again into the woods, and soon having selected a terrapin, backed him and got to the boat soon after night fall. All were overjoyed to see him again in safety and heartily welcom[d] him to the boat.

After having remain[d] at this island four days and procur[d] one hundred and eighty terrapin, we again set sail. Hoods Island is in 1[deg]:20[m] south lattitude and 89[deg]:40[m] west longitude. We now directed our way towards Charles [Santa María] Island[,] one of the same groupe. This island was a famous resort for Capt Porter in the frigate Essex during our last war with England. At this island we arrived the next morning about nine o'clock. There is an excellen[t] harbour on the southwest side of the island. The trees, to the southward of the anchorage show to be of good growth, and things about indicate a good soil.

We obtain^d one hundred terrapins at this island but found them to be very scarce. The terrapin of this island, are the most rich flavour^d and delicious meat I have ever met with. It was not unfrequently that we took from them eight to ten lbs. of fat. This was as clear and pure as the best of yellow butter and of a rich flavour. We took one of those animals onboard which weight six hundred lbs and took six of our men to carry him to the beach with cross poles[.] He appear^d very old and we gave him the name of the Commodore but as he never came quick at the call we presume he didnot fully appreciate the cognomen.

There is at those islands a curious animal called the guano.[29] There are two kinds, the land guano and the sea guano. The one is amphibious and seems to live amongst the rocks whilst the land guano is a different sort of animal and resembles something our lizards but grow to a much larger size[.] They have four legs and grow to about two feet in length. They look very old and ugly. Their colour resembles the burned rocks of that country, which has a dirty yellowish cast. Their skin looks very rough and uneven. I have known many persons eat them with a gusto and pronounce them excellent food.

The pelicans of this island are very numerous and worthy of some notice. They have a large bill perhaps a foot long, with a natural bag reaching from the throat to near the end of the bill. Beneath it the under jaw is so formed that it can be spread open and thus forms a net. The bag will expand and contain more than half a peck. With this net they supply themselves and their young with food. They make a very clumsy and awkward appearance when in the act of diving for fish, as they then extend their wings[,] open the mouth and spread the wide and awkward foot. Green turtle are found here in abundance. The whalers make little or no use of them as the terrapin are so far preferable for the table that the green turtle stand but a poor chance for a choice.

This island has a better soil upon it than any other island of the groupe but I think two hundred acres of good land would be a large calculation for it[,] the remainder being burned snuffy soil or parched climpers and loose rock. At this time there was no inhabittants upon Charles Island and of course no cultivation.

We had with us an Englishman[,] a boatstearer named Thomas Chappel. He was very wild and fond of fun at whatever expence it might be produced. This lad took with him a tinder box, onshore unknown to any one and set fire to the underbrush and trees. This being the dry season it spread with fearful rapidity and burned freely crossing our paths in every direction and cutting off our retreat to the boats. On our return we were compell^d to run the gauntlet there being no alternative. We were many of us forced to drop our heads and run through the blazing brush for many yards. Tis true we got a little singed in our hair and clothing but all came off with a whole skin. And it was well for him that we didnot know at the time whose trick it was, for I can assure you it took our lads some time to cool off, and the captain's wrath knew no bounds, swearing vengeance upon the head of the incendiary should he be discover^d.

There can be no estimate of the destruction caused by this fire to the animal creation. On my return to this place many years afterwards the ruin was still visible, wherever the fire raged. Neither trees, shrubbery, nor grass have since appeard, and judging from the extent of desolate ground, there must have been thousands upon thousands of terrapin, birds, lizards, and snakes destroyed and it probably burned untill the rainy season again set in.

At day light on the morning of October the 23^d we weighed our anchor, set all sails and again put to sea, and at sunset having lost sight of the island could still see the reflection from the blazing element.

We now directed our course towards the western or as it is termed, the off shore whaling ground. Nothing occurred worthy of note during this passage with the exception of occasionally chasing a wild shoal of whales to no purpose untill the morning of the 16th November. Then being in 1^{deg}:00^m south lattitude & 118^{deg}:00^m west longitude a shoal of whales was descried from the mast head. All hands was summon^d to prepare the boats and persue the whales. The boat of chief mate being more fleet than the others speedily came alongside of a large whale and having call^d up his harpoons-man to throw his dart, when quick as thought the whale turned upon his side and dashed the boat litterally in pieces, and we all found ourselves quickly thrown into the sea but strange as it may appear, none were injured by it. All were taken safely into an other boat and taken to the ship.

[CHAPTER 9TH]

We mourn indeed; that grief, and toil, and strife
Send one deep murmur, from the walks of life,
That yonder sun, when evening paints the sky,
Sinks beautious, on a world of misery.
The course of wide obstruction to withstand,
We lift our feeble voice—our trembling hand,
But still bowed low, or smitten to the dust;
Father of mercies; still in thee we trust;
Through good or ill, in poverty, or wealth,
In joy, or woe; in sickness, or in health,
Meek piety thy awful hand surveys;
And the faint murmur turns to prayer and praise.
We know whatever evils we deplore,
Thou hast permitted, and we know no more.

BOWLES.[30]

WE NOW COME TO give an account of the shipwreck of the Essex and subsequent sufferings of the crew whilst lingering in their whale boats.

Nothing occurred from our last untill the morning of the 20th November when all hands was suddenly aroused by a cry from the man at the mast head of ["]Whales.["] The boats were instantly lower^d and in full persuit. The boat of the chief mate soon came up with and attacked a small whale, when with the flourish of its tail the boat was badly stoven on one side, and was filling very rapidly with water when each of us in the boat strip^d off our shirts and cram^d [them] into the hole which was broken. This prevented the boat from sinking and gave us an opportunity to return to the ship in our own boat.

The other two boats had alreadey got amongst the whales in an other direction and had fasten^d to two of them, being then about

139

two miles to le[e]ward from the ship. In the mean time we had got our broken boat to the ship having hoisted her upon the cranes and the mate at work repairing the breach temporarily, when I being then at the helm and looking on the windward side of the ship saw a very large whale approaching us.

I call[d] out to the mate to inform him of it. On his seeing the whale he instantly gave me an order to put the helm hard up, and steer down towards the boats. I had scarcely time to obey the order, when I heard a loud cry from several voices at once, that the whale was coming foul of the ship. Scarcely had the sound of their voices reached my ears when it was followed by a tremendous crash. The whale had struck the ship with his head directly under the larboard fore chains at the waters edge with such force as to shock every man upon his feet.

The whale then setting under the ships bottom came up on the starboard side and directly under the starboard quarter. This last position gave the mate a fine opportunity to have kill[d] him with a throw of his lance. His first impulse was to do so, but on a second look observing his tail directly beneath the rudder his better judgment prevail[d] lest a flourish of the tail should unhang the rudder and render the ship unmanagable. But could he have foreseen all that so soon followed he would probably have chosen the lesser evil and have saved the ship by killing the whale even at the expense of losing the rudder. For as we will show all wasnot yet over.

Instead of leaving the ship, the monster took a turn off about three hundred yards ahead, then turning short around came with his utmost speed and again struck the ship a tremendous blow with his head upon the larboard bow and with such force as to stave in the whole bow at the waters-edge.

One of the men who was below at the time, came running upon deck saying the ship is filling with water. The first order was to try the pumps, but of this they were spared the trouble, for on going to the hatchway it was discover[d] that alreadey had the water appe[a]red above the lower deck, which on discovering we turned our attention to getting clear the boat, which was stowed overhead and bottom upwards, that being the only boat left us, with which we could expect to escape.

This was no easey task, under the present excitement. Neverthe-

less we succeeded in getting her out without injury, although the
ship was waterlog[d], and fast falling upon her side.

In the mean time the steward hadnot been idle. He had twice enter[d] the cabin under the most trying circumstances and at his peril,
had bro[t] out the trunks of the captain and mate and also two quadrants and two of Bowditch[s] Practical Navigators. These, with the
two compasses taken from the binnacle, was all, that we had an opportunity of getting into the boat, and get in ourselves when the
ship capsized, with the mast heads in the water.

The scene at this moment—no one can ever realize to its extent,
unless they have been in such a situation under simalar circumstances. What an association of ideas flashed across our minds on
the instant. Here lay our beautiful ship, a floating and dismal
wreck,—which but a few minutes before appeard in all her glory,
the pride and boast of her cap[t] and officers, and almost idolized by
her crew, with all sails neatly set and trim[d] to the breeze presenting
to the eye the fac similie of a ship about to leave the harbour on a
summers day under the admiring gaze of hundreds to witness such
a scene.

Here she now lays, snatched untimely from her stateliness, into a
mere shadow of what she was, and our selves deprived of the home
which her goodly sides had so long afforded us. Now at the least six
hundred miles from the nearest land and that land too, in a direction
rendering it impossible of approach being directly to the windward
of us and as the trade winds blow in the same direction the whole
year around of course left us no hope in that direction, and our only
chance was in a more distant land in a more favourable position.

The boats of the captain and second mate at the time of the accident were as I have before stated about two miles to the leeward
of the ship, and each fast to a whale seperately. Their first intima-
tion of the loss was the boatstearers looking in direction of the ship,
cried out to the captain ["]Look, look, what ails the ship, she is
upsetting.["]

He describes it as bearing the appearance at first sight of a ship
caught in a sudden and hard squall or gust of wind with the sails
flying in all directions, and the vessel nearly turned upon one side.
In a twinkling all eyes were turned in that direction, but judge
of their surprise for {on} looking, no ship was to be seen. They of

course could have no just conception of what had taken place. There were many conjectures as to the cause of the loss but none for a moment thought of a whales having done the work. They however lost no time in disengaging themselves from their fish, and making toward the direction in which the ship was last seen. They hadnot gone {far} before they discovered the hulk floating upon her side and presenting the appearance of a rock.

On coming up to the ship and making some little inquiry the captain's first order was to cut away the masts and try if possible to get the ship more upright and scuttle the decks with the hope to get at some provisions and water. They then got upon the ships side and cut away the laniards.

This done the main mast broke off about twenty feet above deck, and also the head of the mizen mast, and fore topmast broke above the cap, when the ship again righted to an angle of 45 degrees, when we commenced to cut open the decks in different parts of the ship. But unfortunately for us our provisions were mostly in the lower hold and couldnot be come at. We could only obtain two casks of ship bread weighing about 500 lbs and two small hogs, which came swimming to the boats from amongst the wreck, and some half dozen terrapin's.

With this little stock of food then, we are forced to be satisfied and thanks be to God, who is ever watching over us, that it is no less. We now turned our attention to getting some of the ships light sails wherewith to make a full suit of sails for our boats. As the boats are now our only ship we must improve something upon them ere we make a final start from the wreck.

I shall now commence my work in form of a sea journal, and am indebted to our chief mate Mr Owen Chase for dates from his pencil[d] log book kept at the time, and which is the only means I have of getting at dates correctly as I wrote no log or journal at the time myself. We shall for convenience write up our work by sea ac[coun]t[.]

November th 21st, 1820

Strong trade winds from the south east, with pleasant weather but very rough sea. Lay the boats during the night a few yards astern of the wreck. At daylight haul^d alongside the wreck and renewed the search for provisions but without further success. We now give over the search, and set to work at making sails for the boats. Fortunately the mate has saved in his trunk, a quantity of twine and sail needles which in our case is invaluable. This is truly a buisy day, and on the whole we see more cheerful faces than we had dared to expect. We find by our observation that we have been driven in a northwest direction by the current since the shipwreck a distance of forty-nine miles.

Our lattitude this day is by observation 00^d:06^{miles} south[,] longitude pr ac^t 119:30 west[.]

November the 22nd

The weather is remarkably fine, and we are cheerfully at work making sails for our boats, and planking them up at the sides to make them more safe in keeping out the sea &c[.] This we do with boat boards in their rough state, which we have been so fortunate as to save from the wreck. One of those boards being lap^d over the other about two inches[,] this when finished will raise the sides of the boats about eighteen inches higher than they were originally and will form an excellent barrier to the sea.

The night is now upon us again, and we have veered our boats again astern of the wreck to await the return of daylight. All hands save myself are wrap^ed in sweet sleep, and seem to be enjoying[,] unconcious of their awful condition, the soft side of a plank. I have been very wakeful through the night, catching occasionally a few moments repose but to the high rolling of the swell and constant tossing of our little boat, the creaking of spars and timbers about the wreck, I must attribute my lack of rest, which others so well enjoy—Well, sleep on ship mates. It will refresh you for the coming day. You will need all your energies for the contest—I cannot expect rest to the body, when the mind willnot be composed[.]

Daylight at length appeared. We hauled our boats again to the wreck, and took a look for provisions but found none[.] Our only hope now, is that something more may come floating from the lower hold amidst the general confusion.

The weather still holds fine and pleasant with its usual south east trade wind. This morning the decks of the ship begins to give way, and there is strong threats of a speedy dissolution. Indeed it seems from the constant working and straining of the vessel that she will soon disappear and leave ourselves and our frail barks alone upon the surface, to point out where she has been. The casks of oil are continually bursting and flowing out from the hold of the ship filling the whole surface of the deep with the fruits of our labour, as far as the eye can reach. How truly heartrending the scene. Here at one view are our blighted prospects and the reward of our toil scatter[d] to the winds.

Having now completed the fitting of our boats, and feeling satisfied that no more provision can be obtain[d] by remaining longer by the wreck, we have determined to set sail immidiately. One of our men now climbed to the top of the foremast of the ship, to take a last look over the horizon to see if perchance any ship may be in view from that elevation, but in vain did his eyes glance anxiously over the surface of the deep for no vessel could be seen, and he was forced to return to us again without bringing to us any new hope of delivery.

It being now near noon the captain wished to remain by the wreck untill that hour for convenience of getting an observation[.] He called the officers togather and held council with them as to the best route to be taken with the boats. His first desire was, that the boats should keep togather and make for the Society Islands, they being in a southwesterly direction and consequently far under our lee. And how truly unfortunately for us all that his first wish was-not complied with, for in ten days at fartherest we could have been landed safely, probably without the loss of a single individual. The officers however differ[d] in opinion upon that point, and urged upon him to go up the coast and when clear of the trade wind, they urged the probability of a speedy passage to the coast of Chili. Not wishing to oppose where there was two against one the Cap[t] reluctantly yealded to their arguments and it was decided that we should go up the coast as they term[d] it. Fatal error. How many warm hearts has ceased to beat in consequence of it.

We now set about dividing our men and forming them into boats crews. Our complement at this time consisted of fourteen whites, men and boys, with six coloured, in all twenty. Of those we distributed as follows. In the captains boat seven, mates boat seven, and in the second mates boat six. And we had saved one musket, two horse pistols and about two lbs of powder. The captain retaining the musket, gave to each officer a pistol, and equally divided the powder[,] provisions and water. Of water we had obtained about two hundred gallons. Thus finding preparations completed and getting our observation at noon [we] were prepared for a start.

We find by observation that the wreck has still been acted upon by a strong WNW current, and that during the night we have crossed the equator. How strange that we have recieved no visit from Neptune, but I fancy he is like the rest of us on those points, courts luxury and shuns miserey.

Our lattitude by observation at noon is 00^d:13^m north, longitude 120^d:00^m west {pr act.}

November th 23^d

We now having every thing in readiness at thirty minutes past 12= [noon] cast off our lines from the ill fated Essex and set all sails upon our boats which we have rig^d as schooners and which makes a very handsome show on this our first start. But now how changed our feeling from yesterday. Now for the first time did the horror of our situation fall fully before us. Now it was that we could realize the slender thread upon which our lives were hung. Now could be seen the pale and wan features, the wild and vacant stare thrown upon each other and ever and anon, turning to view the fast receding remnant of the hulk, which had borne us so gracefully over the bosom of the ocean, as though it were possible that she could yet relieve us from the fate that seemed to await us, untill at last it sunk from our view beneath the horizon.

It now seemed to us that all had been relieved from a spell by which we had been bound and every countenance lit up as each involuntaryly utter^d ["]Farewell, farewell.["] Very soon all resumed their natural cheerfulness, and now, that our minds were made up for the worst, half the struggle was over.

The wind by this time began to freshen and the sea to run very high and irregular which compell^d us to reduce our sails by reefing, and through the night the wind increased to a gale, and the sea making a continued breach over us, kept us constantly wet through to the skin, wetting and injureing our little stock of provisions. Add to this our boat had sprung a leak, so rapidly as to keep one hand constantly bailing out the water.

Toward^s noon the wind had abated and the sea became more smoothe. The sun also shone out pleasantly, giving us an opportunity to dry our wet clothing. We find by observation that we have made since leaving the wreck seventy one miles to south giving us new hopes, having recross^d the equator[.] Lattitude by obs^n = oo^d:58^m = south

November th 24th

The wind has again arisen and the sea breaks very high and our situation begins to be truly uncomfortable[.] The sea constantly breaking into the boats, makes the prospect of preserving our little stock of provisions less and less probable. At 1 PM a heavey sea broke into our boat filling it half full of water, and entirely saturating our stock of bread with salt water. The bread being our only dependence gave to us on the whole rather a cheerless prospect but with perseverance in attending to it and constant spreading and drying when the weather would permit, saved it from utter ruin. We this day arranged our allowance of food and water, and gave it out for the first time. It consisted for the present in one cake of biscuit and a pint of water to each man, for the 24 hours.

During the night the wind and sea still continued and as we were constantly wet left us no possibility of repose. In the morning we found that the captain's boat had met with the same misfortune as ourselves[,] having had his bread also well soaked. This day being very rugged and the spray continually flying to all parts of the boat renders it utterly impossible to obtain an observation.

November th 25th

The wind has not abated in the least, and although a good comfortable ship to be here, would consider this no more than what they would choose to call a good strong trade wind, yet to us, in our crippled state, it answers the purpose of a gale, and keeps us constantly wet and chilled through. We were suddenly [alarmed?] to day by our boat springing a new leak[.] We immidiately tore up the ceiling of the boat in search for the leak, when we discover^d in the bow that one of the wood ends had bursted off[31] and the water rushing in with great rapidity. As the wound lay below the surface of the sea, it required no little ingenuity to come at on the outside and make the repairs, necsasary. We first hove the boat upon the opposite tack, thus bringing the leak as near to the waters edge as possible, and by placing the men all on the leeward side and thus we were enabled to make our repairs much easier than we had anticipated.

This little incident although it may seem small, was capable of causing amongst us the greatest excitement. It served to show to us in how frail a bark, lay all our hope of safety, and plainly too, could we trace the hand of providence, for had we not have saved by mere accident a small handfull of nails the writer would probably have adorned a tale rather than told it.[32] This spread a gloom over our little company not easily effaced. This evening we had prayers and a few hymns sung by a pious old colour^d man named Richard Peterson which for a time drew our minds from our present miseries to seek deliverance from a higher power.

Again we are without observation from the effects of bad weather[.]

November th 26th

We are now favour^d with some little abatement in the wind but the sea is high and irregular. We are enabled however to spread out our wet bread around the boat and therby save it from total destruction. We have also been enabled to set all sails again upon the boats. We have been pleased to see the wind has hauld to east north east therby giving us a more favourable course, and again the faces around begin to wear a more cheerful aspect.

November th 27th

The sea has become something more smoothe but the wind having again veered to east caused the boats to head off to SSE, which togather with the rapid current running to the westward at all times in those seas gives to us the prospect of making but slow progress to the south, and again our hearts are fill^d with sadness.

November ^th 28th

Our prospects still unfavourable and the wind has again hauled to s. east which again drives us to the south west and again the wind has increased causing us to reduce our sails with two reefs. The night set in awfully dark and tempestuous and we very much feard being seperated from the boats. We however by constant watching and care on part of the captain and officers [managed?] to keep togather by sailing in a line keeping the mates boat ahead and the captains boat in the middle with the second mates boat astern.

About eleven o'clock this night we were suddenly aroused by a cry from the captains boat. We listned for a moment, and could distinctly hear the cap[t]ain call upon the second mate for assistance whose boat was nearer to him than our own. We, of course made all possible haste toward^s him, and on enquiry what was the matter he replied ["]I have been attacked by some sort of a fish, very large, which has stoven the boat.["]

The extreme darkness of the night prevented them from ascertaining what sort of fish it had been, but we believe it to have been what is known by the name of thresher or as the whalemen call them, a killer. It remain^d and played around the boat for a few minutes as if to renew the attack, but finally disappear^d. It seemed to have been twelve to sixteen feet in length. They gave him a few severe punches in the side, with a sprit pole the only weapon at hand which drove him off, but he had made a large breach in the bow of the boat through which the water was pouring very fast when we came up. We took out all their provisions & weight to lighten the boat, which prevented their again getting wet and gave them an opportunity to repair damages.

We lay by him untill daylight {when} he soon repair^d the damage by pressing the broken boards back to their place, and nailing strips of the same material acrossways. All finished we again reloaded his boat, and set sail on our way. The wind and sea becoming more favourable we again made tolerable good progress. We now found that our scanty allowance of water was insufficient to allay our burning thirsts and the torture became almost insupportable[.] This probably arose from having eaten of the bread, so recently soaked with salt water and dried in the sun.

Still we darenot to increase our allowance of water for we had only commenced our journey, nor could we conjecture when or where it would end. We therfore were resolved to endure as long as human nature could hold out with the hope that some means of relief would be offer^d ere long.

November ^the 29th

We still continue to progress slowly to the southward with a high sea causing our boats to labour and strain themselves to an alarming extent. Our own boat in particular being old and crazy complains of a general weakness through[h]out the whole frame, and were we at home we wouldnot feel safe to go ten miles in her. What did I say home, yes home. Can it be possible that such poor objects as we, have a home. Reach me my allowance of bread Bill, and let me partake whilst I think that I have a home[.] It may go farther and nourish better.

Our old boat has an excellent doctor in the mate[.] He being an active and ingenious man lets no opportunity pass wherby he can add a nail by way of strengthning plaster.[33] We have to day a shoal of dolphins playing around us, and in the hope and expectation of catching some of them we have made fishing lines, and made use of all our persuasive powers of argument to induce them to come onboard, but all efforts have failed. They continue to swim around us seemingly as tenacious of their existance as ourselves. The weather now wears a milder aspect, and although our progress has been slow, our men are more cheerful.

November ^th 30th

We are now cheered with serene and beautiful weather and our evenings are cheered by divine service headed by the aforementioned negro Peterson. Indeed, his conduct on those occasions

would do honor to a chaplain. We have this day kill[d] one of our terrapins of which we had two. All seemed quite impatient of an opportunity to drink the warm blood as it came oozing from the
wound of the sacrificed animal.

Although the cravings of hunger upon our stomachs was most
acute, yet some there were who revolted at sight of the blood nor
could they make up their minds to taste it. We divided about one
gill to those who wished it, and cooked the meat, dividing it equally
with all, of which we made a delicious meal not rejecting the entrails. After which our men seemed greatly refreshed and it gave to
all an increase of spirits and cheerfulness. We find by our observation this day that we have made about five hundred miles on our
way, and our observed lattitude is 7[d]:53[m] south[.]

December [th] 1st & 2nd

We had nothing very remarkable on those days save that the
weather has been very fine, and our boats have kept well togather.
The wind too, haul[d] to north east and we are making well on our
way, and there seems amongs[t] us a degree of repose and careless-
ness which would scarcely be looked for amid persons in our forlorn and hopeless situation[.]

December [th] 3[d]

The first part of this day and evening were very pleasant; attended
our usual prayer meeting. After which the sky became suddenly
overcast and the night very dark, making it very difficult to see the
boats and keep each others position. At ten o'clock we very suddenly miss[d] the boat of the second mate, and we were alarmed at so
sudden disappearance lest something had destroyed them. We however struck a light, and on hoisting it to the mast head of the boat,
to our great joy saw it answer[d] by the missing boat a short distance
to the leeward of us. Ever after this we found it very difficult to
keep our boats togather owing to the darkness of the nights. Much
time was lost in looking each other up, being compell[d] sometimes to

tack frequently during the search, but for all that none were willing to separate for it is well known that misery loves company.

December ᵗʰ 4ᵗʰ

Nothing worthy of note.

December ᵗʰ 5ᵗʰ

This day we have a strong S.east wind, with very thick and dark weather which continued through the night. During this night we were seperated from the other boats for a time but after having fired our pistols a few times we again got togather and steered along on our way.

December ᵗʰ 6ᵗʰ and 7ᵗʰ

The winds blew very strong, and more unfavourable and our boats leaking badly, frequently taking onboard large quantities of water, keeping one hand constantly at work bailing it out and they suffered very much from being constantly wet.

December the 8ᵗʰ

This day the wind has hauled to east south east, with torrents of rain falling, and at midnight had increased to an awful gale with a frightful sea, which seems to threaten our total anihilation. We had kept gradually reducing our sails as the wind had increased, untill we were compelld to strike our masts also. The boats laying to very badly every sea seemed to threaten our destruction, but having done all in our power we threw ourselves down in the bottom of the boat to await the fate of sailors as became men, and trusting in our Maker to dispose of us as seemed best in his sight. The sky was blackened past conception to those who have not witnessd the same.

The constant and vivid lightning seemed to envelope us in a fearful blaze, and the awful thunder of an angry element threatened every moment our final extermination. Nothing but an overruling hand of a Creator could have saved our frail barks from the horrors of that dreadful night, or from the vengeance of that pittiless storm. Towards noon the storm began to abate, and we again step^d our masts, and got the boats head to the southward and they could lay more safely to the sea[.]

During the storm of course our men couldnot sleep for a moment, and now that it was abating nature seemed to give way, and it was with much difficulty as the sea went down, that they could be prevailed on to set more sail. We had providentially kept togather during the gale without any effort of our own, and at noon we were once more near each other to make a fresh start and be cheered with each others presence.

December the 9th

At noon the gale had so far abated that we were enabled to set all sails upon the boats, but the sea being very high caused us to proceed slowly along. Our boat too had started a fresh leak and it became necsasary to keep one hand constantly at work to bail the boat to keep out the water.

By our meridian observation this day we were in the lattitude 17^d:40^m south having now the Society Islands directly to leeward and not more than six hundred miles to the west of us. We were in the influence of a brisk trade wind from S.east and of course could have landed probably in five or six days at fartherest safely with every man in good health. I presume the enquiry will now arise why did you not steer for them instead of attempting the dangerous voyage to the distant coast of Chili which to any reasonable mind must appear almost impossible to attain in such weak and unseaworthy boats. In answer I can only say there was gross ignorance or a great oversight somewhere which cost many a fine seamen their lives.

December the 10th

The winds and the weather seemed something more favourable, and we were making fair progress[.] As the time advanced since having left the wreck our bodies had become more and more wasted and our appetites more importunate and had increased in us a desire to solicit an addition to our daily allowance of bread, but a little reflection convinced us, that an application of that sort would be unmanly and useless for the mate had taken the whole under his protection and slept at the door of the bread room with a loaded pistol at his side. And as the arrangement had been made by himself as to the manner of allowance, I think nothing but violence to his person could have induced him to increase it. To his strict attention to this, as well as keeping up a degree of discipline, I think may be attributed our ultimate relief and final safety.

Whilst sailing along on our course this day we pass[d] through a small shoal of flying fish[.] Four of them in their efforts to escape us flew against the sails and fell into the boat. It was quite laughable to see the excitement this created among our little company, each man eager to catch his fish. They were devour[d] as soon as caught and without regard to cleansing or cooking were consider[d] as a dainty morsel but of course didnot go far towards filling an empty stomach.

Decr [th] 11th & 12th

We had very light winds with frequent calms and our progress in consequence was very slow. We kill[d] our last remaining terrapin which again fill[d] us with new life and vigour. At this time the weather was very hot and having no means of screening ourselves from its piercing rays our sufferings became most intolerable as our short allowance of water was barely enough to support life.

Decr [th] *13* [th]

We this day were again favour[d] with a light breeze from the northward[.] This gave us new hopes of delivery for we now supposed
we had pass[d] the limits of the trade wind and would now be in the
way of a fair proportion of fair winds, but alas this too was but a
passing vision and transitory relief[.] All was like a dream from
which we were too soon to awake, for this wind died gradually
away and at night was succeeded by a total calm. This calm continued through the 14 to 16th Dec[r] inclusive.

During this trying state of affairs the mate proposed reducing
our allowance of provisions one half whilst the calms continued. All
submitted with forbearance and fortitude to this wise decision and
as our stock of water was about equal with our food it was thought
proper not to alter it. Indeed we couldnot have reduced our allowance of water for alreadey we hadnot sufficient to keep our
mouths in moisture. We frequently applied salt water to our
parched lips with the hope to quell the fever that raged there but
that only served to increase our thirst so much that some were compell[d] to seek relief in their own urine. Our sufferings during these
hot days almost exceed belief and the heart again bleeds at the bare
recital. Some of the men were induced to hang themselves over the
side of the boat into the sea, to cool their bodies and it was with the
utmost difficulty that they were enabled to haul themselves again
into the boat through debility and weakness.

This day our boat continued to leak badly, and on searching we
found the leak in the very lowest or garboard streak of the boat. To
remedy this it was absolutely necsasary to get at the bottom of the
boat. As the only means of doing this our boatstearer Benjamin
Lawrence volunteered to tie a rope fast to his waist and with a
hatchet in hand decend under the boat and clench the nails as they
were driven through from the inside therby drawing the planks
more closely togather. Thus again our crazy boat was rendr[d] com-
paritively tight.

Our lattitude was this day by observation 21:42 south[.] By this
observation we ascertained that our boats had been driven directly
out of our course to the northward by the current and swell ten

miles which served again to arouse us to a sense of our imminent danger and strongly demanded some mitigating expedient. The cap[t] now made to us a proposition which was agreed to by all—which was to take a double allowance of bread and water and commence rowing our boats to the southward with the hope that by changing our position a few miles would be the means of obtaining for us a breeze of wind.

When the sun had gone down we man[d] our owers [oars] and commenced to perform our laborious occupation, but our late privations had so far reduced our {strength}, that a few hours sufficed and proved to us the utter impossibility of making farther progress by this means[.] It was given over accordingly, and we again threw ourselves upon the chances of catching a breeze of wind for a further advancment[.]

Dec [th] 17th

With the sunrise this morning a breeze sprung up from the SE[d] and although directly ahead was welcomed by all with feelings of gratitude and joy.

Dec [th] 18th

The breeze continued to increase[,] veering from SE to ESE, and by midnight had increased to a gale and we were compell[d] to reduce our sails and heave the boat too, being again driven to leeward widely from our course.

Dec [th] 19th

The weather again moderated so as to admit of setting all sails upon the boats and soon again the elements became tranquil and the weather once more moderate and pleasant.

December th 20th

The night having been something squally with the showers of rain
falling frequent caused us to rest very uncomfortably but as the day
was followed by such joyful prospects that the gloom of the past
night was entirely dispell^d. At seven oclock this morning whilst we
were sitting in the bottom of our little boat quite silent and dejected
one of our companions named William Wright on rising to stretch
his limbs, casting his eyes along the horizon cried out suddenly
there is land. We were all up in an instant and stretching our eyes to
the leeward could distinctly see that it was no visionary delusion
but in reality land ho as described. All seemed to be reanimated and
instantly to possess a new existance. The first appearence of the island was that of a low white sand beach spread along the horizon
before us and each man seemed to greet it as a final end to his long
confinement and sufferings.

We remain^d hove too in order to get the boats to come togather
when after a short deliberation of cap^t and officers, the boats were
steer^d toward this new land of promise.

Never has any eyes rested on anything so pleasingly beautiful
(save the one whose name is not in these pages) as did this little island at this moment appear. We might indeed make some feeble attempt to describe to the reader our feelings upon this occasion but
on the whole could but faintly succeed in the picture, and indeed
would give but a sorry delinaeation. Fear, gratitude, surprise and
expectation held momentary possesion of us forming new impulse
to our exertions.

This island was to all appearance about six miles long and three
broad with steep and rugged cliffs and high perpendicular rocks,
whilst its shores was surrounded on all sides by shelving rocks a
little beneath the surface of the sea, at about one hundred yards
from the shore over which the sea is constantly breaking. The top
of the island looked green and beautiful being coverd with trees and
underbrush.

The numerous swarms of sea birds that surrounded the shores
gave to us proof that the island was uninhabited, and was a great relief to our minds for in our present state we could have made but
feeble resistance to an attack from natives had the island proved in-

habited[.] And to have again put to sea without having effected a landing would have been sentence of death to each man in our then exhausted state as regards water for no quantity however reduced could have made it hold out to any known land.

We at first mistook this island for Ducies Island judging from our observation of the day previous but it subsequently proved to be [an] island discover[d] by Cap[t] H. King of the whaling ship Elizabeth of London some twelve or fifteen months preveous to our visiting it, to which he gave the name of Elizabeths Island in memory of his ship. This island lies seventy miles distant to the west of Ducies, and in the same degree of lattitude viz 24:40 south 125:50 west[.]

We now sail[d] along the shore at about one hundred yards distant, and frequently firing a pistol as we glided past some valley or nook in the woods to arouse its inhabitants should there be any within hearing but neither friend nor foe appear[d].

At length being about the centre of the island on the leeward side and finding a sort of bend in the shore, this seemed the most promising position we had seen to make an attempt to land with our boats[.] We came to a halt and it was agreed upon to land some few of the party preveous to landing with the boats, therby securing to us a retreat in case we should unexpectedly find savages in ambush. But all delay and caution proved of no use to us, as the island proved unpeopled.

The chief mate with three seamen having armed themselves soon effected a landing and made a short excursion into the bush, when finding themselves much exhausted by this little exercise through debility and want of exercise in the boats they were compell[d] to lay down upon the greensward for refreshment, whence they soon struck off into the woods to reconnoitre and kept a good look out for a spring of water. The mate having occasion to cross an inlet of the sea, discovered a fish of about one foot and a half in length swimming near him when he struck him with the butt of his gun which crippled the fish so that he swam under a shelving rock near the shore from whence he was easily taken by aid of his ramrod and quickly devour[d] by the little scouting party.

After their little repast finding themselves refreshed they set off over the hills. They started much refreshed and in good spirit, occasionally scaling some perpendicular cliff at the expense of torn hands and at the imminent peril of their necks, but all in vain for not the least moisture could be seen to ooze from the hills nor rocks after the most diligent search. As the tide was rising rapidly they were compell^d to give over the search and return to the boats.

When they returned and made report, it was agreed to land and hauled the boats upon the green under the woods. We then turned them bottom upwards thus forming a protection from the night dews or rain under which we could sleep comfortably and enjoy dreams of home and friends which most of our wretched shipmates were never to realize.

December t^h 21st

After enjoying a good nights sleep, we awoke in the morning finding ourselves greatly refreshed and quite able to start about the island and renew the search for the article of water of which became now of vital importance to obtain. This now seem^d to be our chief desire as our very lives were involved in the issue. Our men now scatter^d over the hills in every direction and traversed the inmost recesses of the forest and over those lonely hills but in vain for after the most diligent search no water could be discover^d and at night fall we were compell^d to return sorrowing and dejected to our little town of boats[.]

In the valley during the day one of our men having chosen a walk along the seashore in the search chanced to see a sort of moisture issue from a rock and clay hillock. The mate taking a chisel and hammer repair^d speedyly to the place and commenced to peck into the rock but without any farther prospect for getting water was compell^d to give over and return to the village.

Since our absence during the day our captain and steward had not been idle. They had gather^d a large number of land crabs, with which this island abounds; and having roasted them upon the coals togather with a few birds which they had caught formed a sufficiency for a magnificent repast. Here everey one seated himself upon the beautiful green grass and perhaps no banquet was ever enjoyed with greater gusto or gave such universal satisfaction.

But we were soon call^d to our senses for we were yet without water and our allowance was so small that our lips became parched and feverish and were quite swollen and cracked and we were no compell^d to reduce even our present scanty allowance. For were we not to find water, how were we to survive to again cross such an extent of ocean as yet roll^d between our island home and a place of probable delivery. We found at this place a sort of pepper grass which was not unpleasant to the taste which after chewing produced a slight moisture in ones mouth by which in some degree our burning thirst was alleviated. This however only remain^d whilst chewing it and left us in much the same state as when we commenced to chew it.

We found here a large sea bird called by seamen boatswains but more properly tropic birds. They were about the size of a hen. They are entirely white having two long feathers projecting from the tail from which probably the name of boatswain was given them as those two feathers somewhat resemble that very useful instrument to the boatswain viz the marlinespike. Of these we caught an abundance for we had only to await untill nightfall when they came in flocks from sea to roost and feed their young when we could pounce upon them with a stick and take them without difficulty and we by this means kept our table supplied without difficulty during our stay.

There was also at this place a species of sea fowl call^d the man of war hawk. This bird used to afford us a great deal of amusement in watching them during their hours of piracy for being too lazy to go off to sea during the day in quest of food they would hover about over the trees, untill the hours for the tropic birds to return to their young bringing a fish in their mouths for their food, when this bird would pounce upon them and beat them with the wings[.] Clinging to the back of the tropic bird with their beak would cause them to drop the fish and often times vomit what they had swallow^d during the day, when they would seize upon it and fly away, leaving the young tropic birds supperless.

We had now decided to try one more day in search of water and should we yet fail we should quit the island without more delay, for every hour now lost was decreasing our little stock and served to render our destruction more sure.

$Dec^{r\,th}\ 22^{nd}$

After the slumbers of an other night we aroused to a sense of our situation, and again struck off in different directions in search of food and water. Our attention was arrested by seeing one man near the beach run carrying a small keg in his hands. We who were upon the hills on seeing this believing water to have been found ran to them when they informed us that a spring of fresh water had been found on the beach. Our joy was unbounded on receiving this new intelligence and we ran in breathless anxiety to the spot. Here in the providence of God had been provided for us a spring indeed most miraculously presented at the latest moment of pure fresh water.

It arose through a small hole in a flat rock over which the tide arose several feet at high water and could only be come at but half an hour during low tide[,] being quite overflowe^d at all other times of the day.

After filling the small kegs and each one treating himself to a good drink, we now lost no time but tended strictly by night and day to the low tide untill we had fill^d all our vessels capable of containing water to take with us. We now began to conceive different notions in regard to our situation[.]

For since we had found this fountain of water we believed that we could remain as long as we pleased upon the island and always find means of getting water from the spring believing that the tide would always recede below the spring. This I have since learned wasnot the fact, for I have since seen ^{Mr} Seth Weeks of Barnstable who was one of our number who chose to remain upon the island, that during a stay of nine months or more afterwards they could never get water from the spring after our boats left the island, although they could at low tide plainly see the spring bubling beneath the sea but in no instance afterward was it left dry.

We next fell too repairing our boats and preparing ourselves for the next perilous enterprise[.] We nail^d our boats as well as it was possible to do with the small quantity of boat nails in our possession in order to prepare them to stand against the boisterous elements which we were again probable to encounter.

Dec th 23^d

The day was chiefly occupied by scouring the hills and woods with a hope to find somthing to replenish our stock of provisions but could find nothing on which to rely. We could indeed catch a few sea fowls which served us for present food, but even these being constantly harrass^d began to forsake the island[.]

Dec th 24th

This day was spent in persuit of game or vegetable without success as before[.] We find a bastard pine apple growing on trees which at first sight look^d tempting but we soon found them not edible being hard as flint.

Dec th 25th

We found after this days search for provisions there hadnot been enough obtain^d to repay us or warrant our longer stay at this place and began again to think of launching our frail boats upon the mighty deep for it occurr^d to us that we oughtnot to remain longer than we could obtain a full supply for our daily wants, for should we resort to our former sea stock we should greatly diminish the probability of a successful termination to our protracted voyage.

The cap^t call^d togather his officers and after a short consultation it was agreed upon that we should leave soon as possible and make for Easter Island, which we knew to be inhabited and lay very near our track but believed the inhabitants to be savages. This island was visited by the celebrated Captain Cook[.] It bore from this island ESE, and is in lattitude 27:09 south and in 109:35 west[.] Suffice it that we only knew that such an island existed but of the nature of its soil or productions we knew nothing[.] At any rate it was a thousand miles nearer to the land of our hopes and should we get there in safety we might perhaps obtain some little stock in addition to our provisions and enable us to go on our way.

Dec$^{r\,th}$ 26th

We employed ourselves this day wholly to making preparations for our departure. Our village was demolished and our boats taken near the spring[.] All casks[,] tubs and buckets &c were quite fill^d with water and all hands call^d togather for a last talk preveous to taking a final departure[.]

At this time and on the very eve of moving the boats three of our number came forward and declared their intention of remaining upon the island. As the plan favoured the whole party of course no one objected to the proposal. We assured them that should anyone of us survive and get to a civilized country again our first care should be to make every exertion in our power for their speedy relief which we faithfully kept. Their names were William Wright and Seth Weeks of Barnstable ^{Mass}, U.S.A. and Thomas Chappel of Plymouth England.

We gave up to them every small article that we could part with and could be of service to them and they were determined to build them a comfortable dwelling soon as possible. The cap^t wrote several letters which he enclosed in a tin box and left suspended to a tree on the west side of the island near the landing place with the hope, that in case those men should die and ourselves no more be seen, that some more fortunate mariner visiting this secluded spot might perchance convey this last sad relic to our mourning friends, informing them of our hapless fate.

On our first landing at this place we found cut on the trunk of a tree the name of the ship Elizabeth {of London} Capt H. King, who had been the discoverer of this island as before mentioned.

Decth 27th

This day at 10 o clock the tide having risen sufficiently to take the boats over the reef we embarked[,] set our sails and when on the eve of departure discoverd that our absent companions hadnot come down to the beach to see us depart, and we left without again seeing them[.]

We sailed around the northwest side of the island and saw a fine

white sand beach on which we expected we could land in safety
with our boats, but on coming near found this also guarded with a
reef so as to prevent the boats from passing over it[.] We came near
enough to a projecting headland and sent onshore several men.
Whilst they were reconnoitering on shore we shoved our boats off
and tried our luck for fish[.] We caught several small fish and saw
many sharks but as they wouldnot bite at our hook of course they
werenot for our net.

We thus occupied our time untill about six oclock in the evening
when the hunters returned from the shore having caught but few
birds of little consequence.

We again set sail, finally to leave this land which had been so
providentially thrown in our way. We had a pleasant breeze from
the northwest through[ou]t the night which permitted us to sail directly upon our course and we lost sight of the receding land much
more cheerful than could have been expected und{er} the existing
circumstances.

We received our scanty pittance which was barely sufficient to
sustain life[.] We made good progress untill

Dec^{th} 30th

when the wind hauled to the ESE and of course directly ahead and
continued for several days without material change after which it
came again to the north and again enabled us to persue a direct
course. Thus we had made tolerable progress untill

January ^{th} 3^{d} [1821]

when the wind changed to WSW with hard squalls which although
they still permitted us to persue our course yet were so rough and
terrific that we fear^{d} that each successive gust would swamp our
boats for it wasnot possible that such frail vessels could long sustain
themselves amid such severe and repeated shocks.

It would be useless to attempt to describe our sensations at this
time. Everey squall was attended with the most vivid flashes of
lightning and awful thunder which seemed to cause the very bosom

of the deep to tremble and threw a cheerless aspect upon the face of the ocean.

The mate had kept a sort of reckoning since leaving Elizabeth's Island by which we discoverd on the

Jany th 4th

that we had passed so far to the southward of Easter Island that with the wind which had changed to the ENE and seemd likely to continue from that quarter so as to prevent our reaching up to that island, all our fowls and fish being now expended making us wholly dependant upon our small stock of the original provisions which consisted of dry bread alone, and even that allowance must soon be reduced, it was deemd prudent to turn our minds toward some other expedient for our final safety. We gave up as hopeless the idea of reaching Easter Island and steered nearly as possible towards the islands Juan Fernandez and Massafuero upon the coast of Chili. They bore ESE from us and were at this time distant twenty five hundred miles.

The wind continued to blow very lightly from the east and our sufferings were intense from the excessive heat of the sun.

January th 7th

This day our wind changed to the northward and we made good progress on our proper course when at noon found by our observation that we were in lattitude 30:18 south and by our act were in longitude 117:29 west.

Jany th 10th

We have the wind yet fair but very light with a smoothe sea[.] Our second officer this day complaind of being quite unwell and expressd a desire to be removed to the captains boat. After his removal and having spent part of the day there finding himself getting worse, expressd a wish to be again removed to his own boat, after which he shortly died without a struggle. His end was hastened without doubt by the exercise in the removal owing to his extreme debility. His loss threw a gloom over us not easily effaced.

Jan^y ^{th} 11th

We this morning buried the remains of our deceased officer in the deep blue sea as decently as our wretched circumstances would admit of[.] Breathing a silent prayer for the future and placing the boat under command of his own boatstearer ^{Mr} Obed Hendricks[, we] again resumed our precarious way.

Jan ^{th} 12th

We had a light breeze in the morning which by night increased to a gale from the northwest. We were compell^d to take in all our sails and keep the boats directly before the wind and sea. The gale drove us along rapidly before it and on our right course making thus good way, even without aid of the sails. So that our situation, notwithstanding we were liable to have our boats upset by each succeeding wave, didnot terrify us in the least.

And although the danger was very great, yet none seemed to dread this, so much as death by starvation and I believe none would have exchanged this terrific gale for a more moderate head wind or a calm. The rain fell in torrents and the flashes of lightning were most vivid. We were apprehensive that during the extreme darkness of the night our boats would get astray from each other nor in this were we disappointed for at 11 oclock our boat being ahead suddenly missed our companions. It was raining very hard at this time, so much so that you couldnot see the distance of fifty yards from the boat. We hove our boat too, and remained about an hour, expecting them to come up with us, when not seeing them we again kept on our course. As soon as daylight appeared every man in our boat raised themselves to their utmost height, searching along the horizon untill their eyes grew dim with the vain hope of again finding our friends, but in this were we again disappointed, nor did we ever meet them again.

We now found on examining our bread locker that our allowance must be again curtail^d or we should soon have nothing left. Our debility increased rapidly not leaving our men sufficient strength to do the necessary duties of our boat and often would the boat drive on for many hours togather without half our sails being set.

We again reduced the allowance to one ounce of bread pr day. Our water bearing a large proportion to the bread we didnot find necessary to reduce which was the fourth of a pint to each man.

By our observation taken this day we were in the lattitude 32:16 south and longitude by account 112:20 west.

Much of the time since our seperation we have been depressed with melancholy reflections and forebodings. We had lost much, in the loss of our companions and this loss too, irreparable. Their presence had done much to alleviate at least our mental distress[.] Their fate too, being to us quite uncertain caused a double anxiety. They might for aught we could know have founder^d during that awful night, and ourselves be the only survivors to tell the tale of woe. And we too might at any moment sink beneath this vast extent of ocean leaving scarcely a momentary buble to mark the spot or tell that we once was. All these reflections rushing over our weakend minds threw us into a despondency which couldnot be easily shaken off.

Jan^{y th} 14th

This also proved another squally day with constant rain. Our spirits flag, and our bodies already debilitated seem no longer able or willing to act in concert with the mind.

We are now nineteen days from the island and have only made the distance of nine hundred miles on our way. And having compared our provision which remains with the distance our hearts seems to sink within us, for without some wonderful interposition of providence, our stock of provisions must be quite exhausted, long ere our journey can be at an end. We were suffering the most extreme sufferings from the exposed state to the rays of the sun, and our wasted forms daily growing more and more feeble.

This night we had some excitement from one of our colour^d men having made an attempt to take bread from our little stock that remain^d but as the vigilance of the mate prevented the theft he was let off, with only a severe reprimand. He was a good old man, and nothing but the cravings of a starved appetite could have induced him to be guilty of so rash an attempt[.]

January th 15th

As we were sailing along with a light breeze and pleasant weather but rather a dark night we were suddenly attacked at the stern of our boat by a large shark. He made several onsets at different parts of the boat in a ravenous manner frequently biting the end of the steering oar. We succeeded however at last in beating him away with the oars of the boat and a lance, nor did he appear afterwards[.]

Jan^{y th} 16th

We had moderate breezes with pleasant weather and passing through a large shoal of porpoises attempted to catch one with the harpoon, but could not muster strength sufficient to pierce through their tough hide, and they soon left us, appearantly in high glee leaping from the water and apparently in full exercise of every enjoyment. Poor devils, how much they are now our superiors and yet not to know it.

Jan^{y th} 18th

Up to this day we have had a continuation of calms and again compell^d to bear the torture of a burning sun, without power to protect our bodies from its scorching rays. We now feel that we are indeed miserable, and that after all our efforts to preserve life, we must soon realize all the horrors of an untimely end. About eight oclock in the evening being perfectly calm, we were suddenly surrounded by a shoal of spermaciti whales. They came foaming and thrashing past us in a most furious manner. We were alarmed at this, and would fain have taken to the oars and rowed the boats away from those lawless intruders. Our men were too weak to make the attempt, and we were soon overjoyed to find they had pass^d quite clear of our boat when we lay down quietly and slept soundly.

Jan^y ^th ₁9th

We had again to encounter a severe thunder storm. This caused us to take in all sails and lay the boat too. The weather continued very changable and unpleasant with sudden gusts. The reader who is not familiar with a sea life will probably think strange that with those frequent showers of rain we had caught no fresh water. To such in answer, I would say that we made frequent attempts to catch water with our sails spread horizontally, but the boats were very low and the sails were constantly wet with salt water and consequently fill^d with salt so as to spoil all the fresh water that fell. And although we used frequently to catch a pail full in a shower yet always found it too salt for use.

Jan^y ^th ₂0th

This day we have the wind more moderate, but yet a strong breeze from ENE is yet blowing causing a high irregular sea. We are however enabled to set some little additional sail upon the boat, and although we cannot sail directly upon our course, yet we are making very fair progress.

This day Richard Peterson a colour^d man and a native of New York State complain^d of general debility and low spirits declaring that he could not survive the day, and indeed his symptoms did indeed threaten a speedy dissolution. He refused his allowance of food saying ["]Keep it, it may be of service to some one but can be of none to me.["] He died without a struggle. He was a man of about sixty years of age and we believe he died a Christian, if frail man can deserve such a name, thus laying before us the sad spectacle which each of us must very soon expect to display. We committed his remains to the deep, breathing his requiem in silence.

Our lattitude was this day by observation 35:07 south and longitude by ac^t 105:46 west[.]

We continued to sail slowly along, the wind prevailing to the eastward untill

Jan th 24th

when it again fell off to calm. Our minds were now fill^d with the most awful conjectures as to the future. With our provisions nearly exhausted, scarcely a hope remained for us to cling to, and all sunk in sullen silence in the bottom of the boat, untill aroused by the cheerful voice of the mate who again wished to remind us that all hopes werenot yet at an end, and that our duty to ourselves and to each other demanded our latest exertion. Even the strong fortitude of this remarkable man seemed to waver, but in no instance did it finally forsake him, untill the day of our delivery.

During our intervals of sleep often did our fever^d minds wander to the side of some richly supplied table groaning as it were under its weight of luxuries and often to some brook or spring of delightful water. Often have I awaked in the act of placing a draught to my lips and burst into crying at the disappointment.

The wind again breezed up from the eastward being again ahead, and we were compell^d to sail in an unfavourable direction.—Nothing could now sustain us but a firm trust in an almighty power. We were resolved now to act more like consistant men whilst life yet remaind to us.—The wind still continued to blow from the same quarter until

January th 28th

This had driven our boats as far south as the lattitude of 36 degrees {S} which was to us a cold and chilly region by which our suffering was extreme having nothing to cover us from those piercing winds but wet and cold canvass which even had it been dry would have been but a poor apology for covering.

The wind this day changed to the westward and we made the

best of it. We were so feeble that we could scarcely crawl about the
boat upon our hands and knees. We however managed to get sufficient sail upon the boat and again made good progress. Thus it continued until

Jan^y ^th 31st

when again changing to the eastward threw us again into despair[.]

February the 1st

The wind changed again to the westward but on the Feb ^th 2nd and
Feb ^th 3^d blew again from the eastward blowing light and variable
untill

Feb ^th 8th

making very little progress when one of our crew named Isaac Cole
a native of Rochester Mas^s became suddenly ill and appear^d de-
ranged[.] The weather during the night had been very squally and
he had over exerted in managing the sails without calling out assistance, who were trying to get some little rest and he wished not to
disturb them. This without doubt hasten^d his death. He now became a spectacle of madness[.] At 10 oclock he became speechless
but being in great agony groaned most piteously[.]

He expired at four oclock this day in the most frightful convulsions. We kept the body through the night. In the morning we
comitted his body to the deep in the most solemn manner[.] Never
yet had man died more deeply lamented than did this man by his
remaining friends.

The death of these two men was the sole means, under God, of
our final deliverance, for by means of the small pittance meted out
for their share formerly enabled us to exist until relieved.

February th *10* th

At about 3 oclock this afternoon we had a fine breeze spring up from the northwest and we made very good progress for several days.

February th *15* th

This day we are about three hundred miles from the island Massafuero and have taken out our last morsel of food which consists of only two cakes of common ship bread to each one and as there are three of us we have each rec[eive]^d an equal share.

Death seems truly to be hovering over us, and staring broadly in our face. But upon a consultation we agreed that let whatever would come, we would never draw lots after our food had quite gone for each others death, but leave all with God. We consented however at this time, in case one should die first the others could if they thought proper subsist upon our remains with the hope that some one might carry the news to our friends. But God designed it should be otherwise and again gave his protecting arm and saved us from the very jaws of death.

Matters were now speedily drawing to a close and our very existance depended wholly upon the continuation of the breeze.

February th *17* th

This afternoon a heavey cloud settled upon the horizon to the eastward which we receive as strong indications of land. This greatly relieved our drooping spirits, and the dark features of our distress seemed to diminish.

We continued to sail along on our course through the night more cheerfully than we had done for many days previous and the morning brought with it a blessing for which we had scarcely dared to hope.

At seven oclock we had the joyful sight of a sail. She was steering along in the same direction with ourselves, and although we were

several miles astern of her we soon ascertained that we sailed faster
{than} she, and was drawing rapidly up to her. The officer of the
deck soon descried us, and made report to the captain who order^d
sail shortend immidiately and let us come up with them.

The captain hailed us on our approach to know who we were,
and from whence we came. On our proper answers being given he
requested us to come alongside the brig, which we did. He seemed
deeply affected with the spectacle now before him, and actually
shed tears on viewing our emaciated bodies. We were taken onboard his vessel and every possible kindness shown to us.

We were taken from the boats in the lattitude of 33:45 south and
long^d 81:03 west. In four hours after our delivery we saw the island
of Massafuero to the eastward and passing to the south of it and on
the following day made the island Juan Fernandez upon which we
sent a boat and obtain a quantity of fine fruit which consisted in
apples[,] peaches and green figs[.]

This brig was call^d the Indian of London commanded by W^m
Crosier Esqr who was a native of Cumberland in England[,] a gentleman who would do honour to any nation. He took our boat in
tow of his vessel with the hope to sell her at Valparaiso towards our
relief, but as a gale came on during the succeeding night the rope
broke and we lost her.

February ^th 25th

We arrived safely this day at Valparaiso and on the following morning received a visit from the governor ^Don Luiz Del Cruz[34] who
wished to make some little enquiry into the history of our shipwreck, for there was a whispering abroad that foul play had been
used by us. Nor was this entirely put down untill the ship arrived a
few days after bringing in port our captain and his companion.

The governor however so far believed our story that he permitted
us to go at large, and kindly offerd us his assistance in case of need.
We found laying in this port our own country ship the U. S. frigate
Constellation C. G. Ridgley Esq commander, who extended to us
every kindness offering to us in person the freedom of his ship.

^Mr Hill[35] acting U. S. consul at this port was also very kind in
providing every necessary means for our board and comfort during

our stay at this place. Indeed all residents American and English seemed determin^d to the utmost to relieve our wants[.] They open^d a subscription on shore and onboard the ships in port wherby more than five hundred dollars were collected and presented to us.

During our stay the U S ship Macedonian arrived Capt Downs[36] who kindly offer^d to us a free passage to America as he was bound directly home having been relieved by the Constellation. The ship Eagle of Nantucket having arrived from a whaling cruize and being bound to our own town we accepted the kind offer of Wm Coffin Esqr her captain and took passage in that ship. The captain of the Essex still remained behind and returned home in the ship Two Brothers. The Eagle after a pleasant passage of 78 days brought us safely home to the bosom of our friends and families.

Captain Pollard thus relates his narrative after our separation—

He says after finding past all doubt that they had lost us, he kept away on his course making all possible progress toward the island Juan Fernandez as was agreed upon but contrary winds prevail^d and the extreme debility of the crew gave him great concern. He was as ourselves much concern^d at the seperation but at first felt every confidence in meeting with us again. On

January th *14*th

the whole stock of provisions of the boat in charge of ^{Mr} Hendricks was exhausted and he was compell^d to give him out a share from his own scanty locker[.] On

Jan^{y th} *15*th

this day a colour^d man named L. Thomas died and his body constituted the food of his surviving companions for several days.

Jan^{y th} *23*^d

A colour^d man named Charles Shorter died, and his body was shared in the two boats for the like purpose[.]

Jany th 27th

This day an other colour^d man named Isaih Sheppard died of extreme debility[.]

Jany th 28th

An other colour^d man named Saml Reed died of the same disease.
    The flesh of those unfortunate men constituted the only food of the survivors whilst it lasted[.]

Jany th 29th

Owing to the darkness of the night and the want of power to manage the boats the two were seperated, never again to meet[.] They were then in lattitude 35:00 south and about the longitude 100:00 west[.]

February th 1st

Having now consumed their last morsel of food the captain with his three surviving companions after a due consultation agreed to cast lots. The awful lot fell upon a young man named Owen Coffin who was a nephew to Captain Pollard, who with great fortitude and resignation cheerfully smiled at his fate at this awful moment. The captain wished to exchange lots with him, but to this Coffin would not listen for one moment. He placed himself in a firm position to receive his death and was immidiately shot by Charles Ramsdell who became his executioner by fair lot.

Feby th 11th

This day Barzillai Ray died of general debility and on these two bodies the two survivors subsisted until the morning of

Feb^{y th} 23rd

when they were rescued by the ship Dauphin of Nantucket commanded by Zimri Coffin.

They were taken onboard that ship and all their necessities cared for, when they subsequently arrived in Valparaiso as before stated, and from thence in due time returned in safety to their friends and to their country.

Upon our arrival at Valparaiso the United States consul had designed to despatch the U S frigate Constellation to the rescue of our companions which had been left upon Elizabeths Island, but on finding the ship Surrey of London bound to Sidney, New South Wales, he formed a contract with that captain for the sum of eight hundred dollars to proceed to Ducies Island and rescue the three men.

On their arrival at Ducies Island they made search for the men by firing signal guns and all other means in their power but no men appear^d, when they gave over the search thinking probably that the men had either all died or been taken off by some passing ship.

They bore up and stood on their course but as the cap^t was poring over his chart [he] glanced his eye upon the small island of the Elizabeth situated in near the same lattitude but a few more miles to the westward, [and] believed it possible that men in our situation may have been mistaken in the position and got the island somewhat confounded and mistaken the one island for the other.

Thither he bent his way, and on his arrival found the men which we had left there. They found the sea breaking violently against its shores and although they made several attempts to land with their boats, they were dashed frequently against the rocks and the boats were much injured. They were on the point of giving up altogather when they called to the men on shore to swim off to them. They were quite feeble and for a long time none dared to make the attempt.

At last having become almost desperate with the thought of being left again upon that desolate spot at this moment Thomas Chappel dashed himself into the sea and succeeded in safely reaching the boat where having rested awhile took the end of a line to shore whence all his companions were soon hauled into the boat. They were taken onboard the Surrey and kindly treated and gladly left this solitary spot perhaps forever.

I have since conversed with Mr Weeks[,] one of the survivors[.] He stated to me that after our having left the island their sufferings became extreme. The birds having been constantly harrassd soon forsook the island. The land crabs were killed off. The fish could rarely be caught. Worse than all strange as it may appear the little submerged fresh water spring was never afterwards left dry so as to be come at, and they had only the means left them to catch water in the holes of the rocks during showers which would soon dry up, and they were left without water untill the next rain came on.

They found a cave on the eastern part of the island during their perambulations[.] They were led by curiosity to enter it, when to their surprise they found seated side by side eight human skeletons, probably some ill fated mariners who had sought a place of safety like ourselves and proved less fortunate.

They had formed a design to again visit this cave with a hope to gain some farther intelligence into their fate by finding some mark either on the hills or sea shore, when they were defeated by the arrival of the Surrey. They were taken to Port Jackson whence Wright and Weeks arrived safely to their homes in the United States and the boatstearer Tho[s] Chappel to his home and friends in England.

The following is a list of the whole crew as they were arranged in the three boats on leaving the wreck.

1ST BOAT

Capt George Pollard	Survived
[Mr] Obed Hendricks {Boat Stearer}	Missing
Barzillai Ray	Died
Owen Coffin	Shot
Samuel Reed (Col [oure][d])	Died
Charles Ramsdell	Survived
Seth Weeks (left on the island)	Survived

2ND, OR MATES BOAT

Owen Chase Chief Mate	Survived
Benjamin Lawrence {Boat Stearer}	d[itt]o
Thomas G Nickerson {Boy}	do
Isaac Cole	Died
Richard Peterson (Col^d)	do
*Wm Wright (left on the island)	Survived

3D OR 2ND MATES BOAT

Mathew P. Joy 2nd Mate	Died
†Thomas Chappel {Boat Stearer}	Survived
Joseph West	Missing
Lawson Thomas (Col^d)	Died
Charles Shorter do	do
Isaih Shepperd do	do
William Bond do Steward	do

---

*Wm Wright since lost in a hurricane at the W. India Islands.
†Thos Chappel since died at the island Timor

Nickerson's Letter to Lewis

The following letter from Thomas Nickerson to Leon Lewis was written in reply to specific questions Lewis had about the disaster after reading Nickerson's narrative. In addition to indicating that Nickerson had, upon Lewis's request, done some additional research respecting the *Essex*'s last voyage, the letter provides a detailed account of what is perhaps the central episode in the ordeal: the sacrifice of Owen Coffin.

The editorial procedures that were followed in the preparation of the text of Nickerson's letter to Leon Lewis, the manuscript of which is among the holdings of the Nantucket Historical Association, were the same as those that were applied to the "Desultory Sketches."

———————

NANTUCKET OCT^R 24TH /76

My dear friend[,]

Your favour of 23^d came to hand last evening. The date is the very date on which I wrote you last which I trust you have had all right. It contained the searching of the records & other matter which makes it important for you to have got them.

I will now try to answer your inquiry. Your 1st is, ["]Are you aware that the missing boat reached Ducies Island[?"] The missing boat, nor no other of our boats, touched at, or ever saw Ducies Island. We all three boats landed safely at Elizabeth Island safely with all hands comparatively well except M. P. Joy. He was very weak and debilitated. This Ducies Island lies in the same lattitude of Elizabeths Island and about seventy miles to the east. All which you will find plainly described in my manuscript. To confirm that it wasnot Ducies Island, I can well satisfy you on that point. The captain of the ship[1] in communicating with his correspondent, he says, ["]As directed I arrived off the island Ducie and finding no landing place I fired guns nearly all day, but finding no one upon the shores to make an appearance I came to the conclusion that Pollard was either mistaken or else that the men had either all died or had been taken off.["] But on looking over his chart he found that a small island lay to the west distant 70 miles and thither they went, which was the island discovered by Capt King in the ship Elizabeth of London. He fired a gun on their arrival which brought them to view as described fully in the manuscript[.]

As regards Pollards reef or shoal,[2] I have just been talking with Captain Thomas Derrick who was chief mate of the ship Martha, which was in trouble with us at the time and which ship saved us and took us to the Sandwich Islands. He agrees with my opinion as regards the reef[.] He as well as myself, believes that this was French Frigate Shoal notwithstanding our two captains believed and reported that this was a new discovery. The lattitudes were very

much the same, and owing to thick weather we had no lunar observation for ten or twelve days, hence the mistake. Your 2nd is as regards Owen Coffin. Of his family I know but very little[.] His
mother I am told has been dead many years, & I know that he had
a brother sailing between New York & Curacoa in the West Indies
in command of the brig Tam O Shanter and died at that island with
consumption shortly after that. I have no farther knowledge of any
of the family.

Now as regards the casting of lots. As I had my information
from Charles Ramsdell, who was one of the survivors of the
cap[t]ains boat: he said that when their last morsel of food was gone
and finding as they were, all must die, and for the sake of their
friends should know their fate[,] I think if my memory serves me,
that he Ramsdell made the first proposition to cast lots. Be that as it
may, Captain Pollard wouldnot listen to it[,] saying to the others
["]No, but if I die first you are welcome to subsist on my remains"
and that Coffin joined in the entreaty to cast lots[.] They then cut
some blank paper checks [and] put them in a hat. The lot fell upon
Coffin, which he distinctly declared to be a fair lot and that he
wished to abide by it. Captain Pollard then declared that he would
take the lot himself, but to this Coffin wouldnot listen for a moment[.] This was a trying moment truly[,] the son of a beloved sister, to fall by their hands. Who can doubt but that Pollard would
rather have met the death a thousand times. None that knew him,
will ever doubt. Neither of his companions but that shrank from
the heart rending tryal. So they were compelld again to cast lots that
who should draw the fatal trigger. As if the fate would have it, the
awful die turned upon Captain Pollard[.] For a long time [he] declared that he could never do it, but finally had to submit.

Coffin then called to them to come near whilst he breathed a
parting message to his dear mother & family[.] Then craving a few
moments in silence he told them that he knew the lots had been
fairly drawn and he submitted to his fate perfectly resigned, and we
know the rest. Let us draw a vail over the fate of a shipmate we all
loved so dearly and so well. Peace to his memory. Capt Pollard was
not nor could he be thought to have dealt unfairly with this trying
matter. On his arrival he bore the awful message to the mother as
her son desired, but she became almost frantic with the thought,
and I have heared that she never could become reconciled to the

capt's presence. Captain Pollard has since lived on the island, greatly respected by all whose buisnes [or] pleasure brought them in contact with and died lamented by a large circle of friends.

You will find on refering to my manuscript that all the men that got to the island with us, left it with us with the exception of Thomas Chappel[,] Wm Wright and Seth Weeks[.] Those three men chose to remain and were subsequently taken off by the Surrey ship. And that our boats never seperated until long after we left Elisabeths Island.

Captain Pollards wife still lives but has become totally blind[.]

You wish to know something about my own history[.] I believe that I was born in the town of Harwich in Massachusetts[,] at least they tell me so, and at the age of six months my parents removed to the island Nantucket into a house in North Water S[t]. At the age of 18 months my parents died and was buried from that house, and their head stones are plainly legible after a lapse of 70 years in the western part of the Gardners burying ground.

I began my carreer as above and after a few years in the schools of this island living in the family of my grandfather Cap[t] Robert Gibson[,] I commenced my sea life in the ill fated Essex followed by the voyage under the same commander in the Two Brothers, belonging to Samuel Mitchel Esqr and others of this town.

Afterward as mate of several vessels in the whaling service[;] that is[,] after I had gone through my degrees in a subordinate capacity and in 1834–5 as chief mate of several ships in the merchant service[,] then as master of many different ships in the employ of various merchants, such as George Sutton Sen[r][,] Moses H. Call, Foster & Giraud, Oliver B Hilliard[,] J H Holcombe &c.[3] And since I quit the sea I have been living in Brooklyn and doing buisness in New York, in the shipping buisness.

I shallnot have time to write much more this time but I would wish to refer you to my manuscript[.] I think you will find all the questions you have asked to be answered in that perhaps more correctly than this, for having parted with my manuscript I now have to write from memory only. I shall not be able to send you all you have desired before next week as I have been a little bothered in collecting them.

I have enclosed a history of a very exciting Coolie voyage[4] which I made and which I think can be made interesting. You can make use of it as you think proper[.] Either use it among the Desultory Sketches or any where that you in your judgement may think fit. I have confined myself to facts and you can handle as you think proper[.]

I think I willnot write to you again untill I hear from you again or know if you are coming[.]

THE CAPTAIN'S STORY

Excerpt from Ridgely's Letterbook

Commodore Charles Goodwin Ridgely, commanding the U.S. frigate *Constellation* stationed at Valparaiso, Chile, recorded in his journal two arresting images of the *Essex* survivors. The first concerns the condition of Captain Pollard and Charles Ramsdell when they were rescued by the crew of the *Dauphin*. As Thomas Heffernan, who quotes from Ridgely's journal in *Stove by a Whale*, points out, Ridgely's information would have come from Obed Starbuck, first mate of the whaleship *Hero*. Ridgely also speaks of the condition of Owen Chase, Thomas Nickerson, and Benjamin Lawrence, who had spent time recuperating in the *Constellation*'s sick bay.

The Penguin text is transcribed from a memorandum included in the Letterbook for the USF *Constellation*, pp. [32–36], among the Papers of Charles Goodwin Ridgely, Naval Historical Foundation Manuscript Collection, Library of Congress, Washington, D.C.

———————

On the 9th March the American ship Hero of Nantucket arrived, the chief Mate reports that a few days previous, while lying at anchor off the Island of St Marys, near Conception that the ship was taken possession by a party of Spaniards & Indians under the command of a Spaniard named Benevides having previously induced the Captain Russel & ten men, to land, whom they made prisoners, that after plundering the ship of a number of articles of provisions &c they got the Ship underway for the purpose of proceeding to some other place that about the same instant a strange sail came in sight which they believed to be a cruiser from Valp° that the plunderers immediately fled in their boats, & that he took advantage of it & immediately made sail for this port leaving the Captain and ten men in possession of the plunderers—the Hero brings the pleasing acct. that the Master of the Essex, Pollard & one boy have been picked up by a Whale ship from New York. They were ninety two days in the boat & were in a most wretched state, they were unable to move when found sucking the bones of their dead Mess mates, which they were loth to part with. On the 15 the English Brig India arrived a prize to Lord Cochrane, she brought in the Mate one man & a Boy of the Ship Essex of Nantucket Pollard master, they stated that ninety two days previous while some of the boats were about striking whale, the ship then in Lat.^d   Long: a large whale attacked the ship stove in her bows, that they had been in the boat eighty six days, a great part of which time they had subsisted on the flesh of those that died, they separated from the Capt in lat^d long: in a squally night that it was their intention to endeavour to reach Esther Island and presumed the Capt had gone there that a few days after the accident they all reach'd and landed on an island called Ducies in lat^d 24°40′ S long: 124°40′ W that it was not inhabited and only water to be had there, they left it with the exception of three, who prefered remaining alth° there was no probability of their being taken off the island[.] the island afforded no article whatever of sustenance & the whole hope left was, the surf might occasionaly throw on shore a dead fish, they had no boats it was the opinion of the mate they could not have survived many days—the

Indian picked up those that were in the boat within half a degree of Juan Fernandes, the Captain had showed them every kind attention, but their appearance bones working through their skins their legs & feet much smaller & the whole surface of their bodies one entire ulcer was truly distressing—I took them on board my ship, supplied them with every article they required and by the attention of my surgeon they entirely recovered—The English ship Surry Cap.⁺ Raines now lying here being on the eve of sailing for New Holland I applied to him to know if he would call at Esther Island & the Island of Ducies & endeavour to relieve these unfortunate men; he consented, and I paid him for his trouble four hundred & thirty dollars—from the character of this gentleman, and having given me security for the performance of his engagement, I have no doubt but he will do so. I should not omit to mention that a subscription was immediately put on foot by the American & English residents of Valp: for the relief of those poor fellows that were brought in & between three & four hundred dollars was procured them, beside which my crew with that thoughtless liberality which is peculiar to seamen, subscribed each a months pay, but as that would have amounted to between two and three thousand Dollars & as these men were not then in want of any thing, & I intended sending them home in the Macedonian where they would have every comfort & no expence I would allow no more than one dollar from each man to be given them—The Macedonian arrived on the 4ᵗʰ March & informed me that the Ship Chesapeake of Baltimore & Brig Warrior of New York were detained at Coquimbo by the Govt. & their situation a very critical one, I therefore determined on going to their relief. After having landed a quantity of surplus stores & spars, and the Purser who was very sick, caulked & painted Ship, sent the arrested officers[1] on board the Macedonian to be carried to the U. States—and also those unfortunate men of the Essex[2] & requesting Cap.ᵗ Downes to go to Aurauco to the assistance of Cap.⁺ Russell & men of the Hero. On the 11ᵗʰ March I sailed for Coquimbo—

Excerpt from Wilkes's Autobiography

In August of 1822, off the western coast of South America, a twenty-four-year-old midshipman in the U.S. schooner *Waterwitch* named Charles Wilkes met Captain George Pollard, then commanding the whaleship *Two Brothers.* Coincidentally, Wilkes had finished reading Chase's narrative of the *Essex* disaster only the night before.

Many decades later, after he had led the U.S. Exploring Expedition to the Pacific and the Antarctic and then become embroiled in the Trent Affair during the Civil War, Wilkes recorded his still vivid memories of his conversation with Pollard. Although he was to misremember Pollard's name as Potter, the young Wilkes was evidently as impressed by the former captain of the *Essex* as Melville would be almost thirty years later.

The Penguin text is from the *Autobiography of Rear Admiral Charles Wilkes, U. S. Navy, 1798–1877*, ed. William James Morgan *et al.* Washington, D.C.: Naval History Division, Department of the Navy, 1978.

———————

We ran down the Coast with the Trade winds and when off Payta [Paita] we fell in with the Whale Ship *Two Brothers*, Captain Potter [Pollard]. I went on board and was kindly received. He was just out from Payta. The day before, I had been reading the account of A Whale Ship that had been struck by a whale and so much injured that she was wrecked, the blow having started some planks. On finding the Captn's Name to be Potter, I asked him, naturally, if he was any relation to the one who met with the disaster. He at once said he was the person. This made a great impression on me, and then he gave me a full account of the disaster which I will now attempt to give in his own language as nearly as I could recollect it.

He had discovered a large school of Whales and had lowered all his boats including his own for the pursuit and capture, leaving but three men on board—the cook, Steward and a Seaman. The weather was very fine and the Sea smooth. While engaged in the exciting occupation of capturing as many of the Whales, he had his attention called to the Ship which was heeling over very considerably. [He] become assured that some accident had happened, called his boats off and all made for the Ship at great speed. Before he reached the Ship, She had turned over on her side and by the time he got to her she was lying bottom up and the Cook, Steward, & Seaman on the Hull. He described himself as almost appalled by the situation—in the middle of the Vast Pacific and far removed from any land. On reaching his ship the boats were unprovided with every Thing. They had no provisions, no clothing, no instruments, no water. The ship lay turned bottom up—these necessaries were to be got at and the only thing to be done was to scuttle the bottom of the Ship and to make their way into the hull to obtain any thing—this without any tools. Through the energy of Captn Potter they succeeded in tearing off the planking and making an entrance, and in this manner they succeeded in obtaining provisions, tools for repairs of the Boats, but the boats were unable to take all they needed. Can any situation be conceived in such circumstances that require so much thought and action as was required within the short space of time allotted to them, to say nothing of the untoward disappointment of the interruption of a successful issue of their hazardous employment, interrupted when their fondest hopes were about to be realized? A well appointed vessel, crew in all respects efficient, and the fondest hopes indulged in of providing for themselves and families in a short hour to be wrecked and they left to grapple for their lives on the broad Ocean.

Through the example of Captn Potter, all were encouraged; the boats well stowed, and [the] needy equipped, their ship filling fast before taking her final plunge into the deep, deep Sea. She finally went down before their eyes, and then came the thought, followed by the determination, to seek the nearest island, supposed to be some 150 miles distance. For this they lost no time in steering for, and reached it in three days. But little did it ameliorate their condition. It was uninhabited, and, moreover, little was to be found on it to sustain life. It was evident they could not remain there, some thirty in number with five boats. These they set about putting in complete repair from the materials they had brought with them, and when complete, took the determination to embark in hopes of reaching the Shores of South America.

Of the boats only one was ever heard of, that of the Captain, who was picked up on the Coast of Chile after being 32 days at sea. The only two saved were the Captn and a boy. They had twice or thrice drawn lots, and intense suffering ensued. I cannot state the narrative of this, it is too horrible to be related as it was told me. The Captain and boy were merely alive when picked up and reached port. Their boat was nearly in pieces and all hope had long before passed from them. The Annals of wrecks at Sea never has given so disastrous a case; it fairly, in contemplation, causes One's heart almost to cease beating, but when narrated by one who had undergone it all, and miraculously, as it were, been preserved, I could not convey an idea of my feelings.

I expressed myself how he could think of again putting his foot on board Ship to again pursue such a calling, or hazard another voyage. He simply remarked that it was an old adage that the lightning never struck in the same place twice. He had recovered and returned home to Nantucket or New Bedford, I forget which, and was offered the *Two Brothers* for another voyage which he accepted. And there he was, bound probably for the Same Area of Ocean where he had encountered so much. It was to be expected that Some effect of his former cruise would have been visible in his manner or conversation, but not so. He was cheerful and very modest in his account, and very desirous to afford us all the aid we might be in want of, presented us with some vegetables, & potatoes especially—of which he had a large store in nettings affixed to his Cabin ceiling.

I took leave of him with hearty wishes for his success and a feeling of respect that I had by accident become acquainted with a hero, who did not even consider that he had overcome obstacles which would have crushed 99 out of a hundred. There was a vividness about his description of the Scenes he had gone through which recurs to me often. And, [I] scarcely can believe that the actor could have been the Narrator, so modest and unassuming was his account, and I feel satisfied most truthful. At the time I saw him I suppose he was about 35 years of age. I have not been able to trace him since, although I have made many inquiries. He was one of three brothers who followed the Whaling business. It is now some fifty years ago and there is little doubt but he is long since dead. I regret that I did not pursue the short Account in the paper which first attracted my notice of him as I have not been able to find any account of the wreck if ever published.

Excerpt from *Tyerman and Bennet's* Journal

Daniel Tyerman and George Bennet were sent by the London Missionary Society to report on the state of the various missions in the Pacific and the Far East. In April 1823 in the harbor of Raiatea, the largest island in the Leeward Group of the Society Islands, Bennet met Captain George Pollard, who had lost his second whaleship the *Two Brothers* only two months before. Bennet's account captures Pollard in the depths of despair. After losing his second whaleship in as many voyages, he knows full well that his whaling career has ended.

The Penguin edition reproduces the text of *Journal of Voyages and Travels by the Rev. Daniel Tyerman and George Bennet, Esq.*, ed. James Montgomery, 2 vols. (London: Frederick Westley and A. H. Davis, 1831), II, 24–29.

———————

April 16 [1823]: In the harbour here [at Raiatea in the Society Islands], we found the American brig Pearl, Captain Chandler, which had put in for repairs, having sprung a leak at sea; and on board of this vessel, to our great joy and surprise, we met with our friends, Mr. and Mrs. Chamberlain, from the Sandwich Islands. We never expected to have seen their faces again in this world. They were, however, for reasons which we had known and approved when we parted with them, on their return with their young family to America. They gave us the most gratifying account of the safe arrival and cordial reception of Mr. and Mrs. Ellis, at Oahu, by our American Missionary friends there, by the king also, the chiefs, and the people—all of whom rejoiced to welcome them as servants of the Most High God, arrived among them to teach a nation, *without any religion,* the only doctrines under heaven worthy of that name.

There were three captains on board this brig, as passengers to America. The ships of two of these had been wrecked, and that of the third condemned. One of them was captain George Pollard, whose singular and lamentable story, in the case of a *former* shipwreck, (as nearly as can be recollected by Mr. Bennet,) deserves to be recorded in his own manner. It was substantially as follows.

"My first shipwreck was in open sea, on the 20th of November, 1820, near the equator, about 118° W. long. The vessel, a South Sea whaler, was called the Essex. On that day, as we were on the look out for sperm whales, and had actually struck two, which the boats' crews were following to secure, I perceived a very large one—it might be eighty or ninety feet long—rushing with great swiftness through the water, right towards the ship. We hoped that she would turn aside, and dive under, when she perceived such a baulk in her way. But no! the animal came full force against our stern-port: had any quarter less firm been struck the vessel must have been burst; as it was, every plank and timber trembled, throughout her whole bulk.

"The whale, as though hurt by a severe and unexpected concussion, shook its enormous head, and sheered off to so considerable a distance that for some time we had lost sight of her from the starboard quarter; of which we were very glad, hoping that the worst was over. Nearly an hour afterwards, we saw the same fish—we had no doubt of this, from her size, and the direction in which she came—making again towards us. We were at once aware of our danger, but escape was impossible. She dashed her head this time against the ship's side, and so broke it in that the vessel filled rapidly, and soon became water-logged. At the second shock, expecting her to go down, we lowered our three boats with the utmost expedition, and all hands, twenty in the whole, got into them—seven, and seven, and six. In a little while, as she did not sink, we ventured on board again, and, by scuttling the deck, were enabled to get out some biscuit, beef, water, rum, two sextants, a quadrant, and three compasses. These, together with some rigging, a few muskets, powder, &c. we brought away; and, dividing the stores among our three small crews, rigged the boats as well as we could; there being a compass for each, and a sextant for two, and quadrant for one, but neither sextant nor quadrant for the third. Then, instead of pushing away for some port, so amazed and bewildered were we that we continued sitting in our places gazing upon the ship, as though she had been an object of the tenderest affection. Our eyes could not leave her, till, at the end of many hours, she gave a slight reel, then down she sank. No words can tell our feelings. We looked at each other—we looked at the place where she had so lately been afloat—and we did not cease to look, till the terrible conviction of our abandoned and perilous situation roused us to exertion, if deliverance were yet possible.

"We now consulted about the course which it might be best to take—westward to India, eastward to South America, or southwestward to the Society Isles. We knew that we were at no great distance from Tahiti, but were so ignorant of the state and temper of the inhabitants that we feared we should be devoured by cannibals, if we cast ourselves on their mercy. It was determined, therefore, to make for South America, which we computed to be more than two thousand miles distant. Accordingly we steered eastward, and, though for several days harassed with squalls, we contrived to keep together. It was not long before we found that one of the boats had started a plank, which was no wonder, for whale-boats are all clinker-built, and very slight, being made of half-inch plank only, before planing. To remedy this alarming defect we all turned to, and, having emptied the damaged boat into the two others, we raised her side as well as we could, and succeeded in restoring the plank at the bottom. Through this accident, some of our biscuit had become injured by the salt-water. This was equally divided among the several boats' crews. Food and water, meanwhile, with our utmost economy, rapidly failed. Our strength was exhausted, not by abstinence only, but by the labours which we were obliged to employ to keep our little vessels afloat, amidst the storms which repeatedly assailed us. One night we were parted in rough weather; but though the next day we fell in with one of our companion-boats, we never saw or heard any more of the other, which probably perished at sea, being without either sextant or quadrant.

"When we were reduced to the last pinch, and out of every thing, having been more than three weeks abroad, we were cheered with the sight of a low, uninhabited island, which we reached in hope, but were bitterly disappointed. There were some barren bushes, and many rocks on this forlorn spot. The only provisions that we could procure were a few birds and their eggs: this supply was soon reduced; the sea-fowls appeared to have been frightened away, and their nests were left empty after we had once or twice plundered them. What distressed us most was the utter want of fresh water; we could not find a drop any where, till, at the extreme verge of ebb tide, a small spring was discovered in the sand; but even that was too scanty to afford us sufficient to quench our thirst before it was covered by the waves at their turn.

"There being no prospect but that of starvation here, we determined to put to sea again. Three of our comrades, however, chose to remain, and we pledged ourselves to send a vessel to bring them off, if we ourselves should ever escape to a Christian port. With a very small morsel of biscuit for each, and a little water, we again ventured out on the wide ocean. In the course of a few days our provisions were consumed. Two men died; we had no other alternative than to live upon their remains. These we roasted to dryness by means of fires kindled on the ballast-sand at the bottom of the boats. When this supply was spent, what could we do? We looked at each other with horrid thoughts in our minds, but we held our tongues. I am sure that we loved one another as brothers all the time; and yet our looks told plainly what must be done. We cast lots, and the fatal one fell on my poor cabin-boy. I started forward instantly, and cried out, 'My lad, my lad, *if you don't like your lot,* I'll shoot the first man that touches you.' The poor emaciated boy hesitated a moment or two; then, quietly laying his head down upon the gunnel of the boat, he said, '*I like it as well as any other.*' He was soon dispatched, and nothing of him left. I think, then, another man died of himself, and him, too, we ate. But I can tell you no more—my head is on fire at the recollection; I hardly know what I say. I forgot to say, that we had parted company with the second boat before now. After some more days of horror and despair, when some were lying down at the bottom of the boat not able to rise, and scarcely one of us could move a limb, a vessel hove in sight. We were taken on board, and treated with extreme kindness. The second lost boat was also picked up at sea, and the survivors saved. A ship afterwards sailed in search of our companions on the desolate island, and brought them away."

Captain Pollard closed his dreary narrative with saying, in a tone of despondency never to be forgotten by him who heard it—"After a time I found my way to the United States, to which I belonged, and got another ship. That, too, I have lost by a second wreck off the Sandwich Islands, and now I am utterly ruined. No owner will ever trust me with a whaler again, for all will say I am an *unlucky* man."

THE BOATSTEERER'S STORY

An Account of the Loss of the Essex

Thomas Chappel of Plymouth, England, was the boatsteerer of Matthew Joy, second mate of the *Essex*. Chappel, along with two sailors from Cape Cod, decided to remain on Henderson Island rather than risk a 3,000-mile voyage to South America. It turned out to be a wise decision. Joy's whaleboat would never be heard from again, and only Nantucketers would make it out of Pollard's and Chase's boats alive.

Chappel and the two others were eventually saved by the *Surry*, sent by Commodore Ridgely as a rescue ship. Chappel returned to London, England, in 1823 and soon after contributed to the following narrative. The Penguin text reproduces that of *An Account of the Loss of the Essex*, Pamphlet No. 579 (London: The Religious Tract Society, [1824]).

The ship Essex, George Pollard, master, sailed from Nantucket, in North America, November 19, 1819,[1] on a whaling voyage to the South Seas.

The Essex was for some months very successful, and procured 750 barrels of oil, in a shorter period than usual.

On the 20th November, 1820, she was on the equator, about 118° west longitude, when several whales were in sight, to the great joy of the crew, who thought they should soon complete their cargo.

The boats were soon lowered in pursuit of the whales: George Pollard, the master, and Thomas Chappel, the second mate, each succeeded in striking one, and were actively engaged in securing them, when a black man, who was in the mate's boat, exclaimed, "Massa, where ship?" The mate immediately looked round, and saw the Essex lying on her beam ends, and a large whale near her: he instantly cut his line and made towards the ship; the captain also saw what had happened, and did the same. As soon as they got on board, to their great astonishment they found she had been struck by a whale of the largest size, which rose close to the ship and then darted under her, and knocked off a great part of the false keel. The whale appeared again, and went about a quarter of a mile off, then suddenly returned and struck the ship with great force. The shock was most violent, the bows were stove in, and the vessel driven astern a considerable distance; she filled with water and fell over on her beam ends. The crew exerted themselves to the utmost, the masts were cut away and the ship righted, but she was a mere wreck and entirely unmanageable; the quantity of oil on board alone kept her from foundering. They did not ascertain whether the whale had received any injury, but it remained in sight for some hours without again coming near them.

When the captain found that it was impossible to save the ship, he directed the three boats to be got ready, and they succeeded in saving a small quantity of water, and some biscuit, which was in a very wet state.

As the Essex appeared likely to float for some days longer, the captain remained by her, hoping that some vessel might come in sight. After three days, finding these hopes were not realized, as the wind blew fresh from the east, he determined on attempting to reach the Friendly Islands.[2] They accordingly steered a south-westerly course, and proceeded rapidly for twenty-three days without seeing land. During this time they had only half a biscuit and a pint of water each man per day. In that warm climate the scanty supply of water was particularly distressing, but they could not venture on a larger allowance; as on leaving the ship their whole stock of provisions was only about one hundred and fifty pounds of bread, and fifty gallons of water; occasionally, however, some showers of rain fell, which gave them considerable relief.

On the twenty-fourth day after leaving the Essex, they saw an island, discovered a few years since, and called Elizabeth's Isle. It is about eight or nine miles round, low and flat, nearly covered with trees and underwood.

The shore was rocky, and the surf high; the crew were very weak, so that they did not land without considerable difficulty. Their first search was for water; and their joy was great at finding a spring of fresh water among the rocks; they were however disappointed on examining the island, as it was almost destitute of the necessaries of life, and no other fresh water could be discovered. These painful feelings were greatly increased the following day, for the sea had flowed over the rocks, and the spring of fresh water could not be seen, and did not again appear. In this extremity they endeavoured to dig wells, but without success; their only resource was a small quantity of water which they found in some holes among the rocks.

For six days they continued to examine the island, when finding their situation desperate, the captain and most of the crew determined to put to sea again. The continent of South America was seventeen hundred miles distant, and in their destitute condition they could scarcely expect to reach land: their hopes were rather directed to the possibility of falling in with some vessel.

Thomas Chappel, the second mate, being in a very weak state, thought he might as well remain on the island, as attempt such a voyage; William Wright and Seth Weeks also determined to remain with him.

On the 26th of December the boats left the island: this was indeed a trying moment to all: they separated with mutual prayers and good wishes, seventeen venturing to sea with almost certain death before them, while three remained on a rocky isle, destitute of water, and affording hardly any thing to support life. The prospects of these three poor men were gloomy: they again tried to dig a well, but without success, and all hope seemed at an end, when providentially they were relieved by a shower of rain. They were thus delivered from the immediate apprehension of perishing by thirst. Their next care was to procure food, and their difficulties herein were also very great; their principal resource was small birds, about the size of a blackbird, which they caught while at roost. Every night they climbed the trees in search of them, and obtained, by severe exertions, a scanty supply, hardly enough to support life. Some of the trees bore a small berry which gave them a little relief, but these they found only in small quantities. Shell fish they searched for in vain; and although from the rocks they saw at times a number of sharks, and also other sorts of fish, they were unable to catch any, as they had no fishing tackle. Once they saw several turtles, and succeeded in taking five, but they were then without water; at those times they had little inclination to eat, and before one of them was quite finished the others were become unfit for food.

Their sufferings from want of water were the most severe, their only supply being from what remained in holes among the rocks after the showers which fell at intervals; and sometimes they were five or six days without any; on these occasions they were compelled to suck the blood of the birds they caught, which allayed their thirst in some degree; but they did so very unwillingly, as they found themselves much disordered thereby.

Among the rocks were several caves formed by nature, which afforded a shelter from the wind and rain. In one of these caves they found eight human skeletons, in all probability the remains of some poor mariners who had been shipwrecked on the isle, and perished for want of food and water. They were side by side, as if they had laid down, and died together! This sight deeply affected the mate and his companions; their case was similar, and they had every reason to expect ere long the same end; for many times they lay down at night, with their tongues swollen and their lips parched with thirst, scarcely hoping to see the morning sun; and it is impossible to form an idea of their feelings when the morning dawned, and

they found their prayers had been heard and answered by a provi-
dential supply of rain.

In this state they continued till the 5th of April[3] following; day
after day hoping some vessel might touch at the island; but day after day, and week after week passed by, and they continued in that
state of anxious expectation which always tends to cast down the
mind and damp exertion, and which is so strongly expressed in
the words of scripture, "Hope deferred maketh the heart sick."[4]
The writer of this narrative says, "At this time I found religion not
only useful but absolutely necessary to enable me to bear up under
these severe trials. If any man wishes for happiness in this world, or
in the world to come, he can only find it by belief in God and trust
in him: it is particularly important that seamen whose troubles and
dangers are so numerous should bear this in mind. In this situation
we prayed earnestly, morning, noon, and night, and found comfort
and support from thus waiting upon the Lord."

This testimony of the benefits to be derived from religion is ex-
ceedingly valuable: hours of trial prove the vanity and uncertainty
of all earthly enjoyments, and show the necessity of looking forward for another and a better world. The experience of believers of
old taught them that they were but "strangers and pilgrims upon
earth," and led them to earnest desires after another and a better
country, that is, an heavenly. See Heb. xi. Prayer is the means which
God has appointed whereby we may draw near to him, asking for
the blessings we need. He has promised to hear and to answer us in
such a manner as shall be for our good: but let us always remember,
that prayer does not consist in merely kneeling down, and uttering
our desires with our lips, but prayer should be the earnest expression of the feeling of the heart, filled with a sense of its own misery
and wretchedness, not only as to the things of this life, but still
more deeply affected as to the concerns of our souls. We may be
miserable in this world, and in the world to come also. We may be
happy in this life and miserable hereafter. The one does not depend
upon the other, nor are they in any way connected with each other.
The prayer of the poor publican (as related in the 18th of St. Luke)
was "God be merciful to me a sinner!" This will always be the first
and principal desire of the soul, when awakened to a knowledge of
its wretched and miserable state by nature and practice, and we

would hope that such was the prayer of these poor men. Our Saviour himself has promised, that he will hear and answer such prayers: he graciously declares, "Come unto me all ye that labour and are heavy laden, and I will give you rest."[5] He has also promised that he will give his Holy Spirit to those that ask him; and the soul that is led by the teaching of the Holy Spirit to draw near to the Saviour will find support under all the troubles of this life. It will find that peace which the world cannot give.

To return to these poor men. On the morning of April 5, 1820, they were in the woods as usual, searching for food and water, as well as their weakness permitted, when their attention was aroused by a sound which they thought was distant thunder, but looking towards the sea, they saw a ship in the offing, which had just fired a gun. Their joy at this sight may be more easily imagined than described; they immediately fell on their knees and thanked God for his goodness, in thus sending deliverance when least expected; then hastening to the shore, they saw a boat coming towards them. As the boat could not approach the shore without great danger, the mate, being a good swimmer, and stronger than his companions, plunged into the sea, and narrowly escaped a watery grave at the moment when deliverance was at hand; but the same Providence which had hitherto protected, now preserved him. His companions crawled out further on the rocks, and by the great exertions of the crew were taken into the boat, and soon found themselves on board the Surry, commanded by captain Raine. They were treated in the kindest manner by him and his whole crew, and their health and strength were speedily restored, so that they were able to assist in the duties of the ship.

When on board the Surry, they were told the deplorable and painful history of their captain and shipmates. After leaving the isle, the boats parted company; the captain's boat was sixty days at sea, when it was picked up by an American whaler: only himself and a boy were then alive. Their scanty stock of provisions was soon exhausted, and life had only been sustained by the dead bodies of their companions. The particulars of their sufferings are too painful to relate, but they were confirmed by proofs which could not be doubted. The ship reached Valparaiso in a few days; when the particulars of the loss of the Essex, and of the men left on the island were immediately communicated to the captain of an American frigate then in the port; who humanely endeavoured to procure a vessel to go to the island, as his own ship was not ready for sea. Captain Raine, of the Surry, engaged to do this, and sailed without loss of time: he had a quick passage; and, by the kind providence of God, the mate and his companions were preserved till thus unexpectedly relieved.

The sufferings of these men were great, and their preservation remarkable: such circumstances afford instruction to every one. If you are inclined to say, there is no probability of your being similarly situated, remember that although not placed in a desert island, or in a small boat, destitute of the means of subsistence, yet all are placed in the midst of many and great dangers, as to this life. But it is of infinitely more importance to remember that there is a great and awful danger, namely, of eternal death, to which we are all alike exposed, if ignorant of the Saviour and his salvation. The subject speaks both to seamen and landmen; are you aware of its importance? Pray earnestly to God for the knowledge of his truth: these men prayed earnestly for deliverance from their sufferings: and can you be less earnest respecting your soul? Again, remember that God has promised to give his Holy Spirit to those that ask, and it is only by his teaching that we can be led to a knowledge of our danger, and of the value of that salvation which is so fully and freely offered unto us, through Christ, who died for our sins, and rose again for our justification.

To return to our narrative. The mate and two survivors of his boat's crew were picked up by another ship, after sufferings similar to those of the captain; but the third boat was never heard of, and its crew are supposed to have perished for want, or to have found a watery grave.

The Surry proceeded to New South Wales, and the mate, Mr. Chappell, returned to London in June, 1823, and furnished the details from which this account has been drawn up. He says, "Before I was cast away, I was like most seamen, I never thought much about religion; but no man has seen more of the goodness of the Lord than I have, or had more reason to believe in him. I trust I am enabled to do so." He also bears a strong testimony to the good resulting from the labours of the missionaries in the islands of the South Sea, and the great change effected in the natives: he says, "There are very many among the poor natives of those isles, who know more of religion, and show more of the effects of it in their conduct, than the greater part of our own countrymen."

We meet with many instances of unexpected dangers and remarkable preservations, but few are more worthy of notice than the one which has been related. May they lead the reader to a more earnest and constant attendance upon the means of Divine grace. Above all, remember, that it is not merely hearing of Divine truths, or bending the knees in prayer, that can save from the sentence of "Depart ye cursed;"[6] which will be pronounced at the last day on all evil and wicked doers; nothing but feeling, deeply feeling our lost and ruined state by nature, the evil of sin, and the necessity of a change of heart, can lead us to look to the Saviour, and to trust in him for pardon and salvation.

Again, remember that ALL, whether seamen or landmen, are passing rapidly along and hastening to eternity! ETERNITY! solemn, awful word! Fearful to those who are pursuing a course of sin and folly, but delightful to the believer in the Lord Jesus Christ; who has been brought out of nature's darkness into marvellous light, and from the power of sin and Satan, to rejoice in the God of salvation; having obtained pardon and sanctification by the blood of the cross, through the influence of the Holy Spirit. And though the believer's course through life may be across a stormy and tempestuous ocean, yet he proceeds with confidence, assured that he shall reach his desired port in safety, because Christ is his Pilot and Saviour.

Excerpt from the Journal of the Surry

The following account has been attributed by Thomas Heffernan to Edward Dobson, first mate of the *Surry,* the vessel that rescued Chappel, Wright, and Weeks from Henderson Island on its way back to Sydney, Australia, from Valparaiso, Chile. Originally directed to sail for Ducie Island, the *Surry*'s Captain Raine had the good sense to realize that the *Essex* survivors might have been mistaken as to their whereabouts. Sure enough, he soon found the survivors on the north shore of nearby Henderson. As Heffernan has pointed out, the events described by Dobson would become the basis of the first published account of the *Essex* disaster in the Sydney *Gazette,* 9 June 1821. The Penguin text is a transcription of the relevant portion of the manuscript journal MS A 131 in the Mitchell Library, Sydney, Australia. The Library ascribes the journal to a different mate of the *Surry,* W. L. Edwardson.

They found it [Ducie Island] a most barren Spot, the Beaches lined with Coral Rocks and Shells, there were a few Bushes among which an immense number of Birds, Kept their nests—there was a large Lagoon in the Middle.—there was not the least appearance of any one ever having landed on this place before no appearance of Fires, no Trees cut, and indeed no Sign whatever—they found a piece of a Spar on the Beach with notches at the ends.—which apparently had been a fender to some Ship.—

Captn Raine took a Meridian observation and found the Latitude of the N.E. end 24°38′ S.—and its Long: 124°24′ W.—being 13 Miles more to the Eastw^d than laid down in chart.—

Captn Raine not finding the 3 Men, thinks this Island has been mistaken for one, More to the Westw^d and accordingly intends to touch at it.—at 5 P.M. made Sail with a pleasant breeze.—

7th Pleasant breeze and fine Weather—70^{miles}

8th Light Winds and cloudy Weather. Sea Smooth 4 P.M. Long. [by Obs.] 126°1′ W. chro. 125°48′ W.—Lat. 24°26′ S.—Keeping a good look out for the Supposed Ducies Island. 119^{miles}

9th Fresh breezes and cloudy Weather, a man at the Mast Head who at 2 P.M. announced the intelligence of Land a head, we immediately steered for the Centre of it and being close in fired a Gun, but not seeing any one hauled on the Starboard tack and stood to the North End, on rounding of which, we opened a Spacious Bay and fired another Gun, in a few minutes to our very great joy we saw the "three poor fellows" come down to the Beach out of the Bush.—Shorten^d Sail and lowered the Boats down immediately lowered down. Captn & Doctor, went in the Gig, and Mr. Powers in Cutter, in about an hour they returned with the Men they found the Surf very high and of course impracticable to land, but having Worked the Boats as close in as possible, the Men then Waded through the Surf, but with great difficulty they were got into the Gig, one of them being very much bruised, by the sharp coral Rocks that line the shore. they were very weak and thin and Captn Raine supposes they would not have weathered it another Month.—their names are Thomas Chappel, Willm Wright and Seth

Weeks—as soon as they came on board, they were taken into the Cabin and treated with every attention and Kindness their situation demanded.—

They told Captⁿ Raine there were some Papers on shore, left by their Captain,—determined on laying on and off the Island for the Night and in the Morning to go on shore again.—

April 10th This Morning at Day light found ourselves something to leeward of the Island, made all Sail and beat up, at Noon being close too, both Boats again went on shore and landed in another Bay, through a very nasty Surf, between a small Crack in the Rocks—they got the Letters (one addressed to the Public, one to the Capt^{n's} Wife and one to the Brother of the Chief Mate). Captⁿ Raine having taken the Letters, left one in their place, giving particulars of the above transactions, he also ordered the name of the ship and his own name, with the date to be cut on some trees,—he having seen the name of a Ship which it seems had touched there before these unhappy Men had landed on this desolate place—the name was the "Elizabeth' Captⁿ H. King"—these Men say in a cave on another part of the Island—they found the skeletons of 8 Men who it appears (as they say) must have been there som[e] time.—

at 4 P.M. both Boats having come on board again quite safe, made Sail from the Island, which Captⁿ Raine calls "Inca[r]nation Island" its Long. 128°20' West and Lat. obs. 24°26' South.—The above place is larger than Ducies Island and the Top is level like a plain with, here and there a Bush or so, it affords very little Water and less food, they were obliged to live on a kind of Berry called a palm and such Sea Birds which they could catch asleep in the Night— they were partaking of a Bird they had just caught and cooked, when they heard the report of our Gun, one run out to see what it was, and the poor fellow told me himself when he saw the Ship, he was so overpowered with the emotions such a sight excited in his breast, he could not go to tell his companions the joyful intelligence—but when they all saw the Ship and knew they were once more on the point of seeing some of their fellow beings—their emotions and feelings at such a time may be better imagined than described.—

The following is the Account they give of their Shipwrack, and subsequent misfortunes.—They sailed from Nantucket, in the American Whaler Essex, of 260 Tons comm^d by Captⁿ Pollard, on the 12th August 1819.—On a Whaling Voyage—they arrived in the South Seas and were pretty fortunate, having procured 750 Barrels of Oil and where [were] in the Lat 00°47′ S.—and Long 118°0′ W. on the 20th Novr. 1820, on which day, they were among many Whales and their Boats were all down, the 2nd Mates Boat had got stove and had returned on board to be repaired, shortly after his being on board, a very large Whale what Whalers term of the 1st Class Struck the Ship and knock^d part of her false keel off, just abreast of her main channels—the Whale then lay along side the Ship, endeavoring to lay hold with her jaws but could not accomplish it, she then turned and went round the Stern and came up on the otherside—went away ahead, turned short round, and again came with great velocity for the Ship—the vessel at this time was going on at about 5 knots, but such was the force say these Men—she had stern way, the Men on Deck all knock^d down and the Water came dashing in the Cabin Windows, and worst of all, the Bows were stove in, under the cathead on the Starboard side, and in less than 10 Minutes, the vessel filled, and went on her Beam ends.—

The Captain and Chief Mate had each got fast to a Whale but upon the misfortune of the Ship—they cut from them and came on board—the Captⁿ ordered the masts to be cut away, upon which she righted.—they then Scuttled the upper Deck, and got some Bread and some Water, which they put in the Boats they staid by the Ship, three days, during which time they made Sails for the Boats.—having taken in the compasses and some Nautical Instruments—they left the Ship and stood away to the Southw^d in hopes of getting into the variables and fine Weather, but the Wind being right in their teeth, they made much leeway on the 20th Dec. 1820.—they made this Island, from which through the humanity of Captⁿ Raine, they have just been taken.—

Captⁿ Pollard remained here one Week, who finding the Island afforded hardly any nourishment of any Description—they all (excepting the above three who preferred staying here to risking their lives again) determined upon venturing to the Coast of S. America in their Boats, and the sequel of their melancholy Story ends, with the Boats Crews suffering unheard of hardships—two of which were pick^d up—one Boat with the Captⁿ and a Boy was brought into Valparaiso—the other was taken on board some other Ship.

From the Appearance of the Island, it is wonderfull how these poor Men have subsisted for such a period nearly 4 Months from the Captain's leaving them.—the whole Island says Capt.ⁿ Raine appears to be a rock of Volcanic Matter and is full of caves of considerable length.—

The following is the letter address^d to the Public and left there by Capt.ⁿ Pollard.—

"Account of the Loss of the Ship Essex of Nantucket in North America commanded by Capt.ⁿ Pollard Jun.ʳ—which shipwreck happened on the 20.ᵗʰ day of November 1820.—in Long 118°0′ W on the Equator, by a large Whale striking her in the Bow with the head, which caused her to fill with Water we got what Provisions &c the Boats would carry and left on the 22.ⁿᵈ Nov. & arrived here this day with all hands—we intend to leave here to morrow which will be the 26.ᵗʰ Dec.ʳ—for the Continent.—I shall leave with this a letter for my Wife and who ever finding it, will have the goodness to forward it, will oblige an unfortunate man and receive his sincere Wishes.—Ducies Island 25.ᵗʰ Dec.ʳ 1820."

EXTRACTS:
MEMORIES AND APOCRYPHA

Extracts: Memories and Apocrypha

Even though Nantucketers were reluctant to discuss the *Essex* openly, the disaster continued to haunt the island throughout the nineteenth century. In particular, it was the figure of the ship's captain, George Pollard, Jr.—forced to preside over the execution of his own young cousin—in whom people appear to have been the most interested. The *Essex* disaster also haunted the imagination of Herman Melville, who would refer to it directly in *Moby-Dick,* and then eventually meet and write about Captain Pollard. The following *Essex* extracts mix selections from Melville with reminiscences from a variety of sources—some of them reliable, some not. In addition to several stanzas from a ballad written by the Nantucket whaleman Charles Murphey, third mate on the ship that rescued Pollard and Ramsdell, there are testimonies from two other Nantucketers—Frederick Sanford, a contemporary of the young Nantucketers aboard the *Essex* who would write extensively about the island's whaling history, and Joseph Warren Phinney, who grew up as part of George and Mary Pollard's extended family on Nantucket. Published here for the first time is a scrap of family lore passed down from Barnabas Sears, a Quaker from Cape Cod with close ties to the island.

———————

But fortunately the special point I here seek can be established upon testimony entirely independent of my own. That point is this: The Sperm Whale is in some cases sufficiently powerful, knowing, and judiciously malicious, as with direct aforethought to stave in, utterly destroy, and sink a large ship: and what is more the Sperm Whale *has* done it.

First: In the year 1820 the ship Essex, Captain Pollard, of Nantucket, was cruising in the Pacific Ocean. One day she saw spouts, lowered her boats, and gave chase to a shoal of sperm whales. Ere long, several of the whales were wounded; when, suddenly, a very large whale escaping from the boats, issued from the shoal, and bore directly down upon the ship. Dashing his forehead against her hull, he stove her in, that in less than "ten minutes" she settled down and fell over. Not a surviving plank of her has been seen since. After the severest exposure, part of the crew reached the land in their boats. Being returned home at last, Captain Pollard once more sailed for the Pacific in command of another ship, but the gods shipwrecked him again upon unknown rocks and breakers; for the second time his ship was utterly lost, and forthwith forswearing the sea, he has never tempted it since. At this day Captain Pollard is a resident of Nantucket. I have seen Owen Chase, who was chief mate of the Essex at the time of the tragedy; I have read his plain and faithful narrative; I have conversed with his son; and all this within a few miles of the scene of the catastrophe. [From Herman Melville, Moby-Dick (1851), Chapter 45, "The Affidavit."]

Only one of the small boats [belonging to the *Essex*] survived, and only after terrible hardships and suffering. The story goes, they drew lots as to who would die for the others, and the man who drew the lot had his place taken by a young boy who insisted on dying instead of the older man, who had a wife and babies. Well, I dont know how true it is. Anyway, there was some mystery about the surviving boat. [From the autobiographical reminiscences of Joseph Warren Phinney (1845–1934), collected by Diana Taylor Brown, his granddaughter, MS leaf 1.]

A tradition still current in Nantucket has it that the lot fell to the captain, whereupon his nephew, already near death, feeling that he could not survive the afternoon, offered and insisted upon taking his uncle's place. I doubt this. [From Cyrus Townsend Brady, "The Yarn of the 'Essex,' Whaler," *Cosmopolitan* (November 1904), p. 72, note.]

The second month, quite early on
The three-and-twentieth day,
From our mast-head we did espy
A boat to leeward lay.

Hard up the helm, and down we went
To see who it might be,
The Essex boat we found it was,
Been ninety days at sea.

No victuals were there in the boat,
Of any sort or kind,
And two survivors, who did expect
A watery grave to find.

The rest belonging to the boat
Ah! shocking to relate,
For want of food and nourishment,
Met an unhappy fate.

We rounded to, and hove aback;
A boat was quickly lowered;
We took the two survivors out,
And carried them on board.

[From Charles Murphey, 3d Mate, on the Voyage, *A Journal of a Whaling Voyage on Board Ship Dauphin, of Nantucket* (Mattapoisett, Mass.: Atlantic Publishing Company, 1877), p. 9.]

We can never forget the Sunday, August 5th, 1821, the day the ship Two Brothers was announced in sight from the watch tower, for she had Capt. Pollard a passenger. In looking back to *that day*, with all its excitements, for there were full fifteen hundred people upon our wharves, we remember the interest manifested by our citizens for these afflicted men of the sea, suffering . . . as none had in any of our long career of whaling life. [From Frederick C. Sanford, "Obituary of Captain Benjamin Lawrence," *Nantucket Inquirer and Mirror*, 5 April 1879.]

My grandmother heard it from her grandfather Barnabas Sears in South Yarmouth. He was concerned about someone on the ship [*Essex*]—a close relative. When he [the relative] returned from the boats, even though he was under twenty, his hair had turned snow white. My memory is he was the cabin boy. [Rosemary Heaman, 4 December 1999.]

There is a traditional . . . story about Pollard in which he is asked by a "stranger" if he ever knew a Nantucketer by the name of Owen Coffin. "Knew him?" Pollard is reputed to have replied, "Why I et him!" [From Nathaniel Philbrick, *Away Off Shore: Nantucket Island and Its People, 1602–1890* (Nantucket: Mill Hill Press, 1994), pp. 251–52.]

Captain Pollard was gum-shoe man of the town. The boys were supposed to be in the house by nine o'clock & he used to make a tour of the town, a long hickory pole with an iron hook at the end, under his arm. He was a short fat man—jolly, loving the good things of life. And they used to say Aunt Mary, his wife, who had been a tailoress, when he needed a new pair of breeches laid him down on the cloth and marked him out on it. When he wore out the knees he turned then round hind side fore' most. Once a year on the anniversary of the loss of "the Essex" he locked himself in his room and fasted. [Phinney, MS leaf 2.]

> A Jonah is he?—And men bruit
> The story. None will give him place
> In a third venture. Came the day
> Dire need constrained the man to pace
> A night patrolman on the quay
> Watching the bales till morning hour
> Through fair and foul. Never he smiled;
> Call him, and he would come; not sour
> In spirit, but meek and reconciled;

> Patient he was, he none withstood;
> Oft on some secret thing would brood.

[Herman Melville, *Clarel* (1876), Part One, Canto 37, lines 90–100.]

Owen [Chase] is insane (will eventually be carried to the insane hospital)[.] they now have a man to take care of him[.] I met with him last summer[.] . . . he called me cousin Susan (taking me for sister Worth)[,] held my hand and sobbed like a child, saying O *my head, my head*[.] it was pitiful to see the strong man bowed, then his personal appearance so changed, did'nt allow himself decent clothing, fear's he shall come to want— [From a letter dated 15 November 1868 from Phebe B. Chace, Owen Chase's cousin, to Winnifred Battie, his former sister-in-law; the letter is the property of Mrs. Howard Chase.]

Many years later, in fact nearly a century after such news [of the ordeal of the crew of the *Essex*] was received, one young woman deeply interested in the story, asked one of the daughters of Benjamin Lawrence, a survivor in Mate Chase's boat, for some details concerning his experience, and the reply was given in a gentle reproof: "Miss Molly, we do not mention this in Nantucket." [Edouard A. Stackpole and Helen Winslow Chase, eds., *The Loss of the Ship "Essex" Sunk by a Whale* by Thomas Nickerson (Nantucket: The Nantucket Historical Association, 1984), p. 78.]

NOTES

THE PADDACK LETTER

1. *Dauphin:* The *Dauphin* had sailed from Nantucket on 4 September 1820.
2. *miles:* The use of *miles* here instead of the customary *minutes* reflects the fact that by definition a nautical mile is equal to one minute of latitude or of any great circle of the earth.
3. *scutling:* Cutting holes in.
4. *s[t]reaks:* Planks.
5. *Ducies Island:* Not Ducie but Henderson Island, an atoll some 200 miles to the southwest of Ducie. Both islands are in the Pitcairn group.

THE MACY LETTER

1. *navigators:* Nathaniel Bowditch's *The New American Practical Navigator,* which ever since its first publication in 1802 has been the indispensable *vade mecum* of American mariners. Included in its nineteenth-century editions were the positions of many of the Pacific islands.

CHASE'S NARRATIVE

1. *a liberal bounty:* The British government long offered specific bounties per ton of whale oil landed by British vessels in British ports; the subsidy was ended in 1824.
2. *Capt. Porter:* David Porter (1780–1843), who, as commander of the U. S. frigate *Essex,* cruised in the Pacific during the War of 1812, protecting American whalers and attacking British shipping. Before the *Essex* was forced to surrender in March of 1814 after a furious battle with two enemy men-of-war, she had destroyed Britain's whale fishery in the Pacific, captured some 4,000 tons of enemy shipping, and taken nearly 400 prisoners.

3. *the struggle between the patriots and royalists:* The revolution against Spanish rule in Latin America broke out in 1810 and raged until its final triumph in 1824.

4. *boat-steerers, and harpooners:* Chase's distinction between boat-steerers and harpooners is odd, for in the American sperm-whale fishery at the time of the voyage of the *Essex,* the two duties were normally performed by the same man. After successfully harpooning the whale, the harpooner/boat-steerer moved to the rear of the boat where, exchanging places with the mate, he took over the management of the steering oar. Meanwhile, the mate took up a position at the bow in order to lance and kill the whale. It should be noted that by his own account (pp. 22 and 24) Chase, as mate, both harpooned and presumably lanced his prey.

5. *the Western Islands:* The Azores.

6. *on her beam-ends:* Said of a vessel when she is lying so much on her side that her beams, the cross-timbers of her frame, are standing nearly on end.

7. *cambouse:* Usually *caboose,* the cookhouse.

8. *Floros:* Usually *Flores.*

9. *Decamas:* Atacames, on the coast of present-day Ecuador.

10. *Hood's Island:* Española.

11. *Charles Island:* Santa María.

12. *fore-chains:* Heavy chains or iron plates by which the shrouds supporting a mast (in this case, the foremast) are attached with bolts to the side of the vessel; also a name for the channels or chain wales, broad planks bolted to the side of the vessel, through which the chain-plates pass in order to widen the angle of the shrouds.

13. *cat-head:* One of two short beams projecting from either side of the bow by which the anchors are fixed in a horizontal position ("catted") when the vessel is under way.

14. *the waist of the ship:* The midsection of a vessel between the forecastle and the quarter deck.

15. *the plank-shear:* The longitudinal plank that caps the timber-heads along the upper sides of a vessel.

16. *the lanyards:* Systems of ropes connecting the shrouds to the chains by which the tension of the shrouds can be adjusted.

17. *for sails to our boats:* The voyage of the *Essex* took place a decade or so before the use of sails in whaleboats became common in the American sperm-whale fishery.

18. *the Sandwich Islands:* The Hawaiian Islands.

19. *clinker built:* Constructed so that the lower edge of each plank overlaps the one below it.

20. *no glass, nor log-line:* In navigation by dead reckoning, speed (and hence distance traveled) is determined by measuring the rate at which the log line is drawn out as it is trailed from the moving ship. The line is knotted at regular intervals, the passage of the knots being timed with a half-minute sand glass.

21. *capacity and endurance:* Although the original reading of the 1821 edition, "capacity of endurance," makes sense, the reading supplied by the errata sheet, "capacity and endurance," would seem the intended one, for it parallels its antithesis in the next sentence, "incapacity and weakness."

22. *the killer-fish species:* The killer whale.

23. *spissy:* Dense, thick. The *Oxford English Dictionary* records the last appearance of this word as 1683 and labels it obsolete and rare.

24. *one of the offices of nature:* Urination.

25. *"The Elizabeth":* Captain Henry King in the English South-Sea trading vessel *Elizabeth* visited Henderson Island in the spring of 1819. Believing the island to be undiscovered, King named it after his own vessel.

26. *the stern-post:* An upright timber rising from the after end of the keel and bracing the transom.

27. *biles:* Boils. The narrative employs a form of the word that dropped out of standard English in the late eighteenth century and now survives only in provincial dialects.

28. *"Who tempers the wind to the shorn lamb":* The source of this scriptural-sounding phrase is Laurence Sterne's *A Sentimental Journey* (1768) in the chapter "Maria."

29. *the captain of the . . . Constellation:* Commodore Charles Goodwin Ridgely (d. 1848), then the senior officer on the Pacific station of the U. S. Navy.

30. *the whale-ship the Eagle:* The *Eagle* had sailed from Nantucket on 17 October 1818.

MELVILLE'S ANNOTATION OF CHASE

1. *Bennett in . . . the Globe"):* Frederick Debell Bennett, *Narrative of a Whaling Voyage round the Globe, from the Year 1833 to 1836* (London: Bentley, 1840).

2. *Judge Shaw:* Lemuel Shaw (1781–1861), chief justice of Massachusetts and Melville's father-in-law.

3. *Mr. Hall:* No evidence links the John Hall of the *Acushnet* with any one of Chase's whaling voyages.

4. *p. 19. of M.S.:* Actually p. 16.

5. *"Wm Wirt" . . . Chace was the Captain:* The *Acushnet* spoke the

William Wirt on 7 May 1841 near the island of Juan Fernandez. Melville could not have seen Owen Chase then or at any time during his Pacific voyaging, for Chase had retired from the sea in early 1840. The identity of the man for whom Melville mistook him is unknown.

6. *a son of Owen Chace:* William Henry Chase (b. 1824). The young Chase was probably a member of the crew of the *Lima,* a Nantucket whaler which the *Acushnet* spoke twice, on 23 July 1841 and again in mid-August.

7. *the* Charles Carroll . . . *several voyages:* Although Chase had served as master of the *Charles Carroll* on two voyages in 1832–40, her captain at the time of Melville's voyage was Thomas S. Andrews.

8. *sometime about 1850–3:* Melville met Pollard on Nantucket on 8 July 1852.

9. *how many more pages the complete narrative contains:* The last six pages of Chase's *Narrative* were missing from Melville's copy.

10. *[illegible]:* Apparently the name of a vessel.

11. *the Captain . . . narrative to read:* A garbled recollection, for Chase would have heard of the infidelity of his third wife, Eunice, in 1838, three years before the *Acushnet* reached the Pacific. Moreover, William Henry Chase was the son of his father's first wife, Peggy, not Eunice.

NICKERSON'S "DESULTORY SKETCHES"

1. *The Corsair:* Byron, *The Corsair* (1814), I.1–18.

2. *Paul Macy Esqr:* In the register of the *Essex* issued 10 August 1819, the name of Paul Macy heads a list of eight owners.

3. *bar:* The sandbar at the entrance to Nantucket harbor imposed a severe limitation on the draft of vessels passing over it. Heavily laden ships like the *Essex* were forced to anchor outside the bar and lighter their cargoes to or from the harbor.

4. *dolphin:* Nickerson refers not to the marine mammal but to the common dolphin or dorado, famous in the imagery of the romantic period for the beauty of its changes of color as it dies.

5. *steering sail:* Studding sail, a rectangular sail extended from a yard by a boom in light or moderate winds.

6. *gangway:* A passageway or entrance.

7. *pay dear for his whistle:* The phrase comes from Benjamin Franklin's bagatelle "The Whistle" (1779).

8. *Cape ^St Augustine:* On the Brazilian coast in latitude 8° 28' south and longitude 35° 33' west near Recife (Pernambuco).

9. *a subsequently made voyage:* In the ship *Two Brothers* of Nantucket.

The voyage ended when the vessel was wrecked on a coral reef near the Hawaiian Islands on 11 February 1823.

10. *lunar observations:* A complex method of determining the longitude without benefit of a chronometer. The navigator measures the angle between the moon and certain fixed stars or the sun. By comparing the angle observed to published tables of the predicted angles against Greenwich time, he can then ascertain the precise Greenwich time of the observation. Finally, by comparing this time with the local time of the observation, he can find the longitude of his position.

11. *train:* Extracted from the blubber by boiling, as in *train-oil.*

12. *stuff:* Deceive, or trick.

13. *cut stick:* Run away. The earliest example of the phrase in the *Dictionary of American Regional English* is dated 1832.

14. *netting:* A rope network in which the staysail is stowed.

15. *Hero of Nantucket and Perseverance {No. 2} of London:* The attack occurred on 27 February 1821. The mate Obed Starbuck and the others made good their escape on 3 March. The number that Nickerson inserted after "Perseverance" is a means of distinguishing that ship from an older vessel of the same name.

16. *Genl Benevido:* Vincente Benavides (1777–1822), a cut-throat who alternately sided with the Royalist and Patriot forces, but chiefly served his own interests from his base at Arauco. He was executed by the Chilean authorities on 23 February 1822.

17. *slip^d the ships cable:* Instead of performing the laborious task of weighing anchor, the pirates made a fast getaway by leaving the cable and anchor behind.

18. *so soon to lay a heap of ruins:* A severe earthquake on 20 February 1835 heavily damaged Concepción.

19. *Lord Cochrane's detatched fleet:* Nickerson refers to Thomas Cochrane (1775–1860), 10th earl of Dundonald. After a brilliant career in the Royal Navy during the Napoleonic wars, Cochrane was dismissed from the service in 1814 for alleged involvement in a stock-market fraud. Appointed an admiral in the Chilean navy, he played an important part in the liberation of Chile and Peru from Spanish rule, clearing their coasts of Spanish shipping in 1819–20.

20. *Captain Daniel Russel:* Russell had commanded and shared in the ownership of the *Essex* on her previous whaling voyage in 1817, in which George Pollard served as chief mate and Owen Chase as a boatsteerer.

21. *the castles of Callao was evacuated by Genl Rodil:* José Ramón Rodil (1789–1853) commanded the Royalist forces at Callao during a long and costly siege by the Patriots that ended with his evacuation of the

city and its "castles," an extensive system of batteries guarding the inner harbor, in early 1825.

22. *Samuel Wright of Salem* ^{Mass.}: The whaler *Samuel Wright* under the command of John Pitman sailed from Salem on 15 June 1833, and returned after a successful voyage on 27 August 1836. Nickerson was her chief mate.

23. *General Flores:* Juan José Flores (1800–64), a commander under Bolívar in the War of Independence and president of Ecuador (1830–34, 1839–45).

24. *General Wright:* Tomas Carlos Wright (1800–68), an Irish-born soldier-of-fortune who served with the Patriots in Ecuador in 1820–22 and later settled in Guayaquil, where he held a number of posts, among them governor-general of the province of Guayas.

25. *Genl Rocheforte:* Vincente Rocafuerte (1783–1847), who led a revolt at Guayaquil against Juan José Flores in 1834 but was defeated and imprisoned. After he and Flores settled their differences, he succeeded Flores as president of Ecuador (1834–39), instituting many liberal reforms.

26. *Lady Adams of Nantucket:* The *Lady Adams* had sailed from Nantucket on 28 February 1820 under the command of Shubael Hussey.

27. *described by C^{om}[modore] Porter:* In *Journal of a Cruise Made to the Pacific Ocean by Captain David Porter* (1815; expanded edition, 1822).

28. *hove down:* Careened on her side in order to clean or repair the bottom.

29. *guano:* The iguana.

30. *Bowles:* William Lisle Bowles, *The Missionary of the Andes* (1813), II.243–256.

31. *one of the wood ends had bursted off:* A plank had sprung at the point of its attachment to the stem.

32. *adorned a tale rather than told it:* "He left the name at which the world grew pale, / To point a moral, or adorn a tale" (Samuel Johnson, "The Vanity of Human Wishes" [1749], lines 221–22).

33. *strengthning plaster:* The plaster of paris that a surgeon applies to the cast around a broken limb.

34. *^{Don} Luiz Del Cruz:* Luis de la Cruz Goyeneche (1786–1829), who had formerly served as supreme director of Chile (1817–18).

35. *^{Mr} Hill:* Henry Hill (b. 1795), acting consul at Valparaiso from 1818 until 1821.

36. *Capt Downs:* John Downs (1784–1854), who was relieved by Charles Ridgely as head of the U. S. Pacific station.

NICKERSON'S LETTER TO LEWIS

1. *The captain of the ship:* Thomas Raine of the *Surry.*
2. *Pollards reef or shoal:* On which the *Two Brothers* was wrecked in 1823.
3. *George Sutton . . . J H Holcombe &c.:* Ship owners of New York City.
4. *Coolie voyage:* Transporting Chinese laborers from the Far East, generally to ports in California or the West Indies.

RIDGELY'S LETTERBOOK

1. *the arrested officers:* Lt. Robert B. Randolph and Lt. John P. Cambreling of the U. S. Navy and Lt. Joseph P. Hall of the Marine Corps, arrested for insubordination and dueling.
2. *also those unfortunate men of the Essex:* The survivors in fact reached home from the Pacific in whaling ships, Pollard in the *Two Brothers,* and the others in the *Eagle.*

AN ACCOUNT OF THE LOSS OF THE ESSEX

1. *November 19, 1819:* Actually 12 August 1819.
2. *Friendly Islands:* Tonga, a group more than 4,000 miles to the southwest of the wreck and in a direction nearly opposite to that in which the survivors in fact intended to go.
3. *5ᵗʰ of April:* The *Surry* reached Henderson Island on 9 April.
4. *"Hope deferred maketh the heart sick":* Proverbs 13:12.
5. *"Come unto me . . . give you rest":* Matthew 11:28.
6. *"Depart ye cursed":* Matthew 25:41.

CLICK ON A CLASSIC
www.penguinclassics.com

The world's greatest literature at your fingertips

Constantly updated information on more than a thousand titles,
from Icelandic sagas to ancient Indian epics, Russian drama to
Italian romance, American greats to African masterpieces

•

The latest news on recent additions to the list, updated
editions, and specially commissioned translations

•

Original essays by leading writers

•

A wealth of background material, including biographies
of every classic author from Aristotle to Zamyatin, plot
synopses, readers' and teachers' guides, useful web links

•

Online desk and examination copy assistance for academics

•

Trivia quizzes, competitions, giveaways, news on
forthcoming screen adaptations

The Last of the Mohicans
James Fenimore Cooper
Introduction by Richard Slotkin
Tragic, fast-paced, and stocked with the elements of a classic Western adventure, this novel takes Natty Bumppo and his Indian friend Chingachgook through hostile Indian territory during the French and Indian War. *ISBN 0-14-039024-3*

Two Years Before the Mast: A Personal Narrative of Life at Sea
Richard Henry Dana, Jr.
Edited with an Introduction and Notes by Thomas Philbrick
Dana's account of his passage as a common seaman from Boston around Cape Horn to California, and back, is a remarkable portrait of the sea-going life. Bringing to the public's attention for the first time the plights of the most exploited segment of the American working class, he forever changed readers' romanticized perceptions of life at sea.
ISBN 0-14-039008-1

Nature and Selected Essays
Ralph Waldo Emerson
Edited with an Introduction by Larzer Ziff
This sampling includes fifteen essays that highlight the formative and significant ideas of this central American thinker: "Nature," "The American Scholar," "An Address Delivered Before the Senior Class in Divinity College, Cambridge," "Man the Reformer," "History," "Self-Reliance," "The Over-Soul," "Circles," "The Transcendentalist," "The Poet," "Experience," "Montaigne: Or, the Skeptic," "Napoleon: Or, the Man of the World," "Fate," and "Thoreau." *ISBN 0-14-243762-X*

The Scarlet Letter
Nathaniel Hawthorne
Introduction by Nina Baym with Notes by Thomas E. Connolly
Hawthorne's novel of guilt and redemption in pre-Revolutionary Massachusetts provides vivid insight into the social and religious forces that shaped early America. *ISBN 0-14-243726-3*

The Legend of Sleepy Hollow and Other Stories
Washington Irving
Introduction and Notes by William L. Hedges
Irving's delightful 1819 miscellany of essays and sketches includes the
two classic tales "The Legend of Sleepy Hollow" and "Rip Van Winkle."
ISBN 0-14-043769-X

The Portable Abraham Lincoln
Abraham Lincoln
Edited by Andrew Delbanco
The essential Lincoln, including all of the great public speeches, along
with less familiar letters and memoranda that chart Lincoln's political
career. With an indispensable introduction, headnotes, and a chronology
of Lincoln's life. *ISBN 0-14-017031-6*

Moby-Dick
Or, The Whale
Herman Melville
Edited with an Introduction by Andrew Delbanco
Explanatory Commentary by Tom Quirk
The story of an eerily compelling madman pursuing an unholy war
against a creature as vast and dangerous and unknowable as the sea
itself, Melville's masterpiece is also a profound inquiry into character,
faith, and the nature of perception. *ISBN 0-14-243724-7*

The Fall of the House of Usher and Other Writings
Edgar Allan Poe
Edited with an Introduction and Notes by David Galloway
This selection includes seventeen poems, among them "The Raven,"
"Annabel Lee," and "The Bells"; nineteen tales, including "The Fall of
the House of Usher," "The Murders in the Rue Morgue," "The Tell-Tale
Heart," "The Masque of the Red Death," and "The Pit and the
Pendulum"; and sixteen essays and reviews. *ISBN 0-14-143981-5*

Uncle Tom's Cabin
Or, Life Among the Lowly
Harriet Beecher Stowe
Edited with an Introduction by Ann Douglas
Perhaps the most powerful document in the history of American aboli-
tionism, this controversial novel goaded thousands of readers to take a
stand on the issue of slavery and played a major political and social role
in the Civil War period. *ISBN 0-14-039003-0*

Walden and Civil Disobedience
Henry David Thoreau
Introduction by Michael Meyer
Two classic examinations of individuality in relation to nature, society, and government. *Walden* conveys at once a naturalist's wonder at the commonplace and a Transcendentalist's yearning for spiritual truth and self-reliance. "Civil Disobedience" is perhaps the most famous essay in American literature—and the inspiration for social activists around the world, from Gandhi to Martin Luther King, Jr. *ISBN 0-14-039044-8*

Nineteenth-Century American Poetry
Edited with an Introduction and Notes by
William C. Spengemann with Jessica F. Roberts
Whitman, Dickinson, and Melville occupy the center of this anthology of nearly three hundred poems, spanning the course of the century, from Joel Barlow to Edwin Arlington Robinson, by way of Bryant, Emerson, Longfellow, Whittier, Poe, Holmes, Jones Very, Thoreau, Lowell, and Lanier. *ISBN 0-14-043587-5*

Selected Poems
Henry Wadsworth Longfellow
Edited with an Introduction and Notes by Lawrence Buell
Longfellow was the most popular poet of his day. This selection includes generous samplings from his longer works—*Evangeline*, *The Courtship of Miles Standish*, and *Hiawatha*—as well as his shorter lyrics and less familiar narrative poems. *ISBN 0-14-039064-2*

Leaves of Grass
Walt Whitman
Edited with an Introduction by Malcolm Cowley
This is the original and complete 1855 edition of one of the greatest masterpieces of American literature, including Whitman's own introduction to the work. *ISBN 0-14-042199-8*

The Education of Henry Adams
Henry Adams
Edited with an Introduction and Notes by Jean Gooder
In this memoir Adams examines his own life as it reflects the progress of the United States from the Civil War period to the nation's ascendancy as a world power. A remarkable synthesis of history, art, politics, and philosophy, *The Education of Henry Adams* remains a provocative and stimulating interpretation of the birth of the twentieth century.
ISBN 0-14-044557-9

Little Women
Louisa May Alcott
Edited with an Introduction by Elaine Showalter
Notes by Siobhan Kilfeather and Vinca Showalter
Alcott's beloved story of the March girls—Meg, Jo, Beth, and Amy—is a classic American feminist novel, reflecting the tension between cultural obligation and artistic and personal freedom.   *ISBN 0-14-039069-3*

Looking Backward
2000–1887
Edward Bellamy
Edited with an Introduction by Cecelia Tichi
When first published in 1888, *Looking Backward* initiated a national political- and social-reform movement. This profoundly utopian tale addresses the anguish and hope of its age, as well as having lasting value as an American cultural landmark.   *ISBN 0-14-039018-9*

Tales of Soldiers and Civilians and Other Stories
Ambrose Bierce
Edited with an Introduction and Notes by Tom Quirk
This collection gathers three dozen of Bierce's finest tales of war and the supernatural, including "An Occurrence at Owl Creek Bridge" and "The Damned Thing."   *ISBN 0-14-043756-8*

The Awakening and Selected Stories
Kate Chopin
Edited with an Introduction by Sandra M. Gilbert
First published in 1899, *The Awakening* shows the transformation of Edna Pontellier, who claims for herself moral and erotic freedom. Other selections include "Emancipation," "At the 'Cadian Ball," and "Désirée's Baby."   *ISBN 0-14-243709-3*

The Red Badge of Courage and Other Stories
Stephen Crane
Edited with an Introduction by Pascal Covici, Jr.
Here is one of the greatest novels ever written about war and its psychological effects on the individual soldier. This edition also includes the short stories "The Open Boat," "The Bride Comes to Yellow Sky," "The Blue Hotel," "A Poker Game," and "The Veteran."   *ISBN 0-14-039081-2*

Personal Memoirs
Ulysses S. Grant
Introduction and Notes by James M. McPherson
Grant's memoirs demonstrate the intelligence, intense determination, and laconic modesty that made him the Union's foremost commander.
     ISBN 0-14-043701-0